T0369996

Certification Study Companion Series

The Apress Certification Study Companion Series offers guidance and hands-on practice to support technical and business professionals who are studying for an exam in the pursuit of an industry certification. Professionals worldwide seek to achieve certifications in order to advance in a career role, reinforce knowledge in a specific discipline, or to apply for or change jobs. This series focuses on the most widely taken certification exams in a given field. It is designed to be user friendly, tracking to topics as they appear in a given exam and work alongside other certification material as professionals prepare for their exam.

More information about this series at `https://link.springer.com/bookseries/17100`.

CompTIA A+ Certification Companion

Hands-on Preparation and Practice for Exams 220-1101 & 220-1102

Kodi A. Cochran

Apress®

CompTIA A+ Certification Companion: Hands-on Preparation and Practice for Exams 220-1101 & 220-1102

Kodi A. Cochran
Poca, WV, USA

ISBN-13 (pbk): 979-8-8688-0866-1   ISBN-13 (electronic): 979-8-8688-0867-8
https://doi.org/10.1007/979-8-8688-0867-8

Copyright © 2024 by Kodi A. Cochran

This work is subject to copyright. All rights are reserved by the Publisher, whether the whole or part of the material is concerned, specifically the rights of translation, reprinting, reuse of illustrations, recitation, broadcasting, reproduction on microfilms or in any other physical way, and transmission or information storage and retrieval, electronic adaptation, computer software, or by similar or dissimilar methodology now known or hereafter developed.

Trademarked names, logos, and images may appear in this book. Rather than use a trademark symbol with every occurrence of a trademarked name, logo, or image we use the names, logos, and images only in an editorial fashion and to the benefit of the trademark owner, with no intention of infringement of the trademark.

The use in this publication of trade names, trademarks, service marks, and similar terms, even if they are not identified as such, is not to be taken as an expression of opinion as to whether or not they are subject to proprietary rights.

While the advice and information in this book are believed to be true and accurate at the date of publication, neither the authors nor the editors nor the publisher can accept any legal responsibility for any errors or omissions that may be made. The publisher makes no warranty, express or implied, with respect to the material contained herein.

Managing Director, Apress Media LLC: Welmoed Spahr
Acquisitions Editor: Susan McDemott
Development Editor: Laura Berendson
Project Manager: Jessica Vakili

Cover designed by eStudioCalamar

Distributed to the book trade worldwide by Apress Media, LLC, 1 New York Plaza, New York, NY 10004, U.S.A. Phone 1-800-SPRINGER, fax (201) 348-4505, e-mail orders-ny@springer-sbm.com, or visit www.springeronline.com. Apress Media, LLC is a California LLC and the sole member (owner) is Springer Science + Business Media Finance Inc (SSBM Finance Inc). SSBM Finance Inc is a **Delaware** corporation.

For information on translations, please e-mail booktranslations@springernature.com; for reprint, paperback, or audio rights, please e-mail bookpermissions@springernature.com.

Apress titles may be purchased in bulk for academic, corporate, or promotional use. eBook versions and licenses are also available for most titles. For more information, reference our Print and eBook Bulk Sales web page at http://www.apress.com/bulk-sales.

Any source code or other supplementary material referenced by the author in this book is available to readers on GitHub (https://github.com/Apress). For more detailed information, please visit https://www.apress.com/gp/services/source-code.

If disposing of this product, please recycle the paper

Table of Contents

About the Author

Kodi A. Cochran is highly invested in the field of cybersecurity, something he has followed as a hobbyist for the past decade and expanded to make it his field of study and work. He has a bachelor's and a master's in Cybersecurity and Information Assurance, in addition to working as an Information Systems Manager for the Networking and Infrastructure team of the Department of Human and Health Resources under the agency of the Office of Management of Information Services at the state of West Virginia.

He's responsible for networking administration, project management, system support, and site support for the state of West Virginia in all state-owned health care facilities, hospitals, and labs. In addition, Kodi holds the following certifications: CompTIA A+, Network+, Security+, Project+, CySA+, and Pentest+. He's currently working on the CompTIA CASP+.

About the Technical Reviewer

Kyle Reis is a dedicated cybersecurity professional currently pursuing a bachelor's degree in Cybersecurity at Champlain College. With a solid foundation in the field, Kyle holds both the CompTIA Security+ and ISC2 Certified in Cybersecurity certifications.

Kyle began his journey in cybersecurity as a hobby in 2013, driven by a passion for understanding and protecting digital environments. Growing up in Los Angeles, California, he later moved to Florida, where he worked as an electrician. His career path then led him to Huntington, WV, where he transitioned into IT, working for AT&T at a call center. Currently, Kyle applies his expertise in IT for Marshall Health Network, ensuring the security and efficiency of healthcare systems.

As a technical reviewer for this book, Kyle has leveraged his extensive knowledge and experience to ensure the accuracy and relevance of its content. His diverse background and commitment to cybersecurity make him a valuable contributor to the field.

CHAPTER 1

Introduction to CompTIA and Certifications

The purpose of this book is to assist readers in their journey into the Information Technology world. It has been carefully crafted to align with the core requirements for the comprehensive CompTIA A+ certification, covering all examination test requirements. Although all requirements of the CompTIA A+ certification exam are covered, they are not listed in the exact ordering CompTIA has set forth. The content of the book has been structured in a logical and easy-to-follow order, allowing readers to build a foundational understanding before delving into more advanced topics.

As someone deeply invested in this field and passionate about seeing others succeed, I aim to make a significant contribution by leveraging my knowledge, skillset, experience, and certifications. Personally, holding a Master of Science in Cybersecurity, along with various industry certifications such as CySA+, Pentest+, CCSP, and SSCP, I am on track to attain the CASP+ and CISSP certifications. My dedication to continuous learning and growth drives me to share my expertise through publications like this.

© Kodi A. Cochran 2024

K. A. Cochran, *CompTIA A+ Certification Companion*, Certification Study Companion Series,
https://doi.org/10.1007/979-8-8688-0867-8_1

This publication marks just one of many endeavors I hope to undertake. I've chosen to prioritize this project because it provides a foundational understanding of the requirements for entry into the field. Whether you're a newcomer to Information Technology or a seasoned professional seeking certification, I trust that you'll find value in the content presented here.

I sincerely hope that you find this book beneficial in your journey. I extend a warm invitation to all readers to connect with me through social media and reach out for additional guidance or to suggest topics for future coverage. I genuinely do mean this; any that are reading are more than welcome to connect with me through social media, and if there is any assistance or insight that I may provide, I am happy to do so. Currently, I am active on LinkedIn for my career and community support, but you may also look for me on Facebook if you are interested more in me as a person (hopefully you love dogs; that page is primarily about my pets). Your feedback and engagement are invaluable, and I am committed to supporting you every step of the way in your pursuit of excellence in Information Technology.

Understanding CompTIA A+

There are a tremendous number of organizations that provide a multitude of certifications within the field. The purpose of certifications is often misled to newer individuals that they are an all-powerful source of employment and income; this is unfortunately not the case. Now with that in mind, certifications do hold tremendous value within the field but not the same as the sales-minded individuals with premium costs. Certifications have one primary purpose, and they fulfill it quite well. They are to prove the individual's knowledge in a range of categories to ensure a baseline level of understanding. This is true with even the most advanced of certifications as it is the entry level. They each have their own requirements, skillsets, and knowledgebase, but the goal is to prove the user's ability in comparison to a predetermined skill level.

Now that we have covered that item, there are a large variety of organizations that offer these highly sought after certifications. Two names tend to rise to the forefront, especially with vendor neutral considerations; those two names are CompTIA and ISC2. Both are wonderful organizations that contribute immensely to the Information Technology world. This book is meant to serve as a guide for CompTIA's A+ certification, which is broken into two examinations. Both examinations are covered in detail within this content.

The CompTIA A+ certification is, at its core, an entry-level certification to the Information Technology world. This certification covers a large portion of topics within the field, as well as many crucial elements that one would require to be successful. Individuals that have passed the exam and hold the A+ certification are often better positioned to find in-field employment, and alternatively, those with prior Information Technology experience will gain a fair amount of additional leverage. Some of the primary topics covered in this certification are

1. **Soft Skills**
    - Effective communication with clients and colleagues
    - Interpersonal skills for collaboration in team environments
    - Customer service techniques for addressing user needs
2. **Computer Hardware**
    - Understanding of motherboard components and architecture
    - Knowledge of CPU types and socket compatibility
    - Familiarity with RAM types, speeds, and installation procedures

3. **Computer Software**
    - Installation and configuration of operating systems
    - Software troubleshooting techniques
    - Familiarity with productivity software suites
4. **Operating Systems**
    - Installation and configuration of Windows, Linux, and macOS
    - Management of system settings and user accounts
    - Understanding of file system structures and permissions
5. **Laptops**
    - Identification of laptop components and peripherals
    - Maintenance procedures for laptops, including cleaning and battery management
    - Troubleshooting common laptop hardware and software issues
6. **Mobile Devices**
    - Configuration of mobile device settings and preferences
    - Understanding of mobile operating systems and app installation procedures
    - Implementation of security measures for mobile devices

7. **Printers**
    - Identification of printer types and printing technologies
    - Maintenance tasks such as ink cartridge replacement and print head cleaning
    - Troubleshooting common printer hardware and software issues
8. **Networking**
    - Basic networking concepts, including IP addressing and subnetting
    - Configuration of network devices such as routers and switches
    - Troubleshooting network connectivity issues
9. **Wireless Networking**
    - Configuration and management of wireless access points
    - Implementation of wireless security protocols such as WPA2 and WPA3
    - Troubleshooting common wireless networking issues
10. **Cloud Computing**
    - Understanding of cloud service models (IaaS, PaaS, SaaS)
    - Deployment and management of virtual machines in the cloud
    - Implementation of cloud security best practices

11. **Security**
    - Recognition of common security threats and vulnerabilities
    - Implementation of security best practices for data protection
    - Incident response procedures for handling security breaches
12. **Basic Troubleshooting**
    - Utilization of troubleshooting methodologies such as divide and conquer
    - Identification and isolation of hardware and software issues
    - Documentation of troubleshooting steps and outcomes

Each of these components will be covered within this publication, as each is required to successfully pass the CompTIA A+ examinations. We will be very thoroughly going over each topic and subtopic to ensure all readers are provided the opportunity to have the knowledge needed to surpass the baseline metrics. I did want to make mention that these outlined topics are not directly the chapters, but each of these will fully be included in all the proper sections.

Career Opportunities with A+

The CompTIA A+ certification stands as a beacon of opportunity in the expanse of the IT industry. With its comprehensive coverage of foundational knowledge and skills, achieving this certification opens doors to a multitude of career paths and professional growth opportunities.

So, why pursue the A+ certification? Let's review some of the benefits for those that obtain this certification. All of these are, of course, in addition to proving a baseline level of understanding through each domain the A+ exam covers, as well as a nice entryway to most technical recruiters.

First and foremost, the A+ certification serves as a testament to your technical prowess and proficiency. By mastering essential concepts in hardware, software, networking, and security, you demonstrate to employers that you possess the fundamental skills necessary to excel in various IT roles. Whether you're troubleshooting hardware issues, configuring operating systems, or securing network infrastructures, the A+ certification validates your ability to tackle real-world IT challenges with confidence and competence. Moreover, obtaining the A+ certification enhances your marketability and credibility in the eyes of employers. In today's competitive job market, certifications serve as valuable differentiators, setting candidates apart from their peers. With the A+ certification prominently featured on your resume, you signal to potential employers that you are a dedicated professional committed to continuous learning and professional development.

But the benefits of the A+ certification extend far beyond mere job prospects. With this credential in hand, you gain access to a vast network of fellow IT professionals and industry experts. CompTIA's global community provides opportunities for networking, collaboration, and knowledge sharing, enriching your professional journey and fostering growth and innovation in the field. Furthermore, the A+ certification serves as a springboard for career advancement and specialization. Armed with a solid foundation in IT essentials, you can pursue more advanced certifications and specialized training programs tailored to your career aspirations. Whether you're interested in cybersecurity, networking, cloud computing, or beyond, the A+ certification lays the groundwork for continued success and professional fulfillment.

In addition to traditional employment opportunities, the A+ certification opens doors to a wide range of freelance and entrepreneurial ventures. With your newfound expertise, you can offer IT consulting services, troubleshoot technical issues for small businesses, or even launch your own IT startup. The possibilities are endless, limited only by your imagination and ambition. The A+ certification empowers you to adapt and thrive in a rapidly evolving technological landscape. With technology advancing at breakneck speed, staying abreast of the latest trends and innovations is paramount to success in the IT industry. The A+ certification equips you with the knowledge and skills needed to navigate this ever-changing terrain with confidence, ensuring your relevance and resilience in the face of technological disruption.

Finally, pursuing the A+ certification is an investment in your future—one that promises not only financial rewards but also personal and professional fulfillment. By honing your skills, expanding your knowledge, and joining a global community of like-minded professionals, you embark on a journey of lifelong learning and growth, fueled by passion, curiosity, and the relentless pursuit of excellence. As you can see, it's much more than just a credential—it's a gateway to endless possibilities and opportunities in the dynamic and rewarding field of Information Technology. Whether you're launching your career, advancing your skills, or exploring new horizons, the A+ certification sets you on the path to success, empowering you to achieve your dreams and make your mark in the world of IT.

Effective Knowledge Retention Techniques

Mastering the diversity of concepts covered in the CompTIA A+ certification requires more than just passive learning—it demands active engagement and strategic approaches to knowledge retention. In this section, we'll explore proven techniques to help you absorb, retain, and recall information effectively, ensuring that you're fully prepared to ace the A+ exams and excel in your IT career. These are tried and proven study methods, and there is no singular one-size-fits-all methodology. Try these out and see which works best for you:

1. **Spaced Repetition**: One of the most effective strategies for long-term retention is spaced repetition. Rather than cramming information all at once, spaced repetition involves revisiting material at increasingly longer intervals over time. By spacing out your study sessions and reviewing material consistently, you reinforce your memory and strengthen neural connections, leading to more durable learning outcomes. As odd and out of place as it may sound, with this method, it is not uncommon for one to take brief naps between study sessions. This allows for your brain to better absorb the studied material and additionally provides a much-needed rest.

2. **Active Learning**: Engaging actively with the material is essential for deepening understanding and retention. Instead of passively reading or listening to lectures, actively participate in your learning process by summarizing key concepts in your own words, creating flashcards for review, or teaching the material to a study partner. Actively engaging with the content promotes deeper processing and enhances memory retention.

3. **Visualization Techniques**: Harness the power of visualization to enhance memory retention. Create visual aids such as mind maps, diagrams, or flowcharts to represent complex concepts visually. Visualizing information in this way helps reinforce connections between ideas and facilitates easier recall during exams. Additionally, mnemonics and acronyms can aid in memorizing lists or sequences of information by associating them with vivid mental images or catchy phrases.

4. **Interleaved Practice**: Rather than focusing exclusively on one topic at a time, distribute your study sessions with a variety of related subjects. Interleaved practice involves alternating between different topics or problem types during your study sessions. This approach promotes deeper learning by forcing your brain to make connections between disparate pieces of information, leading to stronger memory consolidation and retention.

5. **Active Recall**: Test your knowledge through active recall exercises to reinforce learning and identify areas for improvement. Instead of simply re-reading notes or textbooks, challenge yourself to recall information from memory without peeking. This could involve creating practice quizzes, explaining concepts aloud, or teaching the material to someone else. Active recall strengthens memory retrieval pathways and enhances long-term retention of information.

Incorporating these proven techniques into your study routine can significantly enhance your ability to retain and recall information effectively, ultimately leading to greater success in mastering the concepts covered in the CompTIA A+ certification. Experiment with different strategies to find what works best for you, and don't be afraid to adapt your approach as needed. With dedication, persistence, and the right study techniques, you'll be well-equipped to conquer the challenges of the A+ exams and embark on a rewarding career in Information Technology.

Study Practices for Success

Preparing for the CompTIA A+ certification requires diligent study and strategic planning to ensure success. In this section, we'll explore a variety of study tips and best practices to help you maximize your learning potential and achieve your goals. These are primarily standard practices but are of significant benefit as they can reduce the overall level of stress and burnout from this learning process.

1. **Create a Study Schedule**: Establish a structured study schedule that fits your lifestyle and commitments. Set aside dedicated time each day or week to focus on exam preparation and stick to your schedule consistently. Breaking down your study sessions into manageable chunks can help prevent burnout and ensure steady progress towards your goals.

2. **Set Clear Goals**: Define specific, measurable goals for your study sessions to keep yourself motivated and on track. Whether it's completing a certain number of practice questions, mastering a particular topic, or achieving a target score on a practice exam, having clear objectives helps guide your study efforts and measure your progress along the way.

3. **Utilize Multiple Resources**: Don't rely solely on one study resource—explore a variety of materials to gain a well-rounded understanding of the exam topics. Supplement your textbook or study guide with online courses, video tutorials, practice exams, and other resources to reinforce your learning and expose yourself to different perspectives and explanations.

4. **Practice, Practice, Practice**: Practice is key to mastering the material and building confidence for the exam. Take advantage of practice questions, simulations, and hands-on labs to reinforce your understanding of key concepts and familiarize yourself with the exam format. Aim to replicate exam conditions as closely as possible during your practice sessions to simulate the real testing environment.

5. **Stay Organized**: Keep your study materials organized and easily accessible to streamline your study process. Create folders or digital notebooks to categorize notes, practice exams, flashcards, and other resources. Having a well-organized study space helps minimize distractions and allows you to focus more effectively on your learning objectives.

6. **Stay Engaged and Active**: Maintain an active and engaged approach to your studies by actively participating in learning activities. Take notes, ask questions, seek clarification on challenging topics, and participate in study groups or online forums to interact with fellow learners and exchange ideas.

Engaging actively with the material promotes deeper understanding and retention of key concepts.

7. **Take Breaks and Practice Self-care**: Don't forget to prioritize your well-being during your study journey. Take regular breaks to rest and recharge, and practice self-care activities such as exercise, mindfulness, and relaxation techniques to alleviate stress and maintain balance in your life. Remember that a healthy mind and body are essential for optimal learning and performance. This is another section that I can recommend putting the book down, albeit briefly, and taking a nap.

8. **Review and Reflect**: Regularly review your progress and reflect on your learning journey to identify areas for improvement and adjustment. Assess your strengths and weaknesses, adapt your study strategies as needed, and celebrate your achievements along the way. Reflecting on your experiences helps reinforce learning and empowers you to make informed decisions about your study approach.

By utilizing these study tips and best practices into your exam preparation routine, you'll be well-equipped to tackle the challenges of the CompTIA A+ certification with confidence and success. Stay disciplined, stay focused, and stay motivated—your hard work and dedication will pay off as you embark on this exciting journey towards achieving your certification goals. If you can master these study methods and improve self-discipline, you are already going to perform better than most.

Summary: Unlocking the Path to Success with the CompTIA A+

In this introductory chapter, we've broken down the transformative power of the CompTIA A+ certification—an essential steppingstone in the dynamic field of Information Technology (IT). We began by reviewing the true purpose and significance of certifications, debunking common misconceptions, and shedding light on their value as tools for validating skills and knowledge in the IT industry. Certifications, including the CompTIA A+ certification, serve a fundamental purpose—to demonstrate an individual's proficiency in a specific set of skills and technologies. They provide a standardized framework for assessing competency and establishing a baseline level of understanding, making them invaluable assets for aspiring IT professionals and seasoned veterans alike.

Amidst a multitude of certification providers, CompTIA and ISC2 stand out as leaders, offering comprehensive and vendor-neutral certification programs that cater to diverse skill sets and career aspirations. The CompTIA A+ certification holds a prominent position as a foundational credential for entry-level IT professionals, covering a wide range of topics essential for success in the field. The benefits of pursuing the CompTIA A+ certification are manifold. From enhancing marketability and credibility to opening doors to diverse career opportunities, the A+ certification offers a pathway to professional growth and advancement in the IT industry. Whether you're seeking employment in traditional IT roles, exploring freelance opportunities, or launching your own IT venture, the A+ certification equips you with the skills and knowledge needed to succeed.

Moreover, obtaining the A+ certification isn't just about passing exams—it's about embarking on a journey of continuous learning and professional development. With access to a global community of IT professionals, ongoing training resources, and opportunities for specialization, the A+ certification lays the groundwork for a fulfilling and rewarding career in IT. Throughout this chapter, we also examined effective knowledge retention techniques and study tips to help you maximize your learning potential and ace the A+ exams. From spaced repetition and active learning to visualization techniques and active recall, these strategies empower you to absorb, retain, and recall information effectively, ensuring that you're fully prepared to conquer the challenges of the certification exams.

As we conclude this chapter, we invite you to embrace the opportunities that lie ahead on your journey towards achieving the CompTIA A+ certification. Whether you're a newcomer to the field or a seasoned professional seeking to expand your skill set, the A+ certification serves as a beacon of opportunity, guiding you towards success in the dynamic and ever-evolving world of Information Technology.

Join us as we continue to explore the intricacies of the CompTIA A+ certification in the chapters ahead, unlocking the secrets to mastering the essentials of IT and paving the way for a fulfilling and rewarding career journey.

CHAPTER 2

Portable Power: A Guide to Laptop Essentials

Let's look at the world of portable computing with a comprehensive exploration of laptops in this enlightening chapter. We'll continue our learning to establish a solid foundation of knowledge, covering all aspects related to laptops. From their compact components to the unique challenges they present, we'll leave no stone unturned in our aim to understand these essential devices. From processors and RAM to storage options and display technologies, we'll explore each element in detail, shedding light on their roles in powering these compact computing machines.

But our exploration won't stop at hardware alone. We'll also review all common features and functionalities that laptops offer, from sleek designs and lightweight construction to versatile connectivity options and ergonomic considerations. By understanding the full spectrum of features available, you'll be equipped to make informed decisions when selecting the perfect laptop for your needs. However, with great power comes great responsibility, and laptops are no exception. Throughout this chapter, we'll also examine the unique challenges and considerations that accompany portable computing.

© Kodi A. Cochran 2024

K. A. Cochran, *CompTIA A+ Certification Companion*, Certification Study Companion Series, https://doi.org/10.1007/979-8-8688-0867-8_2

But fear not—our journey doesn't end with challenges alone. We'll also explore the vast number of opportunities and possibilities that laptops unlock in both professional and personal spheres. Whether you're a student seeking mobility and convenience or a professional on the go, laptops offer unparalleled flexibility and productivity enhancements that can revolutionize your daily workflow. Join us as we continue this enlightening exploration of laptops, uncovering their secrets, unraveling their complexities, and discovering the transformative power of portable computing.

At the end of this chapter, you'll emerge with an appreciation for these indispensable devices and the knowledge to harness their full potential in your own life and endeavors.

Understanding Laptop Components

From the sleek exterior to the compact internal circuitry, we'll extensively break down the anatomy of these portable powerhouses, unraveling their secrets and uncovering the technology that drives them forward. Laptops are inherently built for mobility, ease of use, and convenience. This, in turn, with the modern, on-the-go lifestyles, creates some unique challenges and differences to what a traditional computer would host. With these considerations in mind, they have all the core components of a standard desktop or workstation, however, certain factors like battery life, heat management, and even weight become concerning factors when considering components.

1. **Processor (CPU):** At the heart of every laptop lies the central processing unit (CPU), a marvel of modern engineering responsible for executing instructions and performing complex calculations. We'll view the inner workings of the CPU, exploring its architecture, clock speed, and cache memory to understand how it powers the entire system.

2. **Random Access Memory (RAM):** As we navigate the digital landscape, we encounter the temporary storage known as random access memory (RAM). Here, data is swiftly accessed and manipulated by the CPU, facilitating multitasking and ensuring smooth performance. We'll learn the role of RAM in enhancing system responsiveness and discuss strategies for optimizing its usage.

3. **Storage Drive:** Beyond the realm of temporary storage, we encounter the need for long-term data storage. Whether it be a traditional hard disk drive (HDD) or a lightning-fast solid-state drive (SSD), the storage drive serves as the repository for our files, documents, and applications.

4. **Motherboard:** As we peer beneath the surface, we encounter the motherboard, the central hub that connects all components of the laptop together. We'll unravel the labyrinth of circuitry and connectors, tracing the pathways that facilitate communication between the CPU, RAM, storage, and peripherals.

5. **Graphics Processing Unit (GPU):** In the realm of multimedia and gaming, the graphics processing unit (GPU) reigns supreme. We'll review the power of dedicated graphics processing, exploring the capabilities of modern GPUs in rendering stunning visuals and immersive gaming experiences.

6. **Display Screen:** Behold the window to the digital world—the display screen. Whether it be a vibrant LCD or a dazzling LED panel, the display screen serves as our portal to productivity and entertainment. We'll discuss the various display technologies, resolutions, and features that define the modern laptop experience.

7. **Keyboard:** As we navigate the digital landscape, we rely on the tactile feedback of the keyboard to input commands and express our thoughts. We'll examine the ergonomic design and layout of laptop keyboards, discussing strategies for efficient typing and ergonomic comfort.

8. **Touchpad/Trackpad:** Alongside the keyboard, we encounter the touchpad/trackpad—a versatile pointing device that allows us to navigate with precision and fluidity. We'll explore the intuitive gestures and multitouch capabilities that make trackpads indispensable companions in our digital journeys.

9. **Battery:** In the realm of mobility, the battery stands as the lifeline, providing power to our laptops when we venture beyond the confines of electrical outlets. We'll discuss the various battery technologies, capacity ratings, and power management strategies that influence battery life and longevity.

10. **Charging Port:** When the battery runs low, we turn to the charging port to replenish our laptop's power reserves. We'll learn the various charging standards and connector types, discussing the importance of compatibility and efficiency in charging solutions.

11. **Connectivity Ports:** As we seek to expand our digital horizons, we encounter a multitude of connectivity ports that enable us to connect external devices and peripherals. From USB and HDMI to Ethernet and audio ports, we'll explore the diverse ecosystem of connectivity options that enhance the versatility and functionality of laptops.
12. **Wireless Network Adapter:** In an increasingly connected world, the wireless network adapter serves as our gateway to the Internet and beyond. We'll discuss the evolution of wireless networking standards, exploring the capabilities of modern Wi-Fi adapters and the importance of signal strength and reliability in wireless connectivity.
13. **Webcam:** In the realm of communication and collaboration, the webcam serves as our digital eyes and ears, enabling video conferencing, streaming, and content creation. We'll review the evolution of webcam technology, discussing the features and capabilities that define modern webcam experiences.
14. **Microphone:** Alongside the webcam, we encounter the microphone—a vital component in capturing clear and crisp audio for voice calls, recordings, and multimedia production. We'll discuss the various microphone types and technologies, exploring strategies for optimizing audio quality and reducing background noise.

15. **Speakers:** As we immerse ourselves in the realm of multimedia and entertainment, we rely on the speakers to deliver rich, immersive audio experiences. We'll explore the evolution of laptop speaker technology, discussing the factors that influence audio quality and the importance of audio enhancements and equalization.

16. **Cooling System:** Behind the scenes, the cooling system works tirelessly to dissipate heat generated by the laptop's components, ensuring optimal performance and reliability. We'll discuss the various cooling solutions employed in laptops, from passive heat sinks to active cooling fans, exploring strategies for managing thermals and mitigating overheating.

17. **Internal Components:** Beyond the components mentioned above, laptops house a myriad of internal components that facilitate their operation. From sensors and controllers to adapters and connectors, we'll explore the inner workings of laptops and the role each component plays in delivering a seamless computing experience.

I know there were many components and peripherals to remember, but take your time to understand each component and its correlating responsibility within a laptop's functional environment. By the end of this chapter, you'll emerge with a newfound appreciation for the craftsmanship and engineering behind modern laptops, equipped with the knowledge to make informed decisions when selecting and optimizing your portable computing companion.

CPU Differences Between Traditional Desktops and Laptops

Although they still maintain the same fundamental purpose of executing instructions and performing calculations, there are slight differences between a laptop's CPU and that of a traditional desktop or workstation. These are primarily due to the physical size of the laptop, the focus on energy efficiency, and the compatibility requirements. Here is a brief overview of the differences between a CPU designed for laptops and that of one for a standard desktop:

1. **Form Factor:** One of the most notable differences is the form factor of the CPU itself. Desktop CPUs are typically larger and have more robust cooling solutions, such as heatsinks and fans, due to the larger chassis and better airflow in desktop computers. In contrast, laptop CPUs are smaller and more compact to fit within the limited space constraints of a laptop's form factor.

2. **Power Consumption:** Laptops prioritize energy efficiency and battery life, so laptop CPUs are designed to consume less power compared to their desktop counterparts. This often means that laptop CPUs have lower thermal design power (TDP) ratings and operate at lower clock speeds to conserve battery life.

3. **Performance:** While desktop CPUs generally offer higher performance capabilities than laptop CPUs due to their larger size and better cooling, advancements in technology have narrowed the performance gap between desktop and laptop

CPUs in recent years. High-end laptops, particularly those designed for gaming or professional use, may feature powerful CPUs that rival desktop performance to some extent.

4. **Integrated Graphics:** Many laptop CPUs include integrated graphics processing units (GPUs) on the same die, allowing for better power efficiency and reduced heat generation compared to discrete GPUs. Desktop CPUs typically do not include integrated graphics, as desktop computers often use dedicated graphics cards for gaming and graphics-intensive tasks.

5. **Socket Compatibility:** Desktop CPUs and laptop CPUs often use different socket designs due to the differences in form factor and power requirements. Desktop CPUs typically use larger sockets such as LGA (Land Grid Array) or PGA (Pin Grid Array), while laptop CPUs use smaller sockets optimized for mobile applications such as BGA (Ball Grid Array) or FP (Flip Chip).

Overall, while desktop and laptop CPUs share many similarities in terms of functionality, there are distinct differences in their design, power consumption, and performance characteristics to suit the specific needs and constraints of each computing platform. Keep these thoughts in mind, particularly with regards to size and power constraints that exist within laptops. Try to imagine how these issues can be addressed and overcome as we progress.

Comparing and Contrasting RAM Designed for Laptops Against Desktops

Once again, we find ourselves looking at some key differences between the unique requirements of a laptop and those of a standard desktop. Where laptops are built to be highly portable, slim, lightweight, and host a strong battery life, traditional RAM does not fit these requirements at all. Laptops utilize a different form factor of RAM, and there are some significant differences. With that in mind, let's break down the differences between traditional RAM and that of the RAM you would see within a laptop.

1. **Physical Size and Form Factor:** Desktop RAM modules are typically larger and longer, utilizing standard DIMM (Dual Inline Memory Module) form factors such as DDR4 DIMMs. In contrast, laptop RAM modules are smaller and more compact to fit within the limited space available in a laptop's chassis. Laptop RAM modules often use smaller form factors such as SODIMMs (Small Outline Dual Inline Memory Modules).

2. **Voltage Requirements:** Laptop RAM modules generally operate at lower voltage levels compared to desktop RAM modules to conserve power and improve battery life. Low-voltage DDR4 RAM (DDR4L) is commonly used in laptops to reduce power consumption, whereas desktop RAM typically operates at standard voltage levels.

3. **Performance:** While both desktop and laptop RAM modules are available in various speeds and capacities, desktop RAM modules often have higher performance capabilities due to their larger physical

size and better cooling. Desktop systems may support faster RAM speeds and larger capacities compared to laptops, allowing for better overall system performance and multitasking capabilities.

4. **Upgradability:** In many desktop systems, RAM modules are easily accessible and can be upgraded or replaced by the user. Desktop motherboards typically have multiple RAM slots, allowing for easy expansion of RAM capacity. In contrast, laptop RAM modules are often soldered directly onto the motherboard or installed in slots that are more difficult to access, making upgrades less convenient and sometimes impossible.

5. **Heat Dissipation:** Desktop RAM modules may feature larger heat spreaders or heat sinks to dissipate heat generated during operation, allowing for better thermal management and stability under heavy loads. In contrast, laptop RAM modules are designed to operate within the thermal constraints of a compact laptop chassis, with less emphasis on elaborate heat dissipation solutions.

6. **Cost:** Due to their smaller size and lower voltage requirements, laptop RAM modules may be slightly more expensive than their desktop counterparts with similar specifications. However, prices can vary depending on factors such as speed, capacity, and brand.

Overall, while desktop and laptop RAM modules serve the same basic function of providing temporary storage for data and instructions, there are differences in their physical design, voltage requirements, performance capabilities, upgradability, heat dissipation, and cost to accommodate the unique needs and constraints of each computing platform. The requirements created by a mobile device result in some interesting alternatives and accommodations.

Various Forms of RAM and Their Comparison

Now that we have reviewed the requirements RAM must adhere to within a laptop, we can begin to break it down further. The form factor of RAM utilized inside a laptop is significantly different from that of a desktop or workstation. Let's compare the different types of RAM (Random Access Memory) used in laptops, including DIMM and SODIMM, considering various factors relevant to the CompTIA A+ certification:

1. **Form Factor:**
    - **DIMM (Dual In-Line Memory Module):** DIMM RAM modules are larger in size and typically used in desktop computers due to their larger chassis and space availability.
    - **SODIMM (Small Outline Dual In-Line Memory Module):** SODIMM RAM modules are smaller in size, specifically designed for laptops and other small form factor devices where space is limited.
2. **Compatibility:**
    - **DIMM:** Desktop computers typically use DIMM RAM modules, and they are not compatible with laptops due to differences in physical size and connector layout.

- **SODIMM:** SODIMM RAM modules are specifically designed for laptops and other small form factor devices, ensuring compatibility with the laptop's memory slots.

3. **Capacity and Speed:**
   - **DIMM and SODIMM:** Both DIMM and SODIMM RAM modules are available in various capacities (e.g., 4GB, 8GB, 16GB, etc.) and speeds (e.g., DDR4 2400MHz, DDR4 3200MHz, etc.). The specific capacity and speed depend on the laptop's specifications and compatibility.

4. **Installation and Upgrade:**
   - **DIMM and SODIMM:** Upgrading or replacing RAM in a laptop usually involves accessing the memory slots located under a panel on the underside of the laptop. It requires removing screws and carefully inserting the new RAM modules into the slots.

5. **Performance and Power Consumption:**
   - **DIMM and SODIMM:** RAM modules contribute to the overall performance of the laptop by providing faster access to data and applications. They consume minimal power and contribute to system stability and responsiveness.

Understanding the differences between DIMM and SODIMM is essential for CompTIA A+ certification candidates, as it helps them diagnose and resolve issues related to memory and storage in laptops. Not only is it a requirement of the exam, but it is significant to the field of Information Technology and will likely be of use later down the road.

Storage Requirements for a Portable Solution

Like some of the other considerations, the requirements inherited from the storage solution are slightly altered. This is primarily due to the concern of reducing battery drainage but also to reduce the amount of heat generated by the device. Some of the key differences between storage solution requirements of desktops and laptops are:

1. **Physical Size and Form Factor:** One of the most noticeable differences is the physical size and form factor of storage devices. In desktop computers, traditional hard disk drives (HDDs) and solid-state drives (SSDs) typically use larger form factors such as 3.5-inch or 2.5-inch drives. In contrast, storage devices for laptops are designed to fit within the smaller form factors of 2.5-inch or M.2 drives to accommodate the space limitations of laptop chassis.

2. **Power Consumption:** Laptops prioritize energy efficiency and battery life, so storage devices for laptops are often designed to consume less power compared to those for desktops. This can affect the type of storage technology used and the power-saving features implemented in laptop storage devices to maximize battery life.

3. **Performance:** While both desktop and laptop storage devices are available at various speeds and capacities, there can be differences in performance characteristics. High-performance desktop HDDs and SSDs may offer faster read/write speeds

and larger capacities compared to their laptop counterparts, although advancements in technology have narrowed this gap in recent years.

4. **Connectivity:** Desktop storage devices typically use standard interfaces such as SATA (Serial ATA) or PCIe (Peripheral Component Interconnect Express) to connect to the motherboard. In contrast, storage devices for laptops may use specialized connectors such as M.2 or mSATA to fit within the limited space available in a laptop's chassis. Additionally, some laptops may use proprietary connectors or storage formats for integrated storage solutions.

5. **Durability and Shock Resistance:** Laptops are often subjected to more movement and physical stress compared to desktop computers, so storage devices for laptops may be designed with enhanced durability and shock resistance features to withstand bumps, vibrations, and impacts. SSDs are inherently more resistant to shock and vibration compared to traditional HDDs, making them a popular choice for laptop storage.

6. **Heat Dissipation:** Laptops have limited airflow and cooling capabilities compared to desktop computers, so storage devices for laptops may be designed with lower heat generation and better thermal management in mind. This can influence the choice of storage technology and the implementation of heat dissipation solutions in laptop storage devices.

Overall, while storage devices for desktops and laptops serve the same basic function of storing data and programs; there are differences in their physical design, power consumption, performance characteristics, connectivity options, durability, and heat dissipation to meet the unique needs and constraints of each computing platform.

Charging Ports and Battery Management in Laptops

In laptop computing, the battery serves as the lifesource of power, enabling users to untether themselves from traditional power outlets and embrace mobility. Paired with charging ports designed to replenish the battery's energy reserves, laptops offer unparalleled flexibility and convenience. In this section, we'll review the necessity of charging ports and battery management in laptops, exploring their design, functionality, and importance in the modern computing landscape.

Charging Ports

At the heart of every laptop lies the charging port, a gateway through which electrical power is supplied to the device. Charging ports come in various shapes, sizes, and configurations, each designed to accommodate different charging standards and connector types. Common charging port standards include

- **DC Barrel Jack:** A cylindrical connector that plugs into the laptop's power input port, commonly found on older laptop models and some budget-friendly devices.
- **USB Type-C:** A versatile connector that supports both power delivery and data transfer, USB Type-C ports have become increasingly common in modern laptops due to their compact size and universal compatibility.

- **Proprietary Connectors:** Some laptop manufacturers use proprietary charging connectors that are unique to their devices, offering specific advantages such as faster charging speeds or additional features.

The choice of charging port can influence factors such as charging speed, compatibility with third-party accessories, and overall user experience. As technology evolves, newer charging standards and connector types continue to emerge, driving innovation in laptop design and charging solutions. With that all said, charging ports are not typically at the forefront of a consumer's mind, but are sometimes considerations with larger enterprise purchases. It is highly unlikely that a charging port will be the deciding factor on a purchase or deployment.

Battery Management

Behind the scenes, sophisticated battery management systems work tirelessly to regulate power consumption, optimize charging efficiency, and prolong battery life in laptops. This is also of importance when considering troubleshooting battery life and is often missed. It is a best practice to ensure that battery management is being properly addressed and is worth continual review. These systems employ a variety of techniques to achieve these objectives, including

- **Charge Controller:** A dedicated microcontroller or charge controller oversees the charging process, monitoring parameters such as voltage, current, and temperature to ensure safe and efficient charging.
- **Battery Health Monitoring:** Laptops often include built-in software utilities that provide insights into battery health, including capacity degradation,

charging cycles, and estimated battery lifespan. Users can leverage these tools to optimize their charging habits and prolong battery longevity.

- **Power Management Settings:** Operating system settings allow users to customize power management preferences, such as battery saver mode, screen brightness adjustments, and sleep settings, to maximize battery life and efficiency.
- **Fast Charging Technologies:** Advancements in battery technology have led to the development of fast charging technologies such as Qualcomm Quick Charge and USB Power Delivery (PD), which enable rapid charging of laptop batteries while maintaining safety and reliability.

Ensuring thorough battery management while also leveraging innovative charging technologies, laptop manufacturers strive to deliver a seamless and reliable user experience. In doing so, this empowers users to stay productive and connected wherever their journeys may take them. This is the assurance that a laptop can maintain its functional level of portability and is an essential factor with laptop computing.

Wi-Fi and It's Contribution to a Portable Device

One of the most significant appeals that a laptop portrays to its users is the ease of portability, freedom of cords, and the influence it has towards an on-the-go lifestyle. This is even further advanced in the consideration that it is largely a standard now that all laptops utilize Wi-Fi technologies and have a wireless network card integrated to provide wireless connectivity as a standard feature. This allows for the user to connect to the network more easily, wherever given the proper credentials and permissions, without the need to provide a cabled connection. There are many benefits that this brings to the table, and each is no more valid than the next, but it is worth understanding as it is the very means that draws users in.

Bluetooth's Support of Wireless Peripherals

Although this is something that can be accomplished through alternative measures, such as utilizing a wireless connector or dongle, Bluetooth acts to further expand upon a truly wireless product. Many devices support Bluetooth connectivity, from gaming headsets, keyboards, and controllers to even peripherals designed for the workplace. With this becoming a more normal and commonplace feature, one can look to pair devices for a much easier connection without the need of additional USB slots being consumed by the wireless adaptors. Keep in mind that Bluetooth is not a network connection nor does it provide Internet connectivity, but it is a common player with peripheral connections.

Laptop Display Technologies a Comparison and Contrast

Due to the unique nature and requirements that a portable device involves, laptops have a few various display technologies, each with their own benefits and detractors. Each of these has its own unique purpose, and it would be difficult to argue one that is best for every situation. Let's continue and review some of the benefits that these various display technologies provide, as well as ensure we understand the differences as these items are often on the A+ exam:

LCD (Liquid Crystal Display):

- **Overview:** LCD displays are the foundation of laptop display technology, utilizing liquid crystals to manipulate light and produce images. These displays consist of layers of polarized glass and liquid crystals that react to electric current, controlling the passage of light to create images on the screen.
- **Features:** LCD displays offer good color reproduction, energy efficiency, and durability, making them a popular choice for laptops across various price points. They typically provide sharp image quality and can display high-resolution content, enhancing the visual experience for users.
- **Applications:** LCD displays are suitable for general computing tasks, multimedia consumption, and productivity applications. They are commonly found in laptops used for office work, web browsing, watching videos, and viewing photos due to their versatile performance and reliability.

LED (Light-Emitting Diode):

- **Overview:** LED displays are a type of LCD display that utilizes light-emitting diodes as backlighting instead of traditional cold cathode fluorescent lamps (CCFLs). LEDs offer improved energy efficiency and can be dynamically controlled to enhance contrast and brightness levels.
- **Features:** LED displays offer improved energy efficiency, brighter images, and better contrast ratios compared to traditional LCD displays. They are also

more environmentally friendly and have a longer lifespan, reducing maintenance and replacement costs over time.

- **Applications:** LED displays are commonly found in modern laptops and offer enhanced visual experiences for users. They are well-suited for multimedia content consumption, gaming, and professional applications where color accuracy and brightness are essential.

OLED (Organic Light-Emitting Diode):

- **Overview:** OLED displays utilize organic compounds that emit light when an electric current is applied, offering superior image quality and flexibility. Unlike LCD displays, OLED panels do not require a backlight, allowing for thinner and more flexible screen designs.
- **Features:** OLED displays boast deeper blacks, better contrast ratios, wider viewing angles, and thinner profiles compared to LCD and LED displays. They also have faster response times, making them ideal for high-speed gaming and multimedia applications.
- **Applications:** OLED displays are increasingly used in high-end laptops and portable devices for their superior visual performance and design versatility. They excel in applications where vibrant colors, high contrast, and immersive viewing experiences are desired.

Touch Display:

- **Overview:** Touchscreen displays enable users to interact with laptops using touch gestures, enhancing user experience and productivity. These displays feature touch-sensitive panels that detect and respond to finger or stylus input, allowing for intuitive navigation and input methods.
- **Technologies:** Touch displays may utilize resistive, capacitive, or infrared touchscreen technologies, each with their own advantages and limitations. Capacitive touchscreens are the most common, offering high sensitivity and multi-touch support for gestures like pinch-to-zoom and swipe.
- **Applications:** Touch displays are widely used in laptops for tasks such as navigation, input, and drawing, catering to diverse user preferences and workflows. They are particularly popular in convertible and 2-in-1 laptops, offering flexibility for both traditional keyboard input and touch-based interactions.

IPS (In-Plane Switching):

- **Overview:** IPS displays offer superior color accuracy, wider viewing angles, and better color consistency compared to traditional LCD displays. These panels utilize a unique arrangement of liquid crystals to minimize color shifts and maintain image quality from various viewing angles.

- **Features:** IPS technology is commonly used in high-end laptops and professional-grade monitors for tasks requiring accurate color reproduction, such as graphic design and photo editing. IPS displays typically have faster response times and higher refresh rates than TN panels, making them suitable for gaming as well.
- **Applications:** IPS displays excel in multimedia consumption, content creation, and professional applications where color accuracy is paramount. They are ideal for tasks such as photo editing, video production, and graphic design, providing users with accurate and consistent color representation for their work.

TN (Twisted Nematic):

- **Overview:** TN displays are known for their fast response times and affordability, making them a popular choice for budget-friendly laptops and gaming monitors. These panels feature twisted nematic liquid crystals that can change orientation quickly, resulting in rapid pixel transitions and reduced motion blur.
- **Features:** TN displays offer fast response times but typically have inferior color accuracy and narrower viewing angles compared to IPS displays. They are well-suited for gaming and multimedia applications where fast response times are prioritized over color accuracy.
- **Applications:** TN displays are suitable for gaming, multimedia, and general computing tasks where fast response times are prioritized over color accuracy. They are commonly found in gaming laptops and budget-friendly monitors, offering high refresh rates and low input lag for immersive gaming experiences.

High Refresh Rate Displays:

- **Overview:** High refresh rate displays refresh the screen more frequently than standard displays, offering smoother motion and reduced motion blur. These panels can refresh at rates higher than the traditional 60Hz, providing users with a more fluid and responsive viewing experience.
- **Features:** High refresh rate displays are ideal for gaming and multimedia applications, providing an immersive and responsive viewing experience. They reduce motion blur and screen tearing, resulting in smoother gameplay and enhanced visual clarity for fast-paced action scenes.
- **Applications:** Gaming laptops often feature high refresh rate displays to deliver fluid gameplay and enhance the gaming experience for users. These displays are also beneficial for multimedia consumption, especially when viewing high-definition content or engaging in graphic-intensive tasks such as video editing or 3D rendering.

By understanding these laptop display technologies, IT professionals can effectively troubleshoot display issues, recommend suitable laptops for specific use cases, and provide valuable support to users in their computing endeavors. The CompTIA A+ certification equips IT professionals with the knowledge and skills needed to navigate the ever-evolving landscape of laptop display technologies with confidence and proficiency.

Step-by-Step Guide: How To Disassemble a Laptop

Disassembling a laptop requires careful attention to detail and adherence to proper procedures to avoid damaging the device or compromising its functionality. In this step-by-step guide, we'll walk through the process of disassembling a laptop, covering essential techniques and precautions recommended by the CompTIA A+ certification. Throughout this process, it is highly recommended to take photos as you go, this will allow you to backtrack more easily, if need be, as well as provide a visual comparison of its prior state.

Step 1: Preparation and Safety

Before beginning the disassembly process, it's essential to prepare the workspace and ensure safety precautions are in place:

- Gather the necessary tools, including screwdrivers, prying tools, and antistatic wrist straps, to prevent electrostatic discharge (ESD) damage.
- Power off the laptop; unplug the AC adapter.
- Work on a clean, flat surface with adequate lighting to facilitate visibility and prevent loss of small components.

Step 2: Removal of External Components

Start by removing any external components or peripherals attached to the laptop:

- Disconnect external devices such as USB drives, external monitors, and peripherals like mice and keyboards.
- Remove any expansion cards, such as SD cards or ExpressCard modules, from their respective slots.

- Carefully remove the laptop's battery by following manufacturer guidelines, usually involving the release of retention clips or screws.

Step 3: Accessing Internal Components

Next, access the internal components of the laptop by removing the outer casing:

- Locate and remove the screws securing the bottom panel or cover of the laptop using a suitable screwdriver. Keep track of the screws and their respective locations to ensure proper reassembly later.
- Use a prying tool or plastic opening tool to gently separate the bottom panel from the laptop's chassis, being mindful of any hidden clips or latches that may secure it in place.
- Once the bottom panel is removed, carefully set it aside, exposing the internal components housed within the laptop.

Step 4: Disassembly of Internal Components

With the internal components accessible, proceed with the disassembly of specific components as needed:

- Start by disconnecting and removing the laptop's hard drive or solid-state drive (SSD), typically secured by screws or mounting brackets.
- Disconnect and remove the laptop's memory modules (RAM) by releasing the retention clips on either side of the module and gently sliding them out of their slots.

- Depending on the laptop model, additional components such as the CPU, GPU, cooling fans, and motherboard may require removal for servicing or replacement. Refer to manufacturer documentation or service manuals for specific instructions.

Step 5: Inspection and Maintenance

As you disassemble the laptop, take the opportunity to inspect internal components for signs of damage, wear, or debris accumulation:

- Check for dust buildup on cooling fans, heat sinks, and vents, and clean them using compressed air or a soft brush to maintain optimal airflow and cooling performance.
- Inspect connectors, cables, and ribbon cables for signs of wear, fraying, or damage, and replace any components showing signs of deterioration.
- Ensure proper reassembly of components by referring to manufacturer documentation or service manuals for detailed diagrams and instructions.

Step 6: Reassembly and Testing

After completing the necessary maintenance or repairs, reassemble the laptop following the reverse order of disassembly:

- Carefully reinstall internal components such as the hard drive, memory modules, and any other removed components, ensuring proper alignment and connection.
- Secure the bottom panel or cover of the laptop by reinstalling the screws removed earlier and ensuring all clips or latches are engaged.

- Reinstall the laptop's battery, plug in the AC adapter, and power on the laptop to verify proper functionality and operation.
- Perform thorough testing of the laptop's components, including the display, keyboard, touchpad, ports, and any other relevant features, to ensure everything is functioning correctly.

By following these step-by-step instructions and safety precautions, you can effectively disassemble a laptop while adhering to the guidelines outlined in the CompTIA A+ certification. Remember to exercise caution and attention to detail throughout the process to prevent damage. A trick to ensure successful reassembly and operation of the device may be to take pictures throughout the disassembly to reference upon reinstallation.

Step-by-Step Guide: How to Replace a Laptop's Screen

Replacing a laptop's screen may become necessary due to damage, malfunction, or upgrading to a higher-resolution display. It's essential to approach this task methodically and with caution to ensure a successful replacement. Here's a step-by-step guide that is aligned to the CompTIA A+ requirements:

Step 1: Preparation and Safety

Before beginning the screen replacement process, gather the necessary tools and ensure a safe working environment:

- Obtain a compatible replacement screen for your laptop model.
- Gather tools such as a screwdriver set, prying tool, and antistatic wrist strap.

- Power off the laptop, unplug the AC adapter, and remove the battery to eliminate the risk of electrical shock.
- Work on a clean, flat surface with adequate lighting to facilitate visibility and prevent damage to components.

Step 2: Removal of Bezel and Screen Frame

Start by removing the bezel or screen frame surrounding the display:

- Use a prying tool or plastic opening tool to gently pry along the edges of the bezel, releasing any clips or adhesive securing it to the display assembly.
- Slowly work your way around the perimeter of the bezel, taking care not to apply excessive force to damage the display assembly.
- Once the bezel is loosened, carefully lift it away from the screen and set it aside, exposing the screen's mounting brackets and securing screws.

Step 3: Removal of Mounting Brackets and Screws

With the bezel removed, locate, and remove the mounting brackets and screws securing the screen to the display assembly:

- Identify the mounting brackets and screws located along the sides or corners of the screen assembly.
- Use a screwdriver to remove the screws securing the mounting brackets to the screen assembly, taking note of their locations for reassembly.
- Carefully detach the mounting brackets from the screen, ensuring all screws are removed and set aside for later reassembly.

Step 4: Disconnecting Display Cables

Before fully removing the screen, disconnect any display cables or ribbon cables attached to the screen:

- Locate the display cable or ribbon cable connected to the back of the screen, typically located near the bottom edge.
- Gently disconnect the cable connector by carefully lifting the locking mechanism or tab and sliding the cable out of the connector.
- Repeat this process for any additional cables or connectors attached to the screen, such as webcam cables or wireless antenna cables.

Step 5: Screen Removal and Replacement

Once all mounting brackets, screws, and cables are disconnected, carefully remove the old screen from the display assembly:

- Hold the screen assembly by its edges and gently lift it away from the display assembly, taking care not to damage any remaining components.
- Place the old screen aside and position the replacement screen in the display assembly, ensuring it aligns with the mounting brackets and connector ports.
- Reconnect the display cables or ribbon cables to the new screen, ensuring they are securely seated and locked in place.

Step 6: Reassembly and Testing

After installing the replacement screen, reassemble the laptop by following the reverse order of disassembly:

- Secure the mounting brackets to the new screen using the previously removed screws, ensuring they are tightened evenly and securely.
- Carefully reattach the bezel or screen frame to the display assembly, applying gentle pressure to snap any clips or adhesive into place.
- Reinstall the laptop's battery, plug in the AC adapter, and power on the laptop to verify the new screen's functionality.
- Perform thorough testing of the screen, including color accuracy, brightness, and touch functionality (if applicable), to ensure everything is functioning correctly.

Following these step-by-step instructions and safety precautions, you can successfully replace a laptop's screen while adhering to the guidelines outlined in the CompTIA A+ certification. Remember to exercise caution and attention to detail throughout the process to avoid damage and ensure a seamless replacement.

Step-by-Step Guide: How to Replace a Wi-Fi Card in a Laptop

Replacing a Wi-Fi card in a laptop may be necessary to upgrade to a faster or more reliable wireless connection or to address connectivity issues. This process is not as difficult as it would sound, here we will go over a comprehensive guide to this component's replacement while also adhering to CompTIA's recommendations. Let's break this down into steps:

Step 1: Preparation and Safety

Before beginning the Wi-Fi card replacement process, gather the necessary tools and ensure a safe working environment:

- Obtain a compatible replacement Wi-Fi card for your laptop model.
- Gather tools such as a screwdriver set and an antistatic wrist strap.
- Power off the laptop, unplug the AC adapter, and remove the battery to eliminate the risk of electrical shock.
- Work on a clean, flat surface with adequate lighting to facilitate visibility and prevent damage to components.

Step 2: Accessing the Wi-Fi Card

Locate the Wi-Fi card compartment on your laptop, typically located on the underside or within the laptop's chassis:

- Use a screwdriver to remove the screws securing the access panel or cover over the Wi-Fi card compartment.
- Carefully lift or slide the access panel away from the laptop to expose the Wi-Fi card and its socket.

Step 3: Removing the Existing Wi-Fi Card

Once the Wi-Fi card is accessible, proceed with removing the existing card:

- Identify the Wi-Fi card within the compartment, noting its orientation and any retaining clips or screws securing it in place.
- If the Wi-Fi card is secured by screws, use a screwdriver to carefully remove the screws and set them aside.

- Gently grasp the edges of the Wi-Fi card and pull it straight out of its socket, taking care not to apply excessive force or damage the socket.

Step 4: Installing the Replacement Wi-Fi Card

Prepare the replacement Wi-Fi card for installation and insert it into the vacant socket:

- Align the replacement Wi-Fi card with the socket, ensuring it matches the orientation of the socket and any alignment notches or guides.
- Carefully insert the Wi-Fi card into the socket, applying even pressure until it is fully seated, and the connectors make contact.
- If the replacement Wi-Fi card is secured by screws, use a screwdriver to reinstall the screws to secure it in place within the compartment.

Step 5: Reassembly and Testing

After installing the replacement Wi-Fi card, reassemble the laptop by securing the access panel or cover:

- Position the access panel or cover over the Wi-Fi card compartment and align it with the mounting points on the laptop.
- Carefully reinstall the screws removed earlier to secure the access panel or cover in place.
- Reinstall the laptop's battery, plug in the AC adapter, and power on the laptop to verify the new Wi-Fi card's functionality.
- Test the Wi-Fi connection by connecting to a wireless network and ensuring stable and reliable connectivity.

Step 6: Driver Installation and Configuration (if necessary)

In some cases, you may need to install drivers or configure settings for the new Wi-Fi card to function properly. Make a note that some devices no longer utilize ethernet ports, and in that situation, it is best to download any necessary drivers to a USB drive or similar. If the laptop cannot connect via hardwire, there would be no option for online connectivity until the drivers are installed and configuration is complete. With that in mind, let's review the procedure:

- If the operating system does not automatically detect the new Wi-Fi card, download, and install the appropriate drivers from the manufacturer's website.
- Access the network settings or device manager on the laptop to configure the Wi-Fi connection and adjust settings as needed.

Step-by-Step Guide: How to Replace a Laptop's Charge Port

Replacing a laptop's charging port may become necessary if the port becomes damaged, loose, or fails to provide a reliable connection for charging. This is one of the most common issues that a laptop user will face over the years and is primarily attributed to improper disconnection of the charging cable, or more plainly speaking, the user's being overly rough. This is not something that would generally be replaced as an upgrade but generally only to remedy a charging issue. Here we will further break down this process in a chronological order to meet all of CompTIA's recommendations:

Step 1: Preparation and Safety

Before beginning the charging port replacement process, gather the necessary tools and ensure a safe working environment:

- Obtain a compatible replacement charging port for your laptop model.
- Gather tools such as a screwdriver set, prying tool, and antistatic wrist strap.
- Power off the laptop, unplug the AC adapter, and remove the battery to eliminate the risk of electrical shock.
- Work on a clean, flat surface with adequate lighting to facilitate visibility and prevent damage to components.

Step 2: Accessing the Charging Port

Locate the charging port on your laptop and assess its accessibility for replacement:

- The charging port may be located on the side, back, or underside of the laptop, depending on the model.
- If the charging port is easily accessible, proceed to Step 3. If not, you may need to disassemble part of the laptop to access it.

Step 3: Removing the Old Charging Port

Once the charging port is accessible, proceed with removing the old port:

- Use a screwdriver to remove any screws or mounting brackets securing the charging port to the laptop chassis.
- If the charging port is attached to a cable or connector, carefully disconnect the cable from the port by gently pulling it away.

- If the charging port is soldered to the motherboard, you may need to desolder it using a soldering iron and desoldering wick or pump.

Step 4: Installing the Replacement Charging Port

Prepare the replacement charging port for installation and attach it to the laptop:

- If the charging port comes with a cable or connector, connect the cable to the appropriate connector on the motherboard or power board.
- If the charging port requires soldering, carefully solder the new port to the motherboard using a soldering iron and solder wire.
- Secure the replacement charging port to the laptop chassis using screws or mounting brackets, ensuring it is firmly seated and aligned properly.

Step 5: Reassembly and Testing

After installing the replacement charging port, reassemble the laptop by following the reverse order of disassembly:

- Reinstall any components or panels that were removed to access the charging port, ensuring all screws are tightened securely.
- Reinstall the laptop's battery, plug in the AC adapter, and power on the laptop to verify the new charging port's functionality.
- Test the charging port by connecting the AC adapter and ensuring the laptop charges properly.

Step 6: Final Checks and Configuration

Perform final checks and configuration to ensure the replacement charging port is functioning correctly:

- Inspect the charging port for proper alignment, secure attachment, and any signs of damage or loose connections.
- Configure any relevant power management settings or drivers on the laptop to optimize charging performance and battery health.

As always, please approach this with both caution and consideration for attention to detail as you work through this process. This is to ensure both your own personal safety and to reduce potential damage to the laptop or its internal components.

Step-by-Step Guide: How to Replace Storage Components Within a Laptop

As our needs for storage expand, over time it is common practice to upgrade our device's internal storage to both meet our needs and ensure timely data retrieval. Laptops will primarily utilize SSD as the form factor for storage solutions, and it is recommended to go with an internal component as opposed to a USB or external storage medium unless timely retrieval is not a requirement. In similar fashion to our prior sections, below we will perform a step-by-step breakdown of this process while also meeting the recommendations of CompTIA.

Keep in mind that these steps are in order to follow the guidelines outlined by the examination; however, there are practical items to follow as well. Primarily, we should look at best practices, like ensuring data backups are taken prior to working with the existing storage components to reduce the risk of data loss.

Step 1: Preparation and Safety

Before beginning the storage component replacement process, gather the necessary tools and ensure a safe working environment:

- Obtain a compatible replacement storage device (e.g., hard drive, solid-state drive) for your laptop model.
- Gather tools such as a screwdriver set, an antistatic wrist strap, and any additional tools required for disassembly.
- Power off the laptop, unplug the AC adapter, and remove the battery to eliminate the risk of electrical shock.
- Work on a clean, flat surface with adequate lighting to facilitate visibility and prevent damage to components.

Step 2: Accessing the Storage Compartment

Locate the storage compartment on your laptop and assess its accessibility for replacement:

- The storage compartment may be located on the underside of the laptop or beneath a removable panel.
- If the storage compartment is easily accessible, proceed to Step 3. If not, you may need to disassemble part of the laptop to access it.

Step 3: Removing the Old Storage Component

Once the storage compartment is accessible, proceed with removing the old storage component:

- Use a screwdriver to remove any screws or mounting brackets securing the storage component to the laptop chassis or storage bay.

- If the storage component is connected via a cable or connector, carefully disconnect the cable from the component by gently pulling it away.
- If the storage component is secured with screws or mounting brackets, remove them, and carefully lift the component out of its slot or bay.

Step 4: Installing the Replacement Storage Component

Prepare the replacement storage component for installation and insert it into the vacant slot or bay:

- Align the replacement storage component with the slot or bay, ensuring it matches the orientation of the connector and any alignment notches or guides.
- Carefully insert the storage component into the slot or bay, applying even pressure until it is fully seated and the connectors make contact.
- If the replacement storage component is secured with screws or mounting brackets, reinstall them to secure it in place within the compartment.

Step 5: Reassembly and Testing

After installing the replacement storage component, reassemble the laptop by following the reverse order of disassembly:

- Reinstall any components or panels that were removed to access the storage compartment, ensuring all screws are tightened securely.
- Reinstall the laptop's battery, plug in the AC adapter, and power on the laptop to verify the new storage component's functionality.

- Test the storage component by accessing files, running diagnostic tests, and ensuring it is recognized by the operating system.

Step 6: Data Migration and Configuration (if necessary)

If you've replaced the primary storage device (e.g., a hard drive with an SSD), you may need to migrate data and configure the new storage device:

- Use disk cloning software to transfer data from the old storage device to the new one, ensuring all files and settings are preserved.
- Configure the new storage device as the primary boot device in the laptop's BIOS or UEFI settings to ensure proper startup and operation.

By following these step-by-step instructions and safety precautions, you can successfully replace storage components within a laptop while adhering to the guidelines outlined in the CompTIA A+ certification.

Step-by-Step Guide: How to Replace RAM in a Laptop

The installation of additional or upgraded RAM (Random Access Memory) is probably the most common upgrade to increase the baseline performance of a laptop. It has become a part of the culture in today's age that the solution to all problems is to add more RAM, which in a lot of cases is well close to the truth of the matter. Let's review the steps needed to add or swap RAM in a laptop:

Step 1: Preparation and Safety

Before beginning the installation process, gather the necessary tools and ensure a safe working environment:

- Obtain compatible RAM modules for your laptop model.
- Gather tools such as a screwdriver set, an antistatic wrist strap, and any additional tools required for disassembly.
- Power off the laptop, unplug the AC adapter, and remove the battery to eliminate the risk of electrical shock.
- Work on a clean, flat surface with adequate lighting to facilitate visibility and prevent damage to components.

Step 2: RAM Installation

- Locate the RAM slots on your laptop, typically found beneath a panel on the underside of the device.
- Open the panel by removing any screws securing it in place and gently lifting it away from the laptop chassis.
- Identify the empty RAM slots and align the notches on the RAM module with the keys in the slot.
- Insert the RAM module into the slot at a 45-degree angle and press down firmly until the clips on either side click into place, securing the module.

Step 3: Reassembly and Testing

- After installing the RAM, reassemble the laptop by securing any panels or covers removed during the installation process.

- Reinstall the laptop's battery, plug in the AC adapter, and power on the laptop to verify the new components' functionality.
- Check the system properties or use diagnostic software to confirm that the RAM is recognized and functioning correctly.

Troubleshooting Common Laptop Issues

Troubleshooting common laptop issues requires a systematic approach to diagnose the problem accurately and identify the root cause. The following are the most-faced issues and their associated troubleshooting measures. It is normal to see these items brought up on either the A+ examination or inside its performance-based questions.

1. **Laptop Not Powering On:**
    - **Diagnosis:** Check if the laptop is receiving power by ensuring the power adapter is plugged in correctly and the battery is charged. Verify that the power indicator lights are illuminated.
    - **Root Cause:** Possible causes include a faulty power adapter, dead battery, defective power jack, or motherboard failure.
    - **Troubleshooting Techniques:** Test the power adapter with a multimeter to ensure it is functioning correctly. Try powering on the laptop with and without the battery. Inspect the power jack for any physical damage or loose connections. If necessary, seek professional assistance for motherboard diagnostics and repairs.

2. **Laptop Overheating:**
    - **Diagnosis:** Monitor the laptop's temperature using diagnostic software or built-in sensors. Check for blocked air vents, excessive dust accumulation, or a malfunctioning cooling fan.
    - **Root Cause:** Overheating can result from prolonged use, inadequate cooling, or hardware/software issues.
    - **Troubleshooting Techniques:** Clean the laptop's air vents and fan using compressed air to remove dust and debris. Place the laptop on a flat, hard surface to ensure proper airflow. Adjust power settings to reduce processor usage and prevent overheating. Update device drivers and BIOS firmware to address any software-related issues contributing to overheating.
3. **Slow Performance:**
    - **Diagnosis:** Determine if the laptop is running slowly during normal use or specific tasks. Check system resources such as CPU, memory, and disk usage using Task Manager or Resource Monitor.
    - **Root Cause:** Slow performance may result from insufficient RAM, outdated software/drivers, malware infections, or a fragmented hard drive.
    - **Troubleshooting Techniques:** Upgrade RAM to improve multitasking capabilities and overall system performance. Update device drivers and operating systems to the latest versions. Perform regular malware scans using reputable antivirus software. Defragment the hard drive or upgrade to an SSD for faster data access speeds.

4. **Screen Display Issues:**

    - **Diagnosis:** Identify the nature of the screen display problem, such as flickering, distorted images, or a blank screen. Check for physical damage to the screen or loose display cables.
    - **Root Cause:** Screen display issues may be caused by a faulty LCD panel, graphics card, display cable, or software-related issues.
    - **Troubleshooting Techniques:** Connect an external monitor to the laptop to determine if the issue is with the internal display or graphics hardware. Adjust display settings and update graphics drivers. If the screen is physically damaged, replace the LCD panel or seek professional repair services.

5. **Connectivity Problems:**

    - **Diagnosis:** Troubleshoot issues related to Wi-Fi, Bluetooth, or other connectivity features by checking network settings, signal strength, and device drivers.
    - **Root Cause:** Connectivity problems may arise from router issues, outdated drivers, signal interference, or hardware malfunctions.
    - **Troubleshooting Techniques:** Reset network settings and reboot the router to resolve Wi-Fi connectivity issues. Update Wi-Fi and Bluetooth drivers from the manufacturer's website. Check for nearby electronic devices or obstacles that may interfere with wireless signals.

6. **Battery Drainage/Charging Issues:**
    - **Diagnosis:** Determine if the battery is not holding a charge, draining quickly, or not charging properly. Check battery health and charging status indicators.
    - **Root Cause:** Battery drainage or charging issues may result from a defective battery, faulty charging port, or power management settings.
    - **Troubleshooting Techniques:** Calibrate the battery to reset its charge capacity and improve accuracy. Clean the charging port and check for debris or corrosion. Adjust power settings to optimize battery life and prevent unnecessary drainage. If the battery is defective, replace it with a compatible replacement.

By employing these troubleshooting techniques and systematically diagnosing laptop issues, users can effectively identify the root cause and implement appropriate solutions to restore their laptop's functionality. Additionally, CompTIA A+ certification candidates should familiarize themselves with these common laptop problems and troubleshooting methods to prepare for certification exams and real-world scenarios.

Summary

In this chapter, we continued our understanding of the foundational aspects of laptops, going deep into their inner workings and common issues faced by users. We began by detailing the essential components of laptops, ranging from the central processing unit (CPU) to the display screen, highlighting the differences between various RAM types and storage devices commonly used in these portable devices. Through detailed explanations and step-by-step guides, readers will obtain valuable insights into the installation and replacement procedures for critical laptop components, ensuring you are equipped with the knowledge to address hardware-related issues effectively.

Moving beyond hardware, we addressed common troubleshooting scenarios encountered by laptop users, providing systematic techniques for diagnosing and resolving issues such as power failure, overheating, slow performance, screen display problems, and connectivity issues. By following our guidance, readers can approach these challenges with confidence, identifying root causes and implementing appropriate solutions to restore their laptops' functionality. Additionally, we emphasized the importance of regular maintenance practices, such as cleaning air vents and updating drivers, to prevent and mitigate potential issues proactively.

As we conclude this chapter, readers are now equipped with a solid understanding of laptops' fundamental components, troubleshooting methodologies, and maintenance best practices. Armed with this knowledge, they are well-prepared to navigate the complexities of laptop technology and address a wide range of issues effectively. Looking ahead to Chapter 3, we will shift our focus to the realm of networking, exploring the intricate systems and protocols that underpin modern communication networks. From wired connections to wireless technologies, we will delve into the intricacies of networking, providing readers with a comprehensive understanding of this essential aspect of Information Technology.

Join us as we embark on the next leg of our journey, uncovering the mysteries of networking and expanding our knowledge horizons in the ever-evolving world of IT.

CHAPTER 3

Networking Fundamentals

Welcome to Chapter 3 of our journey through the field of Information Technology. In this chapter, we will review the foundational concepts and components of networking, laying the groundwork for understanding how devices communicate and share resources in interconnected environments. Networking forms the backbone of modern IT infrastructure, enabling organizations and individuals to access and exchange data efficiently and securely. Throughout this chapter, we will learn the purpose and significance of networking, emphasizing its role in facilitating communication and collaboration across diverse devices and platforms. We will view the various network standards and topologies, examining the different configurations and structures that define network architectures. From wired connections to wireless technologies, we will break apart the fine details of networking and provide insights into the principles that govern data transmission and communication.

In addition, we will cover the most common security measures to be considered within this context. Understanding the fundamentals of network security is essential for safeguarding data integrity, confidentiality, and availability in today's interconnected world. By the end of this chapter, readers will have gained a solid understanding of networking fundamentals, laying the groundwork for further exploration into advanced networking concepts and technologies. As with our prior

© Kodi A. Cochran 2024

K. A. Cochran, *CompTIA A+ Certification Companion*, Certification Study Companion Series,
https://doi.org/10.1007/979-8-8688-0867-8_3

chapters and those to come, this section has been written to meet the requirements set forth by CompTIA for the A+ certification examination. This chapter seeks to thoroughly prepare all readers to not only succeed in the field but also to aid in accomplishing higher certification.

Let's keep pace and continue our learning experience with the realm of networking, where we will detail the interconnected systems and empower readers with the knowledge to navigate the complexities of modern IT infrastructure.

Overview of Networking Concepts

Networking, at its core, is the web of connections that link devices together, enabling the seamless exchange of data and resources across various platforms and environments. This chapter serves as a gateway to understanding the complexities of networking, laying the groundwork for readers to navigate the intricacies of interconnected systems with confidence and clarity.

First and foremost, we review the details of network types, each with its scope and purpose. From the local confines of LANs to the expansive reach of WANs and the specialized domains of MANs and PANs, we explore the nuanced architectures that define the boundaries of communication networks. Through detailed explanations and illustrative examples, readers gain insights into the unique characteristics and applications of each network type, equipping them with a deeper understanding of their role in modern IT infrastructure.

Building upon this foundation, we will comprehensively cover network topologies, where the arrangement of devices and connections shapes the flow of data within a network. From the centralized hub of a star topology to the decentralized mesh of interconnected nodes, we unravel the complexities of network architectures, exploring the advantages, limitations, and practical considerations of each topology. Furthermore, we detail all essential components of network architecture, shedding light on the critical roles played by nodes, links, and networking hardware in facilitating communication and resource sharing. From end devices such as computers and smartphones to intermediary devices like routers and switches, we examine the diverse array of components that comprise a network ecosystem, illustrating their functions and interactions with clarity and precision.

As we continue onward with networking, we uncover the vital role played by network protocols in governing data transmission and communication. From the ubiquitous TCP/IP protocol suited to specialized protocols such as HTTP, DNS, and DHCP, we review the mechanisms that build the seamless exchange of information within a network. Through detailed discussions and practical examples, readers will gain a comprehensive understanding of how protocols enable devices to communicate effectively and reliably across diverse platforms and environments. We will additionally learn about the critical concepts of IP addressing and routing, exploring how devices are identified and located on a network, and how data packets are directed to their intended destinations. From the allocation of unique IP addresses to devices to the dynamic routing algorithms used to determine the optimal path for data transmission, we demystify the complexities of addressing and routing, empowering readers to understand the underlying mechanisms that enable efficient communication in modern networks.

As we conclude this overview of networking concepts, readers are encouraged to reflect on the foundational knowledge acquired in this chapter and prepare to further their understanding of advanced networking topics and technologies. From network security and management to emerging technologies such as SDN and IoT, the journey through the world of networking promises to be both enlightening and enriching.

The Various Types of Networks

Within the context of networking, there are different forms of network implementations that each serve their purpose. Understanding the distinctions between these network types is essential for designing and implementing effective communication infrastructures. These can be intertwined, and no infrastructure is limited to any one deployment model. Let's explore the key characteristics of each network type and compare their advantages and limitations:

1. **Local Area Networks (LANs):**
    - **Scope:** LANs typically cover a small geographical area, such as a single building or campus. They facilitate communication and resource sharing among devices within proximity, promoting collaboration and efficiency in local environments.
    - **Topology:** Common LAN topologies include star, bus, and ring configurations, with devices connected to a central hub or switch. Each topology offers advantages in terms of scalability, redundancy, and ease of management, catering to diverse network requirements.
    - **Advantages:** LANs offer high-speed communication and low latency, making them ideal for local resource sharing and collaborative work environments. They enable efficient data transfer, seamless access to shared resources such as printers and servers, and support for multimedia applications and real-time communication.

- **Limitations:** LANs are limited in scope and may require additional infrastructure to connect geographically dispersed locations. Managing and securing LANs can also pose challenges, particularly in larger networks with numerous connected devices and complex configurations.

Wide Area Networks (WANs):

- **Scope:** WANs span large geographical areas, connecting multiple LANs across cities, countries, or continents. They establish communication links over long distances, enabling global connectivity and access to remote resources.
- **Topology:** WANs often use point-to-point or mesh topologies, with data transmitted over long-distance communication links. This topology provides flexibility and resilience, allowing data to traverse multiple paths and adapt to network failures or congestion.
- **Advantages:** WANs provide extensive coverage and global connectivity, enabling organizations to establish communication links across vast distances. They support a wide range of applications, including remote access, cloud services, and distributed computing, facilitating collaboration and data sharing on a global scale.
- **Limitations:** WANs may suffer from higher latency and lower bandwidth compared to LANs, requiring robust infrastructure and protocols to ensure reliable communication. They are also susceptible to security threats and network disruptions, necessitating measures such as encryption, VPNs, and redundancy to mitigate risks.

2. **Metropolitan Area Networks (MANs):**

    - **Scope:** MANs cover the geographical area of a city or metropolitan area, bridging the gap between LANs and WANs. They provide high-speed connectivity within urban environments, facilitating data transmission and communication over medium-sized geographical areas.

    - **Topology:** MANs typically use ring or mesh topologies, with interconnected nodes providing high-speed communication within urban areas. This topology enhances network resilience and scalability, enabling efficient data exchange and access to shared resources.

    - **Advantages:** MANs offer high bandwidth and low latency, making them suitable for applications requiring fast data transmission over medium-sized geographical areas. They support services such as video streaming, online gaming, and financial transactions, enhancing connectivity and productivity in urban settings.

    - **Limitations:** MANs may require substantial investment in infrastructure and maintenance, particularly in densely populated urban areas. They are also vulnerable to congestion and network congestion, requiring efficient traffic management and optimization to ensure optimal performance.

3. **Personal Area Networks (PANs):**

    - **Scope:** PANs are designed for personal or individual use, connecting devices within a short range, such as a room or personal space. They enable seamless connectivity and data sharing among personal devices, promoting convenience and accessibility in everyday life.
    - **Topology:** PANs often use star or mesh topologies, with devices interconnected via wireless technologies such as Bluetooth or Zigbee. This topology facilitates easy setup and configuration, allowing devices to communicate directly or through intermediary nodes.
    - **Advantages:** PANs provide convenient connectivity for personal devices such as smartphones, tablets, and wearable devices, enabling seamless data sharing and communication. They support a wide range of applications, including file sharing, audio streaming, and device synchronization, enhancing the user experience and productivity.
    - **Limitations:** PANs are limited in range and bandwidth, making them unsuitable for large-scale communication or data-intensive applications. They may also be susceptible to interference and security risks, requiring measures such as encryption and authentication to protect sensitive data and ensure privacy.

By comparing these network types, organizations and individuals can determine the most suitable network architecture to meet their communication needs and infrastructure requirements. Whether establishing a local network for office collaboration or connecting geographically dispersed locations via a wide-area network, understanding the strengths and weaknesses of each network type is essential for building robust and reliable communication systems.

Cabled Networks in Comparison to Wireless

Although this will be covered further in much greater detail, there are various considerations and use cases when considering a wired or wireless network. Cabled and wireless networking are two distinct approaches to establishing communication links between devices, each offering unique advantages and considerations from a technical standpoint. Let's examine the key differences between these two networking technologies:

1. **Physical Infrastructure:**

    - **Cabled Networking:** Cabled networks rely on physical cables, such as Ethernet or fiber-optic cables, to transmit data between devices. These cables are typically installed within buildings or infrastructure, providing reliable and high-speed communication.

    - **Wireless Networking:** In contrast, wireless networks use radio frequency (RF) signals to transmit data wirelessly between devices. This eliminates the need for physical cables and allows for flexible connectivity within a specified range.

2. **Data Transmission:**

    - **Cabled Networking:** Cabled networks offer dedicated and predictable bandwidth, allowing for consistent data transmission speeds and minimal interference. Data travels through the cables with minimal latency, making cable networks suitable for applications requiring high-speed and reliable communication.

- **Wireless Networking:** Wireless networks may experience fluctuations in bandwidth and latency due to environmental factors such as interference from other devices, physical obstacles, and distance from the access point. While wireless technology has advanced significantly in recent years, it may not always provide the same level of performance and reliability as cabled networks.

3. **Security:**

   - **Cabled Networking:** Cabled networks are generally considered more secure than wireless networks, as physical access to the network infrastructure is required to intercept data transmission. This makes it more challenging for unauthorized users to gain access to sensitive information.

   - **Wireless Networking:** Wireless networks are inherently more vulnerable to security threats, as data is transmitted over the airwaves and can be intercepted by unauthorized devices within range. Implementing robust security measures such as encryption and access control is essential to mitigate these risks and protect sensitive data.

4. **Scalability and Mobility:**

   - **Cabled Networking:** Cabled networks may be more cumbersome to scale and reconfigure, as they require the installation of additional cables and infrastructure to accommodate new devices or changes in network layout. However, once installed, cable networks offer stable and reliable connectivity.

- **Wireless Networking:** Wireless networks offer greater flexibility and mobility, allowing users to connect to the network from anywhere within range of the access point. This makes wireless technology ideal for environments where mobility and flexibility are essential, such as offices, campuses, and public spaces.

Difference Between the Internet and the Extranet

The Internet and extranet are both critical components of modern communication infrastructure, facilitating the exchange of information and collaboration among users. While they share some similarities, they serve distinct purposes and have unique characteristics. Let's break down what exactly it is that separates these two:

1. **Scope and Accessibility:**

    - **Internet:** The Internet is a global network of interconnected devices and servers, accessible to users worldwide. It provides access to a vast array of resources, including websites, applications, and services, enabling global communication and information sharing.

    - **Extranet:** In contrast, an extranet is a private network that extends beyond the boundaries of an organization, allowing authorized users, such as partners, suppliers, or customers, to access specific resources or services. Unlike the Internet, which is publicly accessible, an extranet is restricted to authorized users and requires authentication to access.

2. **Security and Access Control:**

    - **Internet:** The Internet is a public network, making it inherently less secure than private networks such as intranets or extranets. While encryption and security protocols help protect data transmitted over the Internet, users must exercise caution when sharing sensitive information online to mitigate security risks.

    - **Extranet:** Extranets typically employ stringent access control measures to restrict access to authorized users only. Authentication mechanisms such as usernames, passwords, and multi-factor authentication help ensure that only approved individuals can access extranet resources, enhancing security and data protection.

3. **Collaboration and Communication:**

    - **Internet:** The Internet serves as a platform for global collaboration and communication, enabling users to connect with others, share information, and collaborate on projects across geographical boundaries. It provides a diverse range of communication tools and platforms, including email, social media, messaging apps, and video conferencing.

- **Extranet:** Extranets facilitate collaboration and communication among authorized users within a specific organization or community. They provide a secure environment for sharing confidential information, collaborating on projects, and coordinating business activities with external partners or stakeholders.

4. **Privacy and Confidentiality:**

    - **Internet:** Privacy and confidentiality on the Internet can be challenging to maintain due to the public nature of the network. Users must take precautions to protect their personal information and sensitive data from unauthorized access or interception by third parties.
    - **Extranet:** Extranets offer a higher level of privacy and confidentiality compared to the Internet, as access is restricted to authorized users only. This enables organizations to share confidential documents, proprietary information, and sensitive data with trusted partners or clients without exposing it to the public domain.

In summary, while both the Internet and extranet play crucial roles in facilitating communication and collaboration, they serve different purposes and have distinct characteristics. The Internet provides global connectivity and access to a vast array of resources, while extranets offer secure collaboration platforms for authorized users within specific organizations or communities. Understanding the differences between these networks is essential for organizations to leverage their capabilities effectively and meet their communication and collaboration needs.

IP Addresses and IPv4, IPv6

IP addresses are fundamental to the functioning of computer networks, serving as unique identifiers for devices connected to the Internet or other networks. In this section, we will cover the different types of IP addresses, exploring the differences between dynamic and static addressing, as well as the transition from IPv4 to IPv6.

It's also a neat fact that the reason IPv6 came to fruition was the history and limitations that IPv4 held. When it was originally being developed, IPv4 was seen as the best option to host all devices that were anticipated to ever reside on the Internet with a unique identifier. However, nobody anticipated just how interconnected we would become as the years progressed. What was once thought of as an unreachable threshold quickly became obsolete, and more unique identifiers were required. IPv6 was the solution to the age-old problem and, theoretically, will be around for many years to come.

Dynamic IP Addresses:

- **Definition:** Dynamic IP addressing involves automatically assigning IP addresses to devices by a DHCP (Dynamic Host Configuration Protocol) server. These addresses are typically leased to devices for a specific period and may change each time a device connects to the network.
- **Advantages:** Dynamic IP addressing simplifies network management by automating the allocation of IP addresses and conserving address space. It is advantageous in environments with many devices that frequently connect and disconnect from the network.

- **Limitations:** Dynamic IP addresses can pose challenges for services that require consistent device identification, such as remote access or networked devices with static configurations. Additionally, frequent changes in IP addresses may impact network performance or security monitoring.

Static IP Addresses:

- **Definition:** Static IP addressing involves manually assigning a fixed IP address to a device, ensuring that the address remains constant over time. These addresses are typically configured directly on the device or assigned by a network administrator.
- **Advantages:** Static IP addressing provides stability and predictability, making it ideal for devices that require permanent or long-term connectivity, such as servers, routers, and networked printers. It also simplifies network management by facilitating device identification and access control.
- **Limitations:** Static IP addressing can be more time-consuming and error-prone to manage compared to dynamic addressing, particularly in large-scale or dynamic environments. Additionally, static IP addresses may lead to address conflicts if not carefully coordinated within the network.

IPv4 (Internet Protocol Version 4):

- **Overview:** IPv4 is the most widely used version of the Internet Protocol, employing a 32-bit address format and supporting approximately 4.3 billion unique addresses. However, the exponential growth of Internet-connected devices has led to address exhaustion, prompting the need for a more scalable solution.

- **Challenges:** The limited address space of IPv4 has necessitated the use of techniques such as Network Address Translation (NAT) and private IP addressing to conserve addresses and enable devices within private networks to communicate with the Internet.
- **Transition:** Efforts to transition from IPv4 to IPv6 have been underway for several years, with IPv6 offering a vastly expanded address space (128 bits) capable of supporting virtually unlimited devices. While the adoption of IPv6 has been gradual, it represents the future of Internet connectivity and addresses the scalability challenges of IPv4.

IPv6 (Internet Protocol Version 6):

- **Overview:** IPv6 is the next generation of the Internet Protocol, designed to replace IPv4 and accommodate the growing number of Internet-connected devices. It employs a 128-bit address format, providing approximately 340 undecillion unique addresses.
- **Advantages:** IPv6 offers several advantages over IPv4, including simplified network configuration, improved security features, and enhanced support for emerging technologies such as IoT (Internet of Things) and mobile networks. It also eliminates the need for NAT and enables end-to-end connectivity without address translation.

- **Adoption:** While IPv6 adoption has been gradual, many organizations and Internet service providers (ISPs) have begun deploying IPv6-enabled networks to future-proof their infrastructure and accommodate the increasing demand for IP addresses.

Understanding the differences between dynamic and static IP addressing, as well as the transition from IPv4 to IPv6, provides valuable insights into the evolving landscape of IP networking and the technologies shaping the future of Internet connectivity. Whether configuring network devices, troubleshooting connectivity issues, or planning for future network expansions, a comprehensive understanding of IP addressing is essential for IT professionals and network administrators alike. This will not only help you with the goal of obtaining the A+ certification, but it will accompany you throughout your time working within the field.

Network Standards and Topologies

Network standards and topologies play crucial roles in shaping the design, implementation, and performance of computer networks. In this section, we explore the significance of standards, the various types of network topologies, their purposes, and how they contribute to redundancy in network architectures.

1. **Explanation of Standards and Network Topologies:**

    - **Standards:** Network standards define the rules and protocols governing communication between devices within a network. These standards ensure interoperability, compatibility, and seamless communication between devices from different manufacturers.

- **Network Topologies:** Network topologies refer to the physical or logical layout of devices and connections within a network. Common topologies include bus, star, ring, mesh, and hybrid configurations, each with its own advantages and limitations.

2. **Network Topology Types: Compare and Contrast:**

   - **Bus Topology:** In a bus topology, all devices are connected to a central cable or bus, with data transmitted in both directions. While simple and inexpensive to implement, bus topologies are susceptible to single-point failures and limited scalability.
   - **Star Topology:** In a star topology, each device is connected to a central hub or switch, forming a centralized architecture. Star topologies offer better performance, scalability, and fault isolation than bus topologies but require more cabling.
   - **Ring Topology:** In a ring topology, devices are connected in a circular arrangement, with data transmitted sequentially from one device to the next. Ring topologies provide efficient data transmission and fault tolerance but may suffer from network degradation if a single link fails.
   - **Mesh Topology:** In a mesh topology, devices are interconnected with multiple redundant paths, ensuring robustness and fault tolerance. Mesh topologies offer high reliability and performance but are complex and costly to implement.

- **Hybrid Topology:** Hybrid topologies combine two or more topology types to leverage their respective strengths. For example, a hybrid topology may incorporate elements of both star and mesh topologies to achieve a balance between performance, scalability, and redundancy.

3. **Purpose of Different Topologies:**

    - Each network topology serves specific purposes based on factors such as scalability, fault tolerance, performance, and cost. For example, star topologies are well-suited for small to medium-sized networks requiring centralized management and fault isolation, while mesh topologies are ideal for mission-critical applications demanding high reliability and redundancy.

4. **How Different Topologies Aid Redundancy:**

    - Redundancy in network topologies refers to the presence of backup paths or connections that can be used in the event of a primary link failure. Topologies such as mesh and hybrid configurations inherently offer redundancy by providing multiple paths for data transmission. This redundancy enhances fault tolerance, resilience, and uptime, ensuring continuous network operation even in the face of failures or disruptions.

By understanding the principles of network standards and topologies, as well as their roles in facilitating communication, redundancy, and fault tolerance, network administrators can design and implement robust and reliable network infrastructures tailored to the specific requirements of their organizations. Whether building a small office network or a large-scale enterprise environment, selecting the appropriate topology and adhering to industry standards are essential for achieving optimal performance and resilience.

Network Security Methodologies

Network security is paramount in safeguarding data, systems, and infrastructure from unauthorized access, malicious attacks, and data breaches. In this section, we cover various security practices and technologies employed to protect networks, including encryption, intrusion detection and prevention systems (IDS/IPS), firewalls (FW), port management, and network monitoring:

1. **Overview of Security Practices in Networking:**

    - Network security encompasses a range of practices, policies, and technologies aimed at protecting the confidentiality, integrity, and availability of network resources. These practices include access control, authentication, encryption, vulnerability management, and incident response, among others.

2. **Encryption:**

    - Encryption is the process of encoding data to prevent unauthorized access or interception by unauthorized parties. In networking, encryption is commonly used to secure data transmitted over the network, such as sensitive information, login credentials, and financial transactions. Common encryption protocols include Secure Sockets Layer/Transport Layer Security (SSL/TLS) for securing web traffic and IPsec for securing IP-based communication.

3. **IDS/IPS/FW (Intrusion Detection and Prevention Systems/Firewalls):**

    - **IDS:** Intrusion Detection Systems monitor network traffic for suspicious or malicious activity and generate alerts or notifications when potential threats are detected. IDS can be signature-based, analyzing patterns and signatures of known attacks, or behavior-based, detecting anomalies or deviations from normal network behavior.

    - **IPS:** Intrusion Prevention Systems go a step further by actively blocking or preventing detected threats from reaching their target. IPS can automatically respond to identified threats by blocking malicious traffic, isolating compromised devices, or triggering alerts for further investigation.

    - **FW:** Firewalls are network security devices that control and monitor incoming and outgoing network traffic based on predefined security rules. Firewalls act as a barrier between trusted internal networks and untrusted external networks, filtering traffic to prevent unauthorized access and mitigate potential threats.

4. **Port Management:**

    - Port management involves controlling access to network services and resources by managing open ports and protocols on network devices. Administrators can restrict access to specific ports and protocols based on security policies, limiting the attack surface, and reducing the risk of unauthorized access or exploitation.

5. **Network Monitoring:**

    - Network monitoring involves continuously monitoring network traffic, devices, and systems to detect and respond to security threats, performance issues, and operational anomalies. Network monitoring tools collect and analyze data from various sources, such as network traffic flows, logs, and security events, providing visibility into the network environment and enabling proactive threat detection and incident response.

The implementation of strong security methodologies and technologies ensures organizations will adequately mitigate the risk of cyber threats, protect sensitive data, and maintain the integrity and availability of their network infrastructure. From encryption and access control to intrusion detection and network monitoring, a layered approach to network security is essential for building resilient and secure network environments in today's evolving threat landscape.

Networking Components and Devices

This section will be more expansive than some of the prior, as we will be viewing all the core components and devices one would find within a network environment and the OSI layers they correlate to. This is one of the most crucial portions of the networking information located within this book, and it is highly advised to pay particular attention to the various layers of the OSI model. Let's break this down a bit to a more granular detail.

Networking Cables

- **Categories:** Networking cables are categorized based on their performance characteristics, with categories ranging from Cat3 to Cat6a, as well as fiber optic cables.
- **Comparison:**
    - **Cat3:** Primarily used for voice transmission, Cat3 cables have a maximum data rate of 10 Mbps and are limited to short distances.
    - **Cat5/Cat5e:** Cat5 cables support data rates of up to 100 Mbps and are suitable for most Ethernet applications. Cat5e (enhanced) cables offer improved performance and reduced crosstalk, supporting Gigabit Ethernet (up to 1000 Mbps).
    - **Cat6:** Cat6 cables support data rates of up to 10 Gbps and feature improved performance and reduced crosstalk compared to Cat5e. They are suitable for high-speed Ethernet applications and are commonly used in modern network installations.

- **Fiber Optic Cables:** Fiber optic cables use light signals to transmit data and offer high bandwidth, low latency, and immunity to electromagnetic interference. They can support data rates exceeding 10 Gbps and can transmit data over much longer distances than copper cables.

Networking Devices

- **Hubs:** Hubs are basic networking devices that operate at the physical layer of the OSI model. They receive data from one port and broadcast it to all other ports, resulting in inefficient use of bandwidth and increased network collisions.
- **Switches:** Switches operate at the data link layer of the OSI model and are more intelligent than hubs. They forward data only to the intended recipient based on MAC addresses, reducing network congestion and improving performance.
- **Routers:** Routers operate at the network layer of the OSI model and are responsible for routing data between different networks. They use routing tables and logical addressing (such as IP addresses) to determine the best path for data transmission, enabling communication between devices on different subnets or networks.

OSI Layers

- **Layer 1 - Physical Layer:** The physical layer deals with the physical transmission of data over the network medium. It includes networking cables, connectors, and hardware devices such as hubs and switches.
- **Layer 2 - Data Link Layer:** The data link layer provides error detection and correction, as well as the framing and addressing of data packets. Switches operate at this layer, forwarding data based on MAC addresses.
- **Layer 3 - Network Layer:** The network layer is responsible for logical addressing, routing, and packet forwarding between different networks. Routers operate at this layer, directing data packets to their destination based on IP addresses.
- **Layer 4 - Transport Layer:** The transport layer ensures reliable and efficient data transmission between devices. It includes protocols such as TCP (Transmission Control Protocol) and UDP (User Datagram Protocol), which provide error checking, flow control, and multiplexing.
- **Layer 5 - Session Layer:** The session layer establishes, maintains, and terminates communication sessions between devices. It manages session synchronization, checkpointing, and recovery in network connections.
- **Layer 6 - Presentation Layer:** The presentation layer is responsible for data translation, encryption, and compression to ensure compatibility between different systems and applications.

- **Layer 7 - Application Layer:** The application layer provides network services and interfaces for user applications, such as web browsers, email clients, and file transfer programs. It includes protocols such as HTTP, SMTP, and FTP for communication between applications.

By understanding the characteristics and capabilities of networking cables, devices, and OSI layers, network administrators can design, deploy, and maintain efficient and reliable network infrastructures to meet the needs of modern business environments. From physical connectivity to logical addressing and data transmission, each component plays a critical role in ensuring seamless communication and connectivity within computer networks.

Common Network Protocols

The following are some of the most common port numbers an IT practitioner will utilize within their professional career. This is also formatted to align with the CompTIA A+ certification requirements and is meant to best assist with remembering each protocol with its associated port number. There are a wide range of common port numbers, and each hosts their own purposes in the field, but for now we will keep to the basics. It is worth researching further if one is interested in working within the field or alternatively looking to expand towards other certifications such as the CompTIA Security+.

1. **TCP/IP (Transmission Control Protocol/Internet Protocol):**
    - TCP/IP is a suite of protocols that provides the foundation for communication on the Internet. TCP ensures reliable, connection-oriented data transmission, while IP handles packet addressing and routing across networks.

2. **HTTP (Hypertext Transfer Protocol) - 80**

    - HTTP is the protocol used for transmitting hypertext documents, such as web pages, over the World Wide Web. It operates over TCP and typically uses port 80 for communication.

3. **HTTPS (Hypertext Transfer Protocol Secure) - 443**

    - HTTPS is a secure version of HTTP that encrypts data transmitted between clients and servers using SSL/TLS encryption. It provides confidentiality, integrity, and authenticity for web communications and typically uses port 443.

4. **FTP (File Transfer Protocol) - 20/21**

    - FTP is a protocol used for transferring files between a client and a server over a network. It allows users to upload, download, and manage files on remote servers and typically uses port 21 for control and port 20 for data transfer.

5. **SSH (Secure Shell) - 22**

    - SSH is a cryptographic network protocol that provides secure, encrypted communication between two computers. It allows users to remotely access and manage systems over an insecure network and typically uses port 22.

6. **SMTP (Simple Mail Transfer Protocol) - 25**

    - SMTP is a protocol used for sending email messages between servers. It defines the rules and procedures for transferring email messages from a sender's email client to a recipient's email server and typically uses port 25.

7. **POP3 (Post Office Protocol version 3) - 110**

    - POP3 is a protocol used by email clients to retrieve email messages from a server. It allows users to download their email messages to their local device for offline access and typically uses port 110.

8. **IMAP (Internet Message Access Protocol) - 143**

    - IMAP is a protocol used by email clients to access and manage email messages stored on a remote server. Unlike POP3, IMAP allows users to view, organize, and synchronize their email messages across multiple devices and typically uses port 143.

9. **DNS (Domain Name System) - 53**

    - DNS is a hierarchical, decentralized naming system that translates human-readable domain names into IP addresses. It enables users to access websites and other online resources using memorable domain names and typically uses port 53 for DNS queries.

10. **Telnet (Telecommunication Network) - 23**

    - Telnet is a network protocol used for remote terminal access to other computers. It provides a virtual terminal connection for users to access and manage remote systems and typically uses port 23.

11. **SNMP (Simple Network Management Protocol) -161**

    - SNMP is a protocol used for network management and monitoring of network-attached devices. It allows network administrators to collect information and manage network devices remotely and typically uses port 161 for SNMP requests.

12. **DHCP (Dynamic Host Configuration Protocol) - 67/68**

    - DHCP is a protocol used for automatically assigning IP addresses and other network configuration parameters to devices on a network. It simplifies network administration by dynamically managing IP address allocation and typically uses port 67 (server) and port 68 (client).

13. **NTP (Network Time Protocol) - 123**

    - NTP is a protocol used for synchronizing the clocks of networked devices. It ensures accurate timekeeping and coordination across distributed systems and typically uses port 123 for time synchronization.

14. **RDP (Remote Desktop Protocol) - 3389**

    - RDP is a proprietary protocol developed by Microsoft for remote desktop access to Windows-based systems. It allows users to interact with remote desktops and applications over a network connection and typically uses port 3389.

15. **SFTP (Secure File Transfer Protocol) - 22**

    - SFTP is a protocol used for secure file transfer over SSH connections. It provides encrypted data transmission and secure authentication for transferring files between clients and servers and typically uses port 22.

16. **SMTPS (SMTP Secure) - 465**

    - SMTPS is an extension of SMTP that uses SSL/TLS encryption to secure email communication between clients and servers. It ensures the confidentiality and integrity of email messages and typically uses port 465.

17. **LDAP (Lightweight Directory Access Protocol) - 389**

    - LDAP is a protocol used for accessing and managing directory information services, such as user authentication and authorization. It provides a standardized method for querying and updating directory data and typically uses port 389 for LDAP queries.

These protocols play crucial roles in various networking tasks, such as web browsing, email communication, file transfer, network management, and system administration. Understanding their functions, port numbers, and usage is essential for network administrators to effectively manage and secure computer networks. Not only will this support you with obtaining the A+ certification, but it is a practical knowledge set that can be fully utilized in the real world.

Internet Features and Services

The Internet, often referred to as the "network of networks," is a global system of interconnected computer networks that use the Internet Protocol Suite (TCP/IP) to link devices worldwide. Here we will break apart the functionality of the Internet, its transformative impact on technology, its evolution over time, and the proliferation of new services that leverage its infrastructure. It's not often that one considers what all the Internet brings to the table or how it has expanded over time, but particularly in this profession, it is a key factor.

1. **Global Connectivity:**

    - The Internet enables seamless communication and data exchange between individuals, organizations, and devices across geographical boundaries. Through its interconnected network of routers and switches, the Internet facilitates real-time communication, collaboration, and information sharing on a global scale.

Information Access:

- One of the defining features of the Internet is its vast repository of information and resources accessible to users worldwide. From websites and online databases to multimedia content and scholarly articles, the Internet provides unparalleled access to knowledge and information on virtually every topic imaginable.

2. **Communication Platforms:**

    - The Internet serves as a platform for various communication tools and services, including email, instant messaging, voice and video calls, social media platforms, and online forums. These communication channels enable individuals and organizations to connect, interact, and collaborate in real time, regardless of their physical location.

3. **E-commerce and Online Transactions:**
    - The Internet has revolutionized commerce and trade through e-commerce platforms and online marketplaces. From purchasing goods and services to conducting financial transactions and banking online, the Internet has transformed the way businesses and consumers engage in commercial activities, offering convenience, accessibility, and global reach.
4. **Entertainment and Media Streaming:**
    - With the rise of streaming services and digital media platforms, the Internet has become a primary source of entertainment for billions of users worldwide. From streaming movies and TV shows to listening to music and playing online games, the Internet offers a diverse array of entertainment options accessible on-demand.
5. **Cloud Computing and Storage:**
    - Cloud computing leverages Internet-based technologies to deliver computing services, such as storage, processing, and software applications, over the Internet. By outsourcing IT infrastructure and services to cloud providers, organizations can scale resources, reduce costs, and improve agility in deploying and managing IT solutions.

6. **Social Networking and Online Communities:**

    - Social networking platforms and online communities enable users to connect with friends, family, colleagues, and like-minded individuals worldwide. These platforms facilitate social interaction, content sharing, and community building, fostering virtual communities and networks across diverse interests and demographics.

7. **Internet of Things (IoT) Connectivity:**

    - The Internet of Things (IoT) connects physical devices, sensors, and objects to the Internet, enabling them to collect, exchange, and analyze data autonomously. From smart home devices and wearable technology to industrial sensors and autonomous vehicles, IoT connectivity is transforming industries, infrastructure, and daily life.

The Internet's pervasive influence on technology, society, and the global economy continues to evolve and expand, driving innovation, connectivity, and digital transformation across all sectors. As new technologies emerge and Internet-enabled services expand, the Internet remains a cornerstone of modern civilization, shaping the way we live, work, communicate, and interact in an increasingly interconnected world.

The Evolution of the Internet

Over time, the Internet has adapted and evolved into a more modernized solution with an immense number of features. Historically, it was meant to allow researchers to exchange data more easily, and it was never expected that it would become what it is today. Even the first variants of malware and similar items were once intended as jokes between friends. Let's run over the highlights of some of the more notable changes the Internet has faced.

1960s – Inception of ARPANET

The concept of the Internet traces its roots to the 1960s with the creation of ARPANET (Advanced Research Projects Agency Network), a pioneering network funded by the US Department of Defense. ARPANET aimed to connect computers to research institutions to facilitate data exchange and collaboration.

1970s – TCP/IP Development

In the early 1970s, the development of TCP/IP (Transmission Control Protocol/Internet Protocol) laid the foundation for modern networking protocols. TCP/IP standardized data transmission across diverse networks, enabling seamless communication between interconnected systems.

1980s – Expansion and Commercialization

Throughout the 1980s, the Internet expanded beyond academic and research institutions to include government agencies and commercial organizations. The introduction of domain names, email, and Usenet newsgroups marked significant milestones in the Internet's growth and accessibility.

1990s – World Wide Web Emergence

The 1990s witnessed the emergence of the World Wide Web, a revolutionary system for organizing and accessing information on the

Internet. Tim Berners-Lee's invention of the HTTP protocol and the first web browser, WorldWideWeb (later renamed Nexus), paved the way for the widespread adoption of the web.

1990s – Dot-Com Boom and E-commerce

The late 1990s saw the rise of the dot-com boom, characterized by the rapid proliferation of Internet-based businesses and the commercialization of online services. E-commerce platforms such as Amazon, eBay, and PayPal transformed the way goods and services were bought and sold, ushering in a new era of digital commerce.

2000s – Social Media and Web 2.0

The early 2000s witnessed the emergence of social media platforms and Web 2.0 technologies, enabling user-generated content, social networking, and online collaboration. Platforms like MySpace, LinkedIn, and later Facebook and Twitter revolutionized communication and social interaction on the Internet.

2010s – Mobile Internet and Cloud Computing

The proliferation of smartphones and mobile devices in the 2010s accelerated the adoption of mobile Internet technologies, leading to a surge in mobile app development and mobile-centric services. Meanwhile, cloud computing technologies, such as Amazon Web Services (AWS) and Google Cloud Platform (GCP), transformed the delivery of IT services and infrastructure, enabling scalable, on-demand computing resources over the Internet.

Present – Internet of Things (IoT) and 5G Connectivity

In the present day, the Internet continues to evolve with the expansion of Internet of Things (IoT) devices and the deployment of 5G wireless networks. IoT devices, ranging from smart home appliances to industrial sensors, are increasingly interconnected, generating vast amounts of data and driving innovation in automation, connectivity, and digitalization.

The Internet's journey from its humble beginnings as a research project to its present-day ubiquity as a global communication and information platform is a testament to human ingenuity, innovation, and collaboration. As we look to the future, emerging technologies such as artificial intelligence, blockchain, and quantum computing promise to further shape the evolution of the Internet and its transformative impact on society, economy, and culture.

Troubleshooting Network Issues

Networking problems can stem from a multitude of sources, ranging from hardware malfunctions and configuration errors to software bugs and security vulnerabilities. To effectively address these issues, it's crucial to understand the underlying causes and employ systematic troubleshooting techniques. In this section, we'll review the most prevalent network issues users encounter and offer comprehensive troubleshooting strategies to diagnose and resolve them. This will likely be like questions found on the A+ certification exam and will also be common topics when working in the field of IT.

1. **Connectivity Issues:**
    - **Symptom:** Inability to connect to the network or access the Internet.

- **Possible Causes:**
  - Faulty network cables or connectors.
  - Misconfigured network settings on the device or router.
  - Issues with the Internet Service Provider (ISP) or modem.
  - Wireless interference from neighboring networks or electronic devices.
- **Troubleshooting Steps:**
  - **Verify Physical Connections:** Check that network cables are securely plugged in and not damaged.
  - **Restart Networking Devices:** Power cycle the router, modem, and any network switches to reset connections.
  - **Verify Network Settings:** Ensure that the device has the correct IP address, subnet mask, gateway, and DNS server settings.
  - **Diagnose Wireless Issues:** Use network diagnostic tools to identify potential sources of interference and adjust wireless settings accordingly.
  - **Contact ISP:** If connectivity issues persist, contact the Internet Service Provider to troubleshoot modem or connection issues.

2. **Slow Network Performance:**
   - **Symptom:** Slow Internet speeds or sluggish network performance.
   - **Possible Causes:**
     - Network congestion during peak hours.
     - Outdated or malfunctioning networking equipment.
     - Malware or background processes consuming bandwidth.
     - Inefficient network configurations or routing issues.
   - **Troubleshooting Steps:**
     - **Check for Bandwidth Usage:** Monitor network traffic using diagnostic tools to identify bandwidth-intensive applications or devices.
     - **Update Firmware:** Ensure that routers, switches, and other networking devices have the latest firmware updates to address performance issues and security vulnerabilities.
     - **Perform Speed Tests:** Use online speed testing tools to measure Internet connection speeds and identify potential bottlenecks.
     - **Optimize Network Settings:** Adjust Quality of Service (QoS) settings to prioritize critical network traffic and minimize latency.
     - **Scan for Malware:** Run antivirus scans on all devices connected to the network to detect and remove any malicious software impacting performance.

3. **Intermittent Connectivity:**

    - **Symptom:** Periodic drops in network connection or intermittent loss of Internet access.
    - **Possible Causes:**
        - Wireless signal interference or signal strength issues.
        - IP address conflicts between devices on the network.
        - Router overheating or hardware malfunctions.
        - Service disruptions from the Internet Service Provider.
    - **Troubleshooting Steps:**
        - **Relocate Networking Equipment:** Position routers and access points away from potential sources of interference, such as microwave ovens or cordless phones.
        - **Assign Static IP Addresses:** Reserve IP addresses for network devices to prevent conflicts and ensure stable connectivity.
        - **Check Router Logs:** Review router logs for error messages or indications of hardware failures that may be causing intermittent issues.
        - **Contact ISP:** Report frequent connectivity issues to the Internet Service Provider to investigate potential service disruptions or line faults.

4. **Device Connectivity Issues:**

- **Symptom:** Inability of devices to connect to the network or communicate with other devices.
- **Possible Causes:**
    - Outdated device drivers or firmware.
    - Configuration mismatch between device settings and network requirements.
    - Security restrictions or access control policies blocking device connectivity.
    - Hardware malfunctions or compatibility issues.
- **Troubleshooting Steps:**
    - **Update Device Drivers:** Ensure that all devices have the latest drivers and firmware updates installed to address compatibility issues and security vulnerabilities.
    - **Check Network Settings:** Verify that device settings, such as IP addressing and subnet masks, are configured correctly to match network requirements.
    - **Review Security Policies:** Check network access control lists (ACLs) and firewall rules to ensure that devices are allowed to communicate on the network.
    - **Test Hardware Components:** Diagnose hardware issues by testing devices on different networks or using diagnostic tools to identify faulty components.

5. **Network Security Concerns:**

    - **Symptom:** Suspicious network activity, unauthorized access attempts, or data breaches.
    - **Possible Causes:**
        - Weak or default passwords on network devices.
        - Unpatched software vulnerabilities exploited by malware or hackers.
        - Insider threats or unauthorized access by employees or third parties.
        - Lack of encryption or inadequate security measures to protect sensitive data.
    - **Troubleshooting Steps:**
        - **Strengthen Passwords:** Enforce strong password policies and use multi-factor authentication (MFA) to secure access to network devices and resources.
        - **Patch and Update Software:** Regularly apply security patches and updates to network infrastructure, operating systems, and applications to mitigate known vulnerabilities.
        - **Monitor Network Traffic:** Use intrusion detection systems (IDS) and network monitoring tools to detect and respond to suspicious activities or security breaches in real time.
        - **Educate Users:** Provide cybersecurity awareness training to employees to educate them about phishing scams, social engineering tactics, and other common security threats.

By systematically diagnosing and addressing common network issues and security concerns, users can ensure stable connectivity, optimal performance, and robust security for their network infrastructure and devices. One recommendation that I would suggest is to make study cards using these troubling topics and the associated resolution steps. This will assist you in learning the steps and processes to address these issues, as well as reinforce the impact these problems place on customers.

Summary

In this chapter, we dove into the foundational concepts of networking, exploring the core principles, components, and troubleshooting techniques essential for building and maintaining reliable network infrastructure. We began by tracing the evolution of the Internet from its inception to its present-day ubiquity as a global communication and information platform, highlighting key milestones and technological advancements that have shaped its development.

Then, we examined networking concepts such as IP addressing, network standards, and topologies, providing a comprehensive overview of the fundamental principles underlying modern networks. We explored the differences between cabled and wireless networking, comparing their respective advantages, limitations, and technical considerations. Additionally, we discussed network security methodologies and common network protocols, emphasizing the importance of robust security measures and adherence to industry standards to protect against cyber threats and ensure data confidentiality, integrity, and availability.

Furthermore, we explored troubleshooting of common network issues, equipping readers with practical techniques and best practices to diagnose and resolve connectivity problems effectively. From troubleshooting no-Internet connection issues to addressing slow network speeds and DNS resolution problems, we provided actionable guidance to help users troubleshoot and resolve common network issues.

As we transition to Chapter 4, we shift our focus to the exciting topic of wireless networking, where we explore the technologies, protocols, and best practices that underpin the wireless revolution. From Wi-Fi and Bluetooth to cellular networks and IoT connectivity, wireless technologies have transformed the way we communicate, collaborate, and interact in an increasingly connected world.

CHAPTER 4

Our Wireless World

As we further progress into the topic of networking, we shift our aim towards the dynamic role of wireless connectivity. In today's digital age, the ubiquity of wireless devices underpins our daily activities, shaping how we communicate, work, and navigate the world around us. From smartphones to smart homes, the prevalence of wireless technology has revolutionized the way we interact with information and each other. However, with the unparalleled convenience and flexibility that a wireless world offers, come unique challenges and security considerations. While wireless connectivity empowers mobility and productivity, it also introduces vulnerabilities that can be exploited by malicious actors. Whether it's a rogue access point intercepting sensitive data or sophisticated man-in-the-middle attack, the wireless environment presents a spectrum of risks that demand vigilance and proactive measures.

In this chapter, we go on a comprehensive journey of learning within wireless networking. We aim to break apart the complexities of wireless technology, shedding light on its fundamental principles, operational dynamics, and security paradigms. By gaining a deeper understanding of wireless connectivity, we equip ourselves with the knowledge and tools necessary to navigate the evolving field of digital communication and safeguard against potential threats. Yet, we will also confront the inherent challenges and vulnerabilities inherent in wireless networks, addressing key concerns such as data privacy, network security, and regulatory

© Kodi A. Cochran 2024

K. A. Cochran, *CompTIA A+ Certification Companion*, Certification Study Companion Series,
https://doi.org/10.1007/979-8-8688-0867-8_4

compliance. Through education, awareness, and proactive measures, we can harness the power of wireless technology to drive innovation, collaboration, and connectivity, while mitigating risks and protecting against potential threats.

Comparison with Wired Networks

In comparing wireless networks to their wired counterparts, it's essential to acknowledge the unique characteristics and trade-offs associated with each option. Wired connections have historically been the bedrock of network infrastructure, renowned for their reliability and stability. Conversely, Wi-Fi has emerged as a groundbreaking alternative, introducing unparalleled mobility, flexibility, and scalability to the networking field. Each has its own benefits and shortfalls they bring to the table, and one is not inherently superior to the other. With that said, it is in the vast majority that within any networking environment, there will be both wired and wireless connections.

Reliability and Stability

Wired Networks: Wired connections, typically Ethernet-based, offer robust reliability and stable performance. Physical cables ensure consistent data transmission, minimizing the risk of signal interference or disruptions.

Wireless Networks (Wi-Fi): While Wi-Fi networks provide impressive flexibility and convenience, they may be susceptible to signal interference, environmental factors, or congestion in densely populated areas, leading to potential fluctuations in connection stability.

Mobility and Flexibility

Wired Networks: Wired connections are inherently stationary, tethering devices to specific locations where Ethernet cables are installed. This limitation restricts mobility and flexibility, particularly in environments where constant movement or device relocation is required.

Wireless Networks (Wi-Fi): Wi-Fi networks liberate users from the constraints of physical cables, enabling seamless connectivity and unrestricted mobility within the coverage area. Users can access the network from anywhere within range, facilitating dynamic work environments and mobile computing.

Scalability and Deployment

Wired Networks: Deploying wired networks often entails substantial upfront costs and infrastructure investments, including cabling, switches, and routers. While wired networks offer unparalleled bandwidth and scalability, expanding or modifying the network infrastructure may require significant time and resources.

Wireless Networks (Wi-Fi): Wi-Fi networks boast incomparable scalability and ease of deployment, allowing rapid expansion and adaptation to changing organizational needs. With wireless access points (APs) strategically positioned, organizations can extend network coverage and accommodate growing user populations with minimal disruption.

Speed and Performance

Wired Networks: Wired connections typically deliver superior speed and performance compared to wireless alternatives. Ethernet cables offer higher bandwidth and lower latency, ensuring fast and reliable data transmission for bandwidth-intensive applications and mission-critical tasks.

Wireless Networks (Wi-Fi): Wi-Fi networks have made significant advancements in speed and performance, with modern standards such as Wi-Fi 6 (802.11ax) offering impressive throughput and efficiency. However, wireless connections may still exhibit latency and throughput limitations compared to wired counterparts, particularly in congested or high-interference environments.

Security

Wired Networks: Wired connections are generally considered more secure than wireless alternatives, as physical access to network infrastructure is required for unauthorized access. However, wired networks are not immune to security threats, and proper safeguards such as network segmentation, encryption, and access controls are essential to mitigate risks.

Wireless Networks (Wi-Fi): Wi-Fi networks introduce unique security challenges, including eavesdropping, unauthorized access, and rogue APs. Implementing robust encryption protocols (e.g., WPA3), strong authentication mechanisms, and regular security audits is critical to safeguarding wireless networks against cyber threats.

Wi-Fi Components

In this section, we will thoroughly review the components that work together to form a wireless networking infrastructure. Each device has its own unique purpose, in addition to pros and cons that it brings along with it. Some devices are no longer in active use and have largely been deprecated with the passing of time, such as hubs. Take the time to thoroughly review the key differences among these items and try to imagine why some did not stand the test of time.

Hubs

Hubs are the most basic device when considering networking components and are primarily no longer in use. The method in which they broadcast information caused numerous collisions and, with that, contributed to networking errors and other deficiencies. It is still something that we must learn and know as it is a requirement of the certification exam and something you may run into in the real world.

- Hubs are basic networking devices that operate at the physical layer of the OSI model.
- They receive data packets from one device and broadcast them to all other devices connected to the network.
- Hubs are characterized by their simplicity and low cost but are inefficient in managing network traffic and prone to collisions.
- Due to their limitations, hubs are rarely used in modern wireless networks and have been largely replaced by more advanced networking devices.

Switches

Switches are a more advanced version of a hub that operates on Layer 2 and sometimes Layer 3 of the OSI model. These devices better route data to reduce many of the issues present when utilizing a hub. It is very common to run into switches within any networking environment, and it is greatly beneficial to learn the fundamentals.

- Switches operate at the data link layer of the OSI model and are essential for managing network traffic efficiently.
- Unlike hubs, switches intelligently forward data packets only to the intended recipient device, minimizing network congestion and collisions.
- Switches offer higher performance, greater scalability, and improved security compared to hubs, making them the preferred choice for modern wireless networks.
- They are widely used in wireless LANs (Local Area Networks) and play a crucial role in ensuring fast and reliable data transmission.

Routers

Routers are seen as a more advanced version of a switch and operate at Layer 3 of the OSI model. These devices can calculate the most efficient method to route data to ensure the best quality of service and speed. In addition to that functionality, they can also even further reduce congestion and nearly eliminate collisions. It is greatly beneficial to all Information Technology practitioners to have a thorough understanding regarding routers.

- Routers operate at the network layer of the OSI model and are responsible for forwarding data packets between different networks.
- They use routing tables and protocols to determine the optimal path for data transmission, ensuring efficient communication across interconnected networks.

- Routers provide network segmentation, security, and traffic management capabilities, making them essential for creating and maintaining complex wireless network infrastructures.
- They are commonly used in wireless WANs (Wide Area Networks) to connect geographically dispersed networks and facilitate Internet access.

Broadcast Methods

Hubs: Broadcasts data packets to all devices connected to the network.

- An example of this would be many individuals in a room and one person attempting to shout over all the others to relay a message. Now imagine if each person were trying to send a message simultaneously. Everyone is yelling over one another, confusion is abundant, and the message was lost in translation.

Switches: Broadcasts data packets only to the intended recipient device based on MAC (Media Access Control) addresses.

- The best example here would be if ten people were in a room and one person (John) wanted to speak to another (Jane). In this situation, John would approach Jane and relay the message directly.

Routers: Do not broadcast data packets; instead, they use routing tables to forward packets to their destination networks.

- The functionality is slightly different here, in that they are not broadcasting information but forwarding it to its destination.

- An example of this would be if I wanted to send a message to someone, but I only had their name, someone would be designated to ensure that messages were delivered to the proper person. Once the message is sent, then I would store that routing information in case of future need.

Modems

- Modems (short for modulator-demodulator) are networking devices that enable communication between digital devices and analog transmission media, such as telephone lines or cable systems.
- They convert digital data into analog signals for transmission over analog channels and vice versa, facilitating connectivity to the Internet and other networks.
- Modems come in various types, including DSL (Digital Subscriber Line), cable, and dial-up modems, each offering different speeds and connectivity options.
- In wireless networks, modems are commonly used to establish Internet connectivity via broadband or cellular networks, providing essential access to online resources and services.

Access Points and Hotspots

- **Access Points (APs)** are wireless networking devices that allow Wi-Fi-enabled devices to connect to a wired network.
- They serve as bridges between wireless clients and the wired infrastructure, providing wireless access within a specific coverage area.
- **Hotspots** are public Wi-Fi access points that provide Internet connectivity to users in locations such as cafes, airports, and hotels.
- They are typically connected to a broadband Internet connection and offer convenient wireless access to the Internet for mobile devices and laptops.

Summary of Components

- Wireless networking components, including switches, routers, modems, access points, and hotspots, play essential roles in creating and maintaining wireless network infrastructure.
- Switches and routers manage network traffic, ensuring efficient data transmission and routing between devices and networks.
- Modems provide connectivity to external networks, such as the Internet, via broadband or cellular connections.

- Access points extend wireless coverage and enable Wi-Fi connectivity for devices within a specific area, while hotspots offer public Wi-Fi access in locations with high user demand.

Together, these components form the foundation of modern wireless networks, providing connectivity, mobility, and access to essential resources and services. Each component is no more important than the next, and they work in unison to create a seamless infrastructure for our technological needs. Many components are utilized whether it is a wireless or wired network, and some of the above may be reviewed further in other chapters.

Wi-Fi Configuration

Now that we have a thorough understanding of the various components residing in a wireless network infrastructure, we are going to review how to configure a wireless network. This section seeks to provide a detailed step-by-step guide on how to configure a wireless network to adhere to CompTIA A+ requirements.

1. **SSID Setup:**
    - The SSID (Service Set Identifier) is the name of your Wi-Fi network, which helps devices identify and connect to it.
    - Choose a unique and memorable SSID that does not reveal personal information.
    - Avoid using default SSIDs, as they can make your network vulnerable to attacks.

- **To set up the SSID:**
    - Access your router's administration interface through a web browser by entering the router's IP address.
    - Navigate to the wireless settings section and locate the SSID field.
    - Enter your desired SSID and save the changes.

2. **Channel Selection:**
    - Wi-Fi operates on different channels within the 2.4 GHz and 5 GHz frequency bands.
    - Choose a Wi-Fi channel with the least interference to optimize network performance.
    - Use Wi-Fi analyzer tools to identify nearby networks and their channel usage.
    - Aim for channels with minimal overlap and interference from neighboring networks.
    - Avoid using the default auto-channel selection feature, as it may not always choose the best channel.
    - **To manually select a Wi-Fi channel:**
        - Access your router's administration interface.
        - Navigate to the wireless settings section and locate the channel selection option.
        - Choose a specific channel based on the analysis from Wi-Fi analyzer tools and save the changes.

3. **Encryption Settings:**

    - Encryption is crucial for securing Wi-Fi networks and preventing unauthorized access.
    - Use WPA2 (Wi-Fi Protected Access 2) encryption, as it provides strong security and is widely supported.
    - Avoid using outdated encryption methods like WEP (Wired Equivalent Privacy), as they are vulnerable to security breaches.
    - Configure a strong passphrase for the Wi-Fi network, consisting of a combination of letters, numbers, and special characters.
    - **To configure encryption settings:**
        - Access your router's administration interface.
        - Navigate to the wireless security settings section and select WPA2 encryption.
        - Enter a strong passphrase and save the changes.

4. **Network Segmentation**

    - Network segmentation involves dividing the Wi-Fi network into separate subnetworks to improve performance and security.
    - Create guest networks for visitors or IoT (Internet of Things) devices to isolate them from the main network.
    - Use VLANs (Virtual Local Area Networks) to separate different types of traffic and enforce access controls.

- Implement network segmentation to reduce the impact of security breaches and minimize network congestion.
- **To set up network segmentation:**
    - Access your router's administration interface.
    - Navigate to the VLAN or guest network settings section.
    - Create separate VLANs or guest networks with their own SSIDs and security settings.
    - Configure access controls to restrict communication between different network segments.

Best Practices for Optimization and Security

- Regularly update your router's firmware to patch security vulnerabilities and improve performance.
- Position your router in a central location to ensure optimal coverage and minimize dead zones.
- Use Wi-Fi extenders or mesh systems to extend coverage in larger spaces.
- Enable MAC (Media Access Control) address filtering to restrict access to authorized devices.
- Disable WPS (Wi-Fi Protected Setup) to prevent unauthorized devices from connecting easily.
- Enable network logging and monitoring to detect and respond to security threats effectively.

By following these steps and best practices, you can configure your Wi-Fi network to ensure optimal performance, reliability, and security. Not only will this enable you to efficiently configure a wireless network, but it also prepares you for the CompTIA A+ certification exam.

Wi-Fi Quality of Service

Quality of Service (QoS) in Wi-Fi networks is a mechanism used to prioritize and manage network traffic to ensure optimal performance for critical applications, such as voice and video communication, online gaming, and real-time streaming. QoS helps maintain consistent and reliable network performance by allocating bandwidth and minimizing latency for high-priority traffic. In modern environments, this has become a common feature that can be toggled on or off and has been gaining significant popularity in recent years.

QoS Mechanisms

1. **Traffic Classification:** QoS begins with the classification of network traffic into different categories based on their priority or type of service. This classification helps routers and switches identify which packets should receive preferential treatment.

2. **Traffic Prioritization:** Once traffic is classified, QoS prioritizes packets based on predefined rules or policies. High-priority traffic, such as voice calls or video conferencing, is given preferential treatment over less time-sensitive data, like file downloads or email.

3. **Traffic Shaping:** Traffic shaping regulates the flow of network traffic to ensure that high-priority packets are transmitted smoothly and without delays. It can involve delaying or buffering lower-priority packets to prevent them from overwhelming the network.

4. **Bandwidth Reservation:** QoS can reserve a portion of the available bandwidth for specific applications or users, guaranteeing them a minimum level of service even during periods of network congestion. This ensures that critical applications always have sufficient bandwidth to operate effectively.

5. **Packet Scheduling:** Packet scheduling algorithms determine the order in which packets are transmitted over the network. QoS uses scheduling techniques like Weighted Fair Queuing (WFQ) or Priority Queuing (PQ) to prioritize high-priority traffic and minimize latency for time-sensitive applications.

Configuration Options

1. **Traffic Classification Rules:** Administrators can define classification rules based on factors such as source/destination IP addresses, port numbers, or application types. These rules determine how traffic is categorized and prioritized within the network.

2. **QoS Policies:** QoS policies specify the treatment of different types of traffic based on their priority levels. Administrators can configure policies to prioritize voice and video traffic over other types of data, ensuring a better user experience for critical applications.

3. **Bandwidth Allocation:** Network administrators can allocate specific amounts of bandwidth to different traffic classes or applications, ensuring that high-priority traffic always receives sufficient bandwidth to meet its requirements.

4. **Traffic Shaping Parameters:** QoS parameters like maximum bandwidth limits, burst rates, and queue sizes can be configured to regulate the flow of traffic and prevent network congestion. Traffic shaping helps maintain consistent performance across the network, even during peak usage periods.

5. **Packet Marking and Tagging:** QoS-enabled devices can mark or tag packets with Differentiated Services Code Point (DSCP) values or IEEE 802.1p priority tags to indicate their priority level. Routers and switches use these markings to prioritize traffic and apply QoS policies accordingly.

By implementing QoS mechanisms and configuring them appropriately, organizations can ensure that critical applications receive the necessary network resources to operate effectively, in addition to optimizing overall network performance and user experience.

Wi-Fi Channel Allocation

Wi-Fi channels are allocated within the 2.4 GHz and 5 GHz frequency bands, which are divided into multiple channels to accommodate simultaneous communication between Wi-Fi devices. Each channel represents a specific range of frequencies over which Wi-Fi signals are transmitted, and these channels, when overlapped, can cause collisions that lead to poor network quality. Below, we will further break down the differences between the 2.4GHz band and the 5 GHz band, as well as the channel ranges included. From there, we will review best practices and recommendations.

Channel Allocation

1. **2.4 GHz Band:** In the 2.4 GHz band, Wi-Fi channels are spaced 5 MHz apart, but due to overlap, only three non-overlapping channels (channels 1, 6, and 11) are recommended for use in the United States. Other countries may have different channel allocations.
2. **5 GHz Band:** The 5 GHz band offers more channels and wider frequency ranges, allowing for higher data rates and reduced interference. Channels in the 5 GHz band are typically spaced at 20 MHz intervals, providing greater flexibility and reduced interference compared to the 2.4 GHz band.

Channel Bonding

Channel bonding allows Wi-Fi devices to combine multiple adjacent channels to increase bandwidth and data rates. In the 5 GHz band, channel bonding is commonly used to achieve higher throughput rates by combining two or more 20 MHz channels into a single 40 MHz or 80 MHz channel. However, channel bonding can also increase susceptibility to interference and reduce overall network performance, particularly in congested environments.

Interference Mitigation Techniques

1. **Automatic Channel Selection (ACS):** Many Wi-Fi routers and access points support automatic channel selection, which periodically scans for the least congested channels and switches to them to minimize interference.
2. **Dynamic Frequency Selection (DFS):** DFS enables Wi-Fi devices to detect and avoid radar signals in the 5 GHz band, reducing the risk of interference from radar systems and improving overall network reliability.
3. **Transmit Power Control (TPC):** TPC adjusts the transmit power of Wi-Fi devices to minimize interference with neighboring networks and optimize signal coverage within the desired area.

Channel Utilization Optimization

1. **Wi-Fi Site Surveys:** Conducting site surveys to identify sources of interference and measure signal strength and quality can help determine the optimal channel configuration for a Wi-Fi network.
2. **Channel Overlapping Analysis:** Analyzing channel overlaps and utilization across neighboring Wi-Fi networks can identify channels with the least interference and maximize throughput.
3. **Channel Planning Tools:** Using Wi-Fi channel planning tools and software applications can automate the process of selecting optimal channels based on real-time data and network conditions.
4. **Manual Channel Selection:** In some cases, manually selecting Wi-Fi channels based on channel utilization and interference levels may be necessary to achieve optimal network performance.

By implementing these techniques and best practices, Wi-Fi network administrators can effectively manage channel allocation, minimize interference, and optimize channel utilization to maximize throughput and overall network performance. For the purposes of the examination, it may be required either on a written or performance-based question to prove understanding of this topic. Keep in mind that the primary goal is to reduce as much overlap as possible, and the standard use channels for a 2.4GHz broadcast are 1, 6, and 11.

Wi-Fi Standards and Protocols

Wi-Fi standards play a crucial role in defining the specifications and capabilities of wireless networking technologies. The Institute of Electrical and Electronics Engineers (IEEE) 802.11 family of standards is the foundation of Wi-Fi technology, with each standard introducing new features, improvements, and advancements to meet the evolving needs of wireless communication. It is likely that these will appear on the certification exam, and it is highly recommended to thoroughly study the differences. Here's an overview of the key Wi-Fi standards and associated protocols:

1. **IEEE 802.11 Standards:**

    - **802.11b:** Introduced in 1999, 802.11b was the first widely adopted Wi-Fi standard, operating in the 2.4 GHz frequency band, and offering data rates up to 11 Mbps.

    - **802.11a:** Also introduced in 1999, 802.11a operates in the less congested 5 GHz frequency band and supports data rates up to 54 Mbps, providing faster and more reliable connections compared to 802.11b.

    - **802.11g:** Released in 2003, 802.11g combines the speed of 802.11a with the compatibility of 802.11b, operating in the 2.4 GHz band and supporting data rates up to 54 Mbps.

    - **802.11n:** Ratified in 2009, 802.11n introduced multiple-input multiple-output (MIMO) technology, which uses multiple antennas to improve signal strength, range, and throughput. It operates in both the 2.4 GHz and 5 GHz bands and supports data rates up to 600 Mbps.

- **802.11ac:** Introduced in 2013, 802.11ac (also known as Wi-Fi 5) builds upon the advancements of 802.11n by offering faster data rates, wider channel bandwidths, and improved multi-user MIMO (MU-MIMO) support. It operates exclusively in the 5 GHz band and supports data rates up to several gigabits per second.
- **802.11ax:** Released in 2020, 802.11ax (Wi-Fi 6) is the latest Wi-Fi standard designed to address the growing demand for high-performance wireless networks. It introduces features such as orthogonal frequency-division multiple access (OFDMA), target wake time (TWT), and uplink and downlink MU-MIMO to increase network efficiency, capacity, and throughput in dense deployment scenarios.

2. **Wi-Fi Protected Access (WPA/WPA2):**

   - **WPA:** Developed in response to security vulnerabilities in the original Wired Equivalent Privacy (WEP) standard, WPA introduced stronger encryption algorithms such as Temporal Key Integrity Protocol (TKIP) and improved authentication mechanisms to enhance Wi-Fi security.
   - **WPA2:** Introduced as the successor to WPA, WPA2 utilizes the more secure Advanced Encryption Standard (AES) encryption algorithm and provides stronger protection against security attacks. It remains the most widely used Wi-Fi security protocol today.
   - WPA3

The evolution of Wi-Fi standards has significantly impacted network performance, reliability, and security. Each new standard has introduced innovations to address the growing demands of wireless communication, enabling faster data rates, increased capacity, and enhanced security features. As organizations continue to adopt Wi-Fi technologies to support their digital initiatives, staying abreast of the latest Wi-Fi standards and protocols is essential for building and maintaining robust wireless networks.

For the CompTIA A+ certification exam, it is highly recommended to learn each of these various standards, as well as to be able to differentiate among them. This is often among the examination's question bank and will very likely come up. There are other security protocols that will be covered throughout the material, but for now, please review the above inclusions. In addition to that, there is a deprecated standard of "WEP or Wired Equivalent Privacy." This should not be used under any circumstances for the CompTIA exam, nor in practical implementations.

Wi-Fi Security Needs

Securing Wi-Fi networks is paramount in today's digital landscape, where the proliferation of wireless connectivity has introduced new security challenges and vulnerabilities. Protecting Wi-Fi networks against unauthorized access and cyber threats requires a multi-layered approach that encompasses encryption, authentication, and security protocols.

Rather than going into detail over it and providing a comprehensive breakdown, if you see the (Wired Equivalent Privacy) WEP encryption standard, it is not to be utilized. This has been deprecated and provides near-zero security within its operational environment. WEP is still often seen on the certification exam, and all we need to remember is that it is not secure and not to be used.

1. **Encryption Standards:**
    - Encryption plays a vital role in protecting data transmitted over Wi-Fi networks from eavesdropping and interception by unauthorized users. Implementing robust encryption standards ensures that data remains confidential and secure.
    - The Advanced Encryption Standard (AES) is widely regarded as the most secure encryption algorithm for Wi-Fi networks. It provides strong encryption capabilities and is used in conjunction with WPA2 and WPA3 security protocols.
    - WPA3, the latest Wi-Fi security protocol, introduces enhancements to encryption algorithms and strengthens security mechanisms to mitigate security vulnerabilities present in previous standards.
2. **Authentication Methods:**
    - Authentication mechanisms validate the identity of users and devices attempting to access the Wi-Fi network, preventing unauthorized access and unauthorized use of network resources.
    - Strong authentication methods, such as Extensible Authentication Protocol (EAP) with Protected EAP (PEAP) or EAP-TLS, provide robust authentication mechanisms that require user credentials or digital certificates for authentication.
    - Implementing strong authentication methods ensures that only authorized users with valid credentials can connect to the Wi-Fi network, reducing the risk of unauthorized access and data breaches.

3. **Security Protocols:**

    - Wi-Fi security protocols such as WPA2 and WPA3 enforce security measures to protect Wi-Fi networks against various security threats and attacks.
    - WPA2 utilizes strong encryption algorithms (e.g., AES) and authentication mechanisms (e.g., 802.1X/EAP) to secure Wi-Fi communications and authenticate users.
    - WPA3 introduces security enhancements such as individualized data encryption, forward secrecy, and protection against brute-force attacks, providing stronger security protections compared to previous standards.

4. **Threat Mitigation:**

    - Wi-Fi networks are vulnerable to various security threats, including eavesdropping, unauthorized access, and man-in-the-middle attacks. Implementing threat mitigation strategies such as network segmentation, intrusion detection/prevention systems (IDS/IPS), and firewalls helps identify and mitigate security threats in real-time.
    - Regular security audits and vulnerability assessments help identify security weaknesses and address them proactively, ensuring the integrity and security of Wi-Fi networks.

By implementing strong encryption standards, authentication methods, and security protocols, organizations can enhance the security posture of their Wi-Fi networks and protect sensitive data from unauthorized access and cyber-attacks. Adopting a proactive approach to Wi-Fi security and staying abreast of emerging threats and security best practices are essential for maintaining a secure and resilient wireless infrastructure. Don't forget, don't implement WEP.

Wireless Certification Programs

Wireless certification programs offered by reputable organizations such as CompTIA and Cisco play a crucial role in validating expertise and advancing careers in wireless networking. These certification programs provide individuals with the opportunity to demonstrate their proficiency in designing, implementing, and managing wireless networks, thereby enhancing their credibility and marketability in the IT industry. Let's review the objectives, requirements, and benefits of pursuing wireless certifications:

1. **Objectives of Wireless Certifications:**
    - Wireless certification programs are designed to equip individuals with the knowledge, skills, and competencies required to plan, deploy, troubleshoot, and secure wireless networks effectively.
    - The objectives of wireless certification programs typically encompass a broad range of topics, including wireless standards and protocols, network infrastructure, RF fundamentals, security protocols, and wireless troubleshooting techniques.

- By focusing on key areas of wireless networking, certification programs aim to ensure that certified professionals possess a comprehensive understanding of wireless technologies and can proficiently address the challenges associated with designing and managing wireless networks.

2. **Requirements for Wireless Certifications:**

    - The requirements for wireless certifications vary depending on the certification level and the certifying organization. Entry-level certifications may have minimal prerequisites, such as basic knowledge of networking concepts and technologies.

    - Higher-level certifications often have more stringent prerequisites, such as relevant work experience, prerequisite certifications, or completion of training courses.

    - Candidates are typically required to pass one or more certification exams that assess their knowledge, skills, and proficiency in wireless networking topics. Exam formats may include multiple-choice questions, simulations, and hands-on practical assessments.

3. **Benefits of Pursuing Wireless Certifications:**

    - **Validation of Expertise:** Wireless certifications validate the expertise and skills of professionals in designing, implementing, and managing wireless networks, providing employers with assurance of their competence.

- **Career Advancement Opportunities:** Achieving wireless certifications can open doors to new career opportunities and advancement within the IT industry. Certified professionals are often preferred candidates for roles such as network administrators, wireless engineers, and security specialists.
- **Enhanced Credibility and Marketability:** Holding wireless certifications enhances an individual's credibility and marketability in the job market. Certified professionals are recognized for their specialized knowledge and expertise in wireless networking, making them valuable assets to employers.
- **Skill Development and Professional Growth:** Pursuing wireless certifications involves rigorous study and hands-on practice, allowing professionals to expand their knowledge, develop new skills, and stay current with evolving technologies and industry trends.
- **Access to Exclusive Resources:** Certified professionals often gain access to exclusive resources, such as online communities, forums, and professional development opportunities, provided by certifying organizations and industry associations.

Troubleshooting Wi-Fi Problems

Identifying and troubleshooting common wireless networking problems is essential for maintaining optimal network performance and reliability. Here are some of the most common issues encountered in wireless networks, along with step-by-step troubleshooting processes for each:

1. **Slow or Intermittent Connectivity:**
    - **Step 1: Check Signal Strength:** Verify the signal strength on the client device by checking the Wi-Fi signal indicator. Move closer to the access point to improve signal reception.
    - **Step 2: Assess Interference:** Identify potential sources of interference, such as other wireless devices, electronic appliances, or physical obstacles. Relocate the access point or adjust its channel settings to minimize interference.
    - **Step 3: Review Network Configuration:** Review the wireless network configuration settings, including channel selection, security protocols, and QoS settings. Optimize these settings for better performance.
    - **Step 4: Update Firmware and Drivers:** Ensure that the access point firmware and client device drivers are up to date. Install any available updates to address compatibility issues and enhance performance.
2. **Connection Drops or Disconnections:**
    - **Step 1: Reset Network Components:** Power cycle the access point, router, and client devices to reset the network connections. Allow the devices to reconnect and establish stable connections.

- **Step 2: Check for Interference:** Investigate potential sources of interference that may disrupt wireless connectivity. Move wireless devices away from sources of interference or relocate the access point to a less congested area.
- **Step 3: Adjust Channel Settings:** Adjust the Wi-Fi channel settings on the access point to minimize channel overlap and reduce interference from neighboring networks.
- **Step 4: Update Firmware and Drivers:** Ensure that the access point firmware and client device drivers are updated to the latest versions. Firmware updates may include bug fixes and performance enhancements that address connectivity issues.

3. **Authentication and Security Issues:**

- **Step 1: Verify Network Credentials:** Double-check the network SSID and passphrase entered on the client device to ensure they match the access point's settings. Correct any typos or discrepancies in the credentials.
- **Step 2: Check Security Settings:** Review the access point's security settings, including encryption protocols (e.g., WPA2-PSK), authentication methods, and passphrase complexity requirements. Adjust the settings as needed to ensure compatibility with client devices.
- **Step 3: Reconfigure Security Settings:** If authentication issues persist, reconfigure the access point's security settings from scratch. Generate a new passphrase and re-enable security features to establish a secure connection.

- **Step 4: Perform a Network Reset:** As a last resort, perform a factory reset on the access point to revert all settings to their default configurations. Reconfigure the network settings and security parameters from scratch.

4. **Limited Range or Coverage:**

   - **Step 1: Check Access Point Placement:** Assess the placement of the access point and ensure that it is positioned centrally within the coverage area. Consider elevating the access point or relocating it to a higher position to improve signal propagation.
   - **Step 2: Install Additional Access Points:** If coverage is insufficient, consider installing additional access points to extend wireless coverage throughout the desired area. Configure the access points to operate on non-overlapping channels to prevent interference.
   - **Step 3: Evaluate Antenna Configuration:** Review the access point's antenna configuration and orientation. Adjust the antenna positioning or upgrade to high-gain antennas to enhance signal strength and coverage.
   - **Step 4: Conduct Site Survey:** Perform a comprehensive site survey to identify dead zones, signal obstructions, and areas of weak coverage. Use professional site survey tools to analyze signal propagation and optimize access point placement.

By following these step-by-step troubleshooting processes, network administrators can effectively diagnose and resolve common wireless networking problems, ensuring reliable connectivity and optimal performance for users. Not only is this practical knowledge that will come of use to those within the field, but it is likely to be included in the exam.

Wi-Fi Emerging Technologies

Emerging technologies in Wi-Fi, such as Wi-Fi 6 (802.11ax), Wi-Fi 6E, and mesh networking, are revolutionizing the wireless networking landscape by introducing advanced features and capabilities that enhance performance, coverage, and reliability. As with all other domains of the Information Technology field, wireless innovation is constantly adapting and evolving, by the day, and it is necessary to understand upcoming changes. Let's explore each of these technologies in detail to further our understanding:

1. **Wi-Fi 6 (802.11ax):**

    - **Features:** Wi-Fi 6, also known as 802.11ax, introduces several key features designed to address the growing demands of modern wireless networks. These features include orthogonal frequency-division multiple access (OFDMA), multi-user multiple input multiple output (MU-MIMO), and target wake time (TWT) scheduling.

    - **Benefits:** Wi-Fi 6 offers significant improvements in throughput, efficiency, and capacity compared to previous Wi-Fi standards. OFDMA enables more efficient spectrum utilization by dividing channels into smaller subchannels, allowing multiple devices to transmit data simultaneously. MU-MIMO enhances network performance by enabling access points to communicate with multiple devices concurrently. TWT scheduling reduces power consumption by allowing devices to schedule their wake times, improving battery life in mobile devices.

- **Applications:** Wi-Fi 6 is particularly well-suited for high-density environments such as stadiums, conference centers, and urban areas where multiple devices compete for network resources. It also benefits IoT deployments, providing better support for many connected devices and improving overall network efficiency.

2. **Wi-Fi 6E:**

    - **Features:** Wi-Fi 6E extends the capabilities of Wi-Fi 6 by leveraging the newly available 6 GHz frequency band. This additional spectrum offers wider channels and less congestion compared to the 2.4 GHz and 5 GHz bands, providing more room for high-speed data transmissions.

    - **Benefits:** By utilizing the 6 GHz band, Wi-Fi 6E networks can achieve higher data rates, lower latency, and better performance in densely populated areas. The availability of additional channels reduces interference and congestion, resulting in improved reliability and throughput for Wi-Fi devices.

    - **Applications:** Wi-Fi 6E is well-suited for bandwidth-intensive applications such as 4K/8K video streaming, virtual reality (VR), augmented reality (AR), and online gaming. It also benefits enterprise environments, enabling seamless connectivity for many users and devices.

3. **Mesh Networking:**

    - **Features:** Mesh networking utilizes multiple access points (nodes) interconnected wirelessly to create a unified Wi-Fi network. Each node communicates with neighboring nodes to extend coverage and create a seamless roaming experience for connected devices.
    - **Benefits:** Mesh networks offer flexible coverage expansion and improved reliability by eliminating dead zones and minimizing signal interference. They provide self-healing capabilities, allowing the network to automatically reroute traffic in case of node failure or signal degradation. Mesh networks also support seamless roaming, allowing devices to switch between access points without interruption.
    - **Applications:** Mesh networking is ideal for large homes, offices, and outdoor areas where traditional Wi-Fi routers may struggle to provide adequate coverage. It is also well-suited for temporary deployments, such as events and outdoor venues, where quick and easy setup is essential.

These emerging technologies in Wi-Fi are poised to transform the way we connect and communicate in the digital age, offering faster speeds, broader coverage, and more reliable connectivity for a wide range of applications. As these technologies continue to evolve, they will play an increasingly important role in shaping the future of wireless networking.

Summary

In this chapter, we covered all requirements of wireless networking as posed by the CompTIA A+ certification requirements, in addition to exploring the latest technologies and trends shaping the wireless world. We began by comparing Wi-Fi to wired connections, highlighting the benefits of wireless networking such as mobility, flexibility, and scalability. Through a comprehensive examination of wireless networking components, including hubs, switches, routers, modems, access points, and hotspots, we gained insights into their functionalities and how they collectively form the infrastructure of modern Wi-Fi networks. We then discussed key configuration aspects, such as SSID setup, channel allocation, encryption settings, and network segmentation, to optimize Wi-Fi performance and security. Quality of Service (QoS) mechanisms were explored to prioritize network traffic and ensure optimal performance for critical applications. Additionally, we examined Wi-Fi channel allocation strategies and the evolution of Wi-Fi standards and protocols, emphasizing their impact on network efficiency and compatibility.

Security considerations took center stage as we delved into encryption standards, authentication methods, and security protocols to safeguard Wi-Fi networks against unauthorized access and cyber threats. We also explored wireless certification programs and troubleshooting techniques to address common Wi-Fi issues effectively. Finally, we explored emerging technologies in Wi-Fi, such as Wi-Fi 6 (802.11ax), Wi-Fi 6E, and mesh networking, highlighting their features, benefits, and potential applications in enhancing wireless performance and reliability.

As we transition into Chapter 5, we will shift our focus to the transformative world of cloud computing. From fundamental concepts to advanced deployment strategies, we will explore the vast opportunities and challenges presented by cloud technologies in the modern digital landscape. Join us as we embark on this exciting journey into the clouds!

CHAPTER 5

Conquering the Cloud

Welcome to Chapter 5 of our venture through the world of IT essentials. In this chapter, we'll define all that is part of cloud computing, a modern element that has revolutionized the way businesses and individuals consume and deliver IT services. Cloud computing offers unparalleled flexibility, scalability, and accessibility, enabling organizations to streamline operations, enhance collaboration, and drive innovation. This chapter was designed to follow the requirements set forth by the CompTIA A+ certification exam and is intended to help all looking forward to furthering their knowledge or tackling the exam.

To make a note and clear some common misconceptions about the nature of the cloud, it is not limited to data centers or any typical geographical location. An individual could very well have physical resources hosted in their closet and utilize them remotely as a "cloud" solution. Although it is much more common and practical to utilize a large entity, such as AWS (Amazon Web Services), rather than to set up a home lab. Keep an open mind as you learn more about the cloud and we progress this chapter. Also try to think of how things can be "Cloud Washed," a term commonly used to add finesse to a product or solution. Cloud washing is an underhanded practice of rebranding a product to be more marketable.

© Kodi A. Cochran 2024

K. A. Cochran, *CompTIA A+ Certification Companion*, Certification Study Companion Series,
https://doi.org/10.1007/979-8-8688-0867-8_5

Overview of Cloud Computing

Cloud computing is a revolutionary technology that delivers computing resources over the Internet on a pay-as-you-go basis. It encompasses a wide range of services and deployment models, providing users with access to virtualized resources, such as computing power, storage, and networking, without the need for on-premises infrastructure. As time continues to progress, more and more items are going to cloud hosting and will likely continue to do so. Cloud services are not always necessarily centralized and can exist within multiple data facilities, often separated by large geographical distances. This alone improves business continuity and disaster recovery efforts but also aids in many other additional benefits. The cloud is seen to have rapid elasticity, in that it is traditionally more of an on-demand or as-needed service. Let's review these different key characteristics that are often unique to the cloud.

Key Characteristics of Cloud Computing

1. **On-Demand Self-service:**

- **Description:** Cloud computing enables users to provision and manage computing resources, such as servers and storage, without requiring manual intervention from the service provider.
- **Benefit:** This self-service capability empowers users to rapidly deploy and configure resources on-demand, facilitating agility and reducing dependency on IT support.

2. **Broad Network Access:**
   - **Description:** Cloud services are accessible over the Internet from any device with an Internet connection, enabling users to access resources from anywhere, at any time.
   - **Benefit:** Broad network access promotes ubiquitous access to cloud services, fostering collaboration, productivity, and flexibility for users across diverse locations and devices.
3. **Resource Pooling:**
   - **Description:** Cloud providers aggregate computing resources, such as servers, storage, and networking, into shared pools that can be dynamically allocated to multiple users as needed.
   - **Benefit:** Resource pooling optimizes resource utilization and enhances scalability by efficiently allocating and reallocating resources based on changing demands, thereby maximizing cost-effectiveness and performance.
4. **Rapid Elasticity:**
   - **Description:** Cloud resources can be rapidly scaled up or down in response to fluctuations in demand, allowing users to dynamically adjust resource capacity to meet changing workload requirements.
   - **Benefit:** Rapid elasticity enables organizations to respond quickly to changing business needs, ensuring optimal performance, resilience, and cost-efficiency without over-provisioning or underutilization of resources.

5. **Measured Service:**

    - **Description:** Cloud usage is metered and billed based on consumption, providing users with transparent pricing models that reflect the actual resources consumed.

    - **Benefit:** Measured service enables cost-effective resource management and budget optimization by allowing users to pay only for the resources they use, thereby eliminating upfront investments and minimizing wastage.

These key characteristics collectively define the essence of cloud computing. This empowers organizations to leverage scalable, flexible, and cost-effective IT solutions. With all of that said, it is worth considering whether a cloud migration might be right for your organization, whether that is to cover one solution or the entirety of the infrastructure. In the majority of instances, the prohibitive factors of a cloud migration are revolving around security or compliance concerns.

Service Models of Cloud Computing

When considering a cloud migration, there are various service models and deployment models to choose from. In this part, we will be covering the three service models that have grown to be the standards of cloud service models. Each of these requires a different amount of involvement, support, and maintenance from the client and as such is largely an important detail. Infrastructure as a Service requires the most upkeep from the client and primarily provides raw computing power to the user. Platform as a Service takes a step back from the full interactive approach and only requires the client to manage software, data, and associated details. Software as a

Service is the most hands-off approach, and commonly used web-hosted applications are SaaS deployments, which could entail an email service or a popular game.

1. **Infrastructure as a Service (IaaS):**

    - **Description:** IaaS delivers virtualized computing resources, such as servers, storage, and networking, as a service over the Internet. Users have complete control over the operating system, middleware, and applications, allowing for maximum flexibility and customization.

    - **Key Features:**

        - **Virtualized Infrastructure:** IaaS providers offer scalable and on-demand access to virtualized computing resources, enabling users to provision and manage infrastructure resources dynamically.

        - **Flexibility and Control:** Users retain control over the configuration, deployment, and management of their virtualized infrastructure, allowing for customization and optimization based on specific requirements.

        - **Pay-Per-Use Billing:** IaaS services typically operate on a pay-per-use or pay-as-you-go pricing model, where users are billed based on their actual resource consumption, providing cost-effective scalability and resource management.

2. **Platform as a Service (PaaS):**

   - **Description:** PaaS provides a comprehensive development platform with tools, libraries, and middleware to facilitate the building, testing, and deployment of applications. Developers can focus on coding and application logic without the burden of managing underlying infrastructure components.
   - **Key Features:**
     - **Development Environment:** PaaS platforms offer integrated development environments (IDEs), frameworks, and runtime environments that streamline the application development lifecycle, from coding to deployment.
     - **Abstraction of Infrastructure:** PaaS abstracts away the complexity of infrastructure management, allowing developers to focus solely on application development and innovation.
     - **Scalability and Integration:** PaaS environments support horizontal and vertical scalability, enabling applications to scale seamlessly based on demand. Additionally, PaaS platforms often integrate with other cloud services and third-party APIs, facilitating interoperability and extensibility.

3. **Software as a Service (SaaS):**

   - **Description:** SaaS delivers software applications over the Internet on a subscription basis, eliminating the need for on-premises installation, maintenance, and management. Users access applications via a web browser or API, with updates and maintenance handled by the service provider.

- **Key Features:**
    - **On-Demand Access:** SaaS applications are accessible anytime, anywhere, via the Internet, providing users with convenient and flexible access to software functionality and data.
    - **Automatic Updates and Maintenance:** SaaS providers are responsible for software updates, patches, and maintenance tasks, ensuring that users always have access to the latest features and enhancements without manual intervention.
    - **Multi-Tenancy and Scalability:** SaaS applications are typically multi-tenant, meaning that multiple users share a single instance of the application, which enables efficient resource utilization and scalability. Providers can scale resources dynamically to accommodate growing user bases and workload demands.

Explanation of Cloud Deployment Models

Cloud deployment models define how cloud services are hosted and managed, with varying degrees of control, security, and customization. These are the different methods of management and access that a client will have to review. Primarily, the most prohibitive factor here is the cost associated with each individual instance. A private cloud may provide the most security and access control; however, it is always going to be the most expensive option. Alternatively, a public cloud will be the cheapest solution but, by its very nature, is a publicly accessible platform. Let's break this down a bit further and review the key elements of each deployment model.

1. **Public Cloud:**
   - **Description:** Public cloud services are provided by third-party vendors and made accessible to the public over the Internet. Resources, including servers, storage, and applications, are shared among multiple users and organizations, enabling cost-effective scalability and flexibility.
   - **Key Characteristics:**
     - **Shared Infrastructure:** Public cloud providers maintain a shared pool of computing resources, allowing multiple users to access and utilize these resources on-demand.
     - **Scalability and Elasticity:** Public cloud environments offer scalability, allowing users to scale resources up or down based quickly and easily on demand. This elasticity ensures that organizations pay only for the resources they consume, optimizing cost efficiency.
     - **Pay-Per-Use Model:** Public cloud services typically operate on a pay-per-use or subscription-based pricing model, where users are charged based on their resource

consumption. This pricing structure offers cost predictability and flexibility, as organizations can adjust their usage and spending according to their needs.

- **Outsourced Management:** Public cloud providers handle the management, maintenance, and security of the underlying infrastructure, relieving organizations of the burden of infrastructure management and allowing them to focus on their core business activities.

2. **Private Cloud:**

- **Description:** Private cloud services are dedicated to a single organization and can be hosted either on-premises within the organization's data center or by a third-party provider. Private clouds offer greater control, security, and customization compared to public cloud environments.
- **Key Characteristics:**
    - **Dedicated Infrastructure:** Private clouds provide dedicated computing resources exclusively for use by a single organization, ensuring that resources are not shared with other users or organizations.
    - **Enhanced Security and Compliance:** Private clouds offer enhanced security controls and compliance capabilities, allowing organizations to maintain strict control over their data and ensure compliance with regulatory requirements.

- **Customization and Control:** Private cloud environments provide organizations with greater customization and control over their infrastructure, allowing them to tailor resources and configurations to meet specific business needs and requirements.
- **On-Premises or Hosted Deployment:** Private clouds can be deployed either on-premises within an organization's data center or hosted by a third-party provider. This flexibility allows organizations to choose the deployment model that best aligns with their budget, security, and compliance requirements.

3. **Community Cloud:**
    - **Description:** Community cloud services are shared among several organizations with similar interests, requirements, or compliance considerations, such as industry-specific regulations or standards. Resources and infrastructure are jointly owned, managed, and accessed by the participating organizations.
    - **Key Characteristics:**
        - **Shared Infrastructure:** Community clouds provide a shared pool of computing resources that are accessible to multiple organizations within a specific community or industry vertically.
        - **Collaboration and Resource Sharing:** Community clouds foster collaboration and resource sharing among organizations with

similar interests or requirements, enabling them to leverage shared infrastructure, applications, and services.

- **Enhanced Security and Compliance:** Community clouds offer enhanced security controls and compliance capabilities tailored to the specific needs and regulatory requirements of the participating organizations.
- **Cost Sharing and Efficiency:** By sharing the costs of infrastructure deployment and management, organizations within a community cloud can achieve cost efficiencies and optimize resource utilization, leading to reduced overhead and operational expenses.

4. **Hybrid Cloud:**

    - **Description:** Hybrid cloud environments integrate public and private cloud infrastructure, allowing organizations to leverage the scalability and cost-effectiveness of public cloud services while retaining control over sensitive data and critical workloads on-premises.
    - **Key Characteristics:**
        - **Integration of Public and Private Clouds:** Hybrid clouds seamlessly integrate public cloud services with private cloud infrastructure, enabling organizations to dynamically distribute workloads and data across both environments based on performance, security, and compliance requirements.

- **Data Portability and Interoperability:** Hybrid cloud environments facilitate data portability and interoperability between public and private cloud platforms, allowing organizations to move workloads and data seamlessly between environments as needed.
- **Flexibility and Scalability:** Hybrid clouds offer flexibility and scalability, allowing organizations to scale resources up or down dynamically to meet changing demand while maintaining control over critical data and applications.
- **Enhanced Security and Compliance:** Hybrid cloud architectures enable organizations to implement granular security controls and compliance measures tailored to the specific requirements of their workloads and data, ensuring that sensitive information remains protected and compliant across both public and private cloud environments.

Cloud Infrastructure Components

Cloud infrastructure comprises various components that work together to deliver computing resources and services to users. Like an on-premises infrastructure, each component serves its own unique purpose. Understanding these components is essential for building and managing cloud environments effectively. Here's an overview of key cloud infrastructure components:

1. **Virtualization:**

    - **Description:** Virtualization is a foundational technology in cloud computing that enables the creation of virtual instances of physical hardware, such as servers, storage devices, and networking equipment. By abstracting physical resources, virtualization allows multiple virtual machines (VMs) to run on a single physical host, optimizing resource utilization and enhancing scalability.

    - **Key Components:**

        - **Virtual Machines (VMs):** Virtual machines are software-based representations of physical computers that run guest operating systems and applications. VMs are created, managed, and executed by hypervisors, which provide the necessary abstraction layer between the hardware and virtualized environments.

        - **Hypervisors:** Hypervisors, also known as virtual machine monitors (VMMs), are software or firmware components that manage and allocate physical resources to virtual machines. Hypervisors enable the creation, execution, and management of VMs, ensuring efficient resource utilization and isolation between virtualized environments.

    - **Benefits:**

        - **Resource Optimization:** Virtualization optimizes resource utilization by consolidating multiple virtual machines onto a single physical host, reducing hardware costs and energy consumption.

- **Scalability:** Virtualization allows for rapid provisioning and scaling of virtual machines to meet changing workload demands, enhancing agility and flexibility in cloud environments.
- **Isolation and Security:** Virtualization provides isolation between virtual machines, minimizing the impact of security vulnerabilities and ensuring data privacy and integrity within virtualized environments.

2. **Hypervisors:**
    - **Description:** Hypervisors, also known as virtual machine monitors (VMMs), are software or firmware components that enable the creation, management, and execution of virtual machines in cloud computing environments. Hypervisors provide the necessary abstraction layer between physical hardware and virtualized guest operating systems, facilitating resource allocation and isolation.
    - **Types of Hypervisors:**
        - **Type 1 Hypervisor:** Type 1 hypervisors, also known as bare-metal hypervisors, run directly on the physical hardware without the need for an underlying operating system. Examples include VMware vSphere/ESXi, Microsoft Hyper-V, and KVM (Kernel-based Virtual Machine).

- **Type 2 Hypervisor:** Type 2 hypervisors, also known as hosted hypervisors, run on top of a conventional operating system and leverage its resources to manage virtual machines. Examples include VMware Workstation, Oracle VirtualBox, and Parallels Desktop.

- **Features:**

    - **Hardware Abstraction:** Hypervisors abstract physical hardware resources, such as CPU, memory, and storage, to create virtualized environments for guest operating systems.
    - **Resource Management:** Hypervisors allocate and manage resources dynamically, allowing for the efficient utilization of hardware resources among multiple virtual machines.
    - **Isolation and Segmentation:** Hypervisors provide isolation between virtual machines, preventing interference and ensuring data privacy and security within virtualized environments.

3. **Storage Systems:**

    - **Description:** Cloud storage systems provide scalable and resilient storage solutions for storing data in cloud computing environments. These systems leverage distributed storage architectures to ensure data durability, availability, and performance.

- **Types of Cloud Storage:**
    - **Object Storage:** Object storage systems store data as objects within a flat namespace, enabling efficient storage and retrieval of unstructured data. Examples include Amazon S3, Google Cloud Storage, and Azure Blob Storage.
    - **Block Storage:** Block storage systems provide raw storage volumes that can be attached to virtual machines as block devices, allowing low-level access to data. Examples include Amazon EBS, Google Persistent Disk, and Azure Disk Storage.
    - **File Storage:** File storage systems offer network-attached storage (NAS) solutions for sharing files and directories across multiple virtual machines. Examples include Amazon EFS, Google Cloud Filestore, and Azure File Storage.
- **Features:**
    - **Scalability:** Cloud storage systems are highly scalable, allowing organizations to scale storage capacity up or down dynamically to accommodate changing data storage requirements.
    - **Resilience:** Cloud storage systems employ redundancy and data replication techniques to ensure data durability and availability, even in the event of hardware failures or network outages.
    - **Accessibility:** Cloud storage systems provide ubiquitous access to data from any location with an Internet connection, enabling seamless data sharing and collaboration among users and applications.

4. **Network Configurations:**

    - **Description:** Network configurations in cloud computing involve the design and management of networking resources to facilitate communication between cloud components and users. This includes configuring virtual networks, subnets, routing, and security groups to ensure secure and efficient data transmission within the cloud environment.

    - **Components of Network Configurations:**

        - **Virtual Networks:** Virtual networks provide isolated network environments within the cloud, allowing organizations to segment and isolate workloads based on security, compliance, or performance requirements.

        - **Subnets:** Subnets divide virtual networks into smaller, logical segments to optimize network traffic management and resource allocation.

        - **Routing:** Routing enables the transmission of data between virtual machines, subnets, and external networks, ensuring connectivity and data exchange within the cloud environment.

        - **Security Groups:** Security groups define firewall rules and access controls to regulate incoming and outgoing traffic to virtual machines and network resources, enhancing network security and compliance.

- **Considerations:**
  - **Performance:** Network configurations impact network performance, latency, and throughput, requiring careful planning and optimization to meet application requirements and user expectations.
  - **Security:** Network security is a critical consideration in cloud computing, requiring robust access controls, encryption, and monitoring to protect data and resources from unauthorized access and cyber threats.
  - **Compliance:** Network configurations must adhere to regulatory and compliance requirements, such as GDPR, HIPAA, or PCI DSS, to ensure data privacy, integrity, and compliance with industry standards and regulations.

Cloud Migration and Deployment

There are many considerations to be made when determining if cloud migration is right for your organization. These range from the level of overhead you are willing to take to costs and all the way through business continuity planning. Once you have determined that a cloud migration is the right fit to suit your operational needs, there are some logical steps to follow:

1. **Planning:** Start by defining the objectives and goals of your cloud migration initiative. Conduct a thorough assessment of your current on-premises infrastructure, including applications, data, and dependencies. Identify the workloads and applications that are suitable candidates for

migration to the cloud based on factors such as performance, scalability, and security requirements. Develop a detailed migration plan that outlines the scope, timeline, resources, and budget for the migration project.

2. **Assessment:** Evaluate your existing on-premises environment to determine the feasibility and readiness for cloud migration. Assess factors such as application dependencies, data volume and complexity, regulatory compliance requirements, and security considerations. Perform a cost analysis to estimate the potential cost savings and benefits of migrating to the cloud compared to maintaining on-premises infrastructure.

3. **Migration Methods:** Choose the appropriate migration method based on your specific requirements and constraints. Common migration methods include

    - **Lift and Shift:** Migrate existing virtual machines or servers to the cloud without making significant changes to the underlying infrastructure. This approach is suitable for applications that can run unchanged in a cloud environment.

    - **Replatforming:** Modify or refactor applications to leverage cloud-native services and capabilities while maintaining compatibility with existing systems. This approach may involve rearchitecting applications to take advantage of cloud-native features such as auto-scaling, serverless computing, and managed services.

- **Rehosting:** Move applications and workloads to the cloud with minimal modifications, typically using automated migration tools provided by cloud providers. This approach is suitable for applications that can be easily migrated without extensive changes or customization.

4. **Post-migration Considerations:** After migrating to the cloud, monitor and optimize your cloud environment to ensure optimal performance, cost efficiency, and security. Implement best practices for managing cloud resources, such as

   - **Continuous Monitoring:** Monitor the performance, availability, and security of your cloud infrastructure and applications using cloud monitoring and management tools. Set up alerts and notifications to detect and respond to any issues or anomalies proactively.

   - **Cost Optimization:** Optimize cloud costs by rightsizing resources, implementing cost allocation, tagging strategies, and leveraging reserved instances or spot instances where applicable. Monitor and analyze cloud spending to identify opportunities for cost savings and optimization.

   - **Security and Compliance:** Implement security best practices, such as encryption, access controls, and identity management, to protect sensitive data and comply with regulatory requirements. Regularly audit and assess your cloud environment for security vulnerabilities and compliance gaps and remediate any issues promptly.

Best Practices for Deploying Applications and Workloads in the Cloud

1. **Scalability:** Design applications and workloads to scale horizontally and vertically to accommodate fluctuating demand and workload patterns. Utilize cloud-native services such as auto-scaling, load balancing, and elastic storage to dynamically adjust resources based on demand.
2. **Elasticity:** Leverage the elasticity of cloud resources to scale up or down in response to changing workload requirements. Implement automated scaling policies and thresholds to ensure that resources are provisioned and deprovisioned dynamically based on demand.
3. **Resource Optimization:** Optimize resource utilization and minimize costs by rightsizing instances, consolidating workloads, and implementing performance optimization techniques. Utilize cloud monitoring and analytics tools to identify inefficiencies and opportunities for optimization and adjust resource allocations accordingly.
4. **High Availability and Disaster Recovery:** Design applications and architectures for high availability and fault tolerance by deploying them across multiple availability zones or regions. Implement disaster recovery solutions such as data replication, backup and restore, and failover mechanisms to ensure business continuity in the event of system failures or outages.

5. **Security and Compliance:** Implement security best practices such as network segmentation, encryption, and identity and access management (IAM) to protect cloud-based applications and data from unauthorized access and cyber threats. Ensure compliance with relevant regulatory requirements such as GDPR, HIPAA, and PCI DSS by implementing appropriate security controls, auditing mechanisms, and compliance frameworks.

By following these best practices, organizations can ensure a smooth and successful migration to the cloud, in addition to optimizing the deployment and management of applications and workloads in the cloud environment.

Cloud Security and Compliance

You may have noticed when speaking of security and compliance requirements that there are a lot of common themes. This is true with most aspects of the Information Technology world; however, the application of compensating measures and controls is vastly different for each scenario. Cloud security encompasses a range of principles and practices aimed at protecting data, applications, and infrastructure in cloud environments. Key security principles include

1. **Data Encryption:** Encrypting data both at rest and in transit to safeguard it from unauthorized access. Encryption algorithms and protocols are used to encrypt sensitive data before it is stored in the cloud and decrypted when accessed by authorized users.

2. **Access Controls:** Implementing access control mechanisms to manage and enforce user permissions and privileges. Role-based access control (RBAC), multi-factor authentication (MFA), and identity and access management (IAM) systems are used to authenticate users and restrict access to authorized individuals or entities.

3. **Identity Management:** Managing user identities, credentials, and access rights across cloud services and applications. Identity management solutions provide centralized control and visibility into user identities, enabling organizations to effectively manage user access and authentication.

4. **Compliance Standards:** Ensuring compliance with relevant regulatory requirements and industry standards, such as the General Data Protection Regulation (GDPR), Health Insurance Portability and Accountability Act (HIPAA), and Service Organization Control (SOC) 2. Compliance frameworks provide guidelines and best practices for protecting sensitive data and maintaining regulatory compliance in cloud environments.

5. **Data Sovereignty:** This is a factor when considering the cloud on particular requirements that certain geographic factors can place. In particular, this is the means of having to follow local, regional, state, and national requirements based on the hosted location of data. As with a lot of aspects in the technological world, location plays a tremendous factor in considering a cloud service provider.

6. **Legal Holds:** Another unique factor when considering the cloud as a provider is that of legal holds. This can be tremendously impactful to your organization, even when your data is not the data being collected. A legal hold occurs when a cloud provider (or client of theirs) is hosted on the same physical machine as your organization's data. When this occurs, the entirety of the physical device is held and brought offline, which in its own will cause disruptions but potentially can result in data loss.

Explanation of Shared Responsibility Model

The shared responsibility model defines the division of security responsibilities between cloud service providers (CSPs) and customers. Under this model, the CSP is responsible for securing the underlying cloud infrastructure, while the customer is responsible for securing their data, applications, and configurations within the cloud environment. Depending on the operational needs of an organization, as well as their desired outcome and levels of involvement, different deployment models may meet individual needs better than others.

Roles of CSPs and Customers

1. **CSP Responsibilities:**

    - Securing the cloud infrastructure, including physical data centers, servers, networks, and storage systems

    - Ensuring the availability, scalability, and performance of cloud services and resources

- Implementing security controls and measures to protect against common threats and vulnerabilities
- Providing compliance certifications and attestations to demonstrate adherence to industry standards and regulations

2. **Customer Responsibilities:**
   - Protecting data and applications stored in the cloud, including encrypting sensitive data, managing access controls, and implementing security policies
   - Configuring and managing cloud services and resources according to security best practices and compliance requirements
   - Monitoring and detecting security incidents and anomalies within the cloud environment and responding to incidents in a timely manner
   - Conducting regular security assessments and audits to ensure compliance with security standards and regulations

By understanding and adhering to the shared responsibility model, both CSPs and customers can collaborate effectively to mitigate security risks and ensure the security and compliance of cloud-based services and applications.

Cloud Management and Monitoring

There are various methods to perform administration and monitoring tasks within a cloud environment. Many of these will be familiar to you, as they are like other domains, but of course, the cloud does have a few unique traits and variables to keep in mind. Let's begin our review and further learn how to manage our newly set-up cloud deployment:

1. **Cloud Management Platforms (CMPs):** Utilize CMPs to centrally manage and orchestrate cloud resources across multiple cloud environments. CMPs provide features such as resource provisioning, automation, and policy enforcement, enabling organizations to streamline cloud management tasks and optimize resource utilization.

2. **Monitoring Tools:** Implement cloud monitoring tools to track the performance, availability, and health of cloud resources and applications. These tools offer real-time monitoring, alerting, and reporting capabilities, allowing organizations to proactively identify and resolve issues before they impact performance or availability.

3. **Performance Optimization Strategies:** Employ performance optimization strategies to optimize cloud resource utilization and improve application performance. Techniques such as right-sizing resources, load balancing, caching, and auto-scaling help organizations maximize the efficiency and cost-effectiveness of cloud deployments.

Overview of Cloud Governance Frameworks and Policies

As we have learned thus far, frameworks and policies are built to support and streamline our workflows. These are not "bad" words that should not be used, but tried and proven procedures that ensure key elements are considered within a particular instance. With this in mind, here is a higher level of some of the various frameworks and policy dependents to consider when working within a cloud environment:

1. **Resource Allocation Policies:** Define policies for allocating cloud resources based on business requirements, workload demands, and budget constraints. Resource allocation policies help organizations optimize resource utilization, minimize wastage, and ensure that resources are allocated efficiently across departments or teams.
2. **Cost Management Policies:** Establish cost management policies to control and optimize cloud spending. Policies may include budget limits, cost allocation tags, reserved instances, and cost optimization best practices to help organizations manage cloud costs effectively and prevent budget overruns.
3. **Compliance Enforcement Policies:** Enforce compliance with regulatory requirements, industry standards, and organizational policies through governance frameworks and policies. Policies may include data governance, access control, encryption, and auditing requirements to ensure data security, privacy, and regulatory compliance in the cloud.

By implementing cloud management and governance frameworks, organizations can effectively manage and monitor cloud resources, optimize performance, and ensure compliance with security and regulatory requirements. These frameworks provide guidelines, policies, and best practices for managing cloud environments and achieving business objectives effectively.

Summary

Chapter 5 aims to be a thorough exploration of cloud computing, covering key concepts, deployment models, infrastructure components, security principles, management techniques, and emerging trends. Over this chapter, we have ticked off all requirements of the CompTIA A+ exam. We began by defining cloud computing and discussing its characteristics and service models, including ***Infrastructure as a Service (IaaS), Platform as a Service (PaaS), and Software as a Service (SaaS).*** We then viewed the various deployment models—***public, private, community, and hybrid clouds***— highlighting their differences and considerations. Throughout the chapter, we examined the essential components of cloud infrastructure, such as ***virtualization***, storage systems, and network configurations, elucidating how they support different ***cloud service models***. We also addressed ***cloud migration*** strategies, deployment best practices, security principles, governance frameworks, and major ***cloud service providers***, providing a comprehensive understanding of ***cloud-native application development***.

As we transition into Chapter 6, we shift our focus from cloud computing to mobile technology. While cloud computing has revolutionized the way we store, process, and access data, mobile devices have transformed how we interact with information and communicate in our daily lives. In this next chapter, we will explore the domain of mobile devices, including their operating systems, components, setup, connectivity, and troubleshooting. We will dive deep into the inner workings of smartphones, tablets, and wearables, uncovering the hardware and software that powers these devices and enables their functionality.

CHAPTER 6

Mastering Mobile Devices

Welcome to Chapter Six of our A+ guide, where we begin to learn the dynamic world of mobile devices. In this chapter, we will explore the details of mobile technology, from the hardware components that power these devices to the software platforms that drive their functionality. As we further our understanding of mobile devices, we will equip you with the knowledge and skills needed to understand, configure, troubleshoot, and secure these ubiquitous gadgets. Mobile devices have become an integral part of our daily lives, revolutionizing the way we communicate, work, and interact with the world around us. From smartphones and tablets to wearables and beyond, these compact yet powerful devices offer unparalleled convenience and connectivity. However, with great mobility comes great complexity, and understanding the inner workings of mobile technology is essential for both personal and professional success.

Our learning experience begins with an exploration of the fundamental components that make up mobile devices. We will dissect these devices, examining the hardware elements such as processors, memory, storage, and batteries that drive their functionality. Understanding the anatomy of mobile devices lays the groundwork for our exploration of their operating systems and software platforms. Next, we will cover the diversity of mobile operating systems, from the most known Android and iOS to the lesser-known Windows and niche platforms. We will compare these operating

© Kodi A. Cochran 2024

K. A. Cochran, *CompTIA A+ Certification Companion*, Certification Study Companion Series,
https://doi.org/10.1007/979-8-8688-0867-8_6

systems, exploring their strengths, weaknesses, and unique features. Whether you're an avid Android enthusiast or a dedicated iOS user, this section will provide valuable insights into the mobile OS ecosystem.

Once we have established a solid foundation of hardware and software fundamentals, we will dive into the practical aspects of setting up and configuring mobile devices. From initial device setup to account creation and security settings, we will guide you through the essential steps to get your mobile device up and running smoothly. Connectivity is a cornerstone of the mobile experience, and in the next section, we will explore the various wireless technologies that enable seamless communication and data exchange. Whether it's Wi-Fi, cellular, Bluetooth, or NFC, understanding how to connect and troubleshoot these wireless connections is essential for staying connected on the go.

As with any technology, mobile devices are not immune to issues and vulnerabilities. In the troubleshooting section of this chapter, we will equip you with the tools and techniques needed to diagnose and resolve common mobile device problems. From battery drain and overheating to software glitches and network issues, we will empower you to tackle these challenges head-on. Security is paramount in the mobile world, and we will dedicate a section to exploring best practices for securing your mobile devices and protecting your personal data. From device encryption and biometric authentication to app permissions and remote wipe capabilities, we will cover all aspects of mobile device security. Finally, we will explore the role of mobile device management (MDM) solutions in enterprise environments, examining the features and benefits of these platforms for managing fleets of mobile devices. Whether you're an individual user or an IT professional responsible for managing mobile devices in your organization, this chapter has something for everyone.

So, grab your smartphone or tablet, and let's continue into the fascinating world of mobile devices. By the end of this chapter, you'll be equipped with the knowledge and skills needed to master the complexities of mobile technology and unleash the full potential of your mobile devices.

Mobile Device Components

Mobile devices have become indispensable tools in our daily lives, seamlessly integrating into our routines and enabling communication, productivity, and entertainment on the go. These devices, whether smartphones, tablets, or wearables, are sophisticated pieces of technology composed of various components working together harmoniously to deliver the user experience we've come to rely on. Understanding the intricacies of these components is essential for both users and technicians, as it provides insights into how these devices function and how to troubleshoot them effectively.

Components of Mobile Devices

1. **Display:** The display is the primary interface between the user and the device, serving as the window into its digital world. It not only presents information but also influences user interaction and satisfaction. Displays come in various forms, including LCD, OLED, and AMOLED, each with its unique characteristics such as resolution, color accuracy, and refresh rate.

2. **Processor (CPU):** Often regarded as the heart of the device, the processor handles all computations and instructions, driving the device's performance. The CPU's architecture, clock speed, and number of cores determine how efficiently the device can execute tasks, impacting overall responsiveness and multitasking capabilities.

3. **Memory (RAM):** RAM provides temporary storage for data and instructions that the CPU needs to access quickly. In mobile devices, RAM plays a crucial role in multitasking, allowing users to switch between apps seamlessly. The amount of RAM affects the device's ability to run multiple apps simultaneously without slowdowns or crashes.

4. **Storage:** Storage encompasses both internal and external memory options, serving as the repository for apps, media, and user data. Internal storage, typically flash memory, holds the device's operating system, apps, and user files, while external storage options like microSD cards offer expandable storage for users with high data needs.

5. **Battery:** The battery powers the device, providing the energy necessary for its operation. Battery life is a critical consideration for users, influencing device usability and portability. Factors such as battery capacity, efficiency, and optimization techniques impact the device's endurance and user experience.

Understanding these components and their interplay is essential for diagnosing issues, optimizing performance, and making informed decisions when selecting or troubleshooting mobile devices. Whether you're a user seeking to maximize device capabilities or a technician tasked with maintaining and repairing mobile devices, familiarity with these components is invaluable in navigating the complexities of mobile technology. Rest assured, this chapter will prepare you for not only the A+ certification exam but also the real-world workings of this field.

Mobile Device Operating Systems

Mobile device operating systems (OS) serve as the foundation for the functionality and user experience of smartphones, tablets, and other portable devices. These operating systems determine how users interact with their devices, manage applications, and access various features. Understanding the nuances of different mobile OS platforms is crucial for IT professionals and users alike, as it enables efficient navigation, customization, and troubleshooting of mobile devices.

1. **Android:**

    - Android, developed by Google, is one of the most widely used mobile operating systems globally. It offers a customizable and open-source platform, allowing device manufacturers and developers to modify and enhance the OS to suit their needs.
    - Key features of Android include a vast app ecosystem through the Google Play Store, seamless integration with Google services, and support for a wide range of devices from various manufacturers.
    - Android versions are named alphabetically after desserts, with recent versions including Android 11 (codenamed "R") and Android 12 (codenamed "S").

2. **iOS:**

    - iOS, developed by Apple, powers iPhones, iPads, and iPod Touch devices. Known for its simplicity, security, and seamless integration with Apple's ecosystem, iOS offers a polished user experience.

- The iOS App Store provides access to a vast selection of high-quality applications tailored for Apple devices, ensuring a consistent and optimized user experience.
- iOS receives regular updates and new feature releases, with the latest version being iOS 15, offering enhancements such as Focus mode, improved FaceTime capabilities, and redesigned notifications.

3. **Windows Mobile:**
   - Windows Mobile, developed by Microsoft, was a mobile operating system primarily used on Windows-based smartphones and PDAs. However, Microsoft ended support for Windows Mobile in 2020, and the platform is no longer actively developed or maintained.
   - While no longer a viable option for new devices, Windows Mobile played a significant role in the evolution of mobile computing and contributed to the development of modern smartphone interfaces and features.

4. **Other Operating Systems:**
   - Beyond Android, iOS, and Windows Mobile, several other mobile operating systems have been developed over the years, including BlackBerry OS, Symbian OS, and Firefox OS. However, these platforms have either been discontinued or have a minimal presence in the current mobile market landscape.

Understanding the characteristics and capabilities of different mobile operating systems empowers users to make informed decisions when selecting devices and allows IT professionals to provide effective support and troubleshooting assistance. All users have their own personal preferences, and it is commonly argued upon which is superior, but in truth, it really is just an opinion. There is no one-size-fits-all operating systems, and as unique as we are, each has its own appeal towards us as individuals.

Setup and Configuration of Mobile Devices

Regardless of the device at hand, its purpose, or how cutting edge of technology it is, you will still need to take the time to properly set up and configure that device, not only to function but to meet individual desires and goals. This is often a fairly simple process, at least from a high level, but can often become more involved depending on the preferences of the user.

1. **Initial Device Setup:**
    - When setting up a new mobile device, users are typically guided through a series of initial setup steps, including language selection, region settings, and Wi-Fi network connection.
    - Users may be prompted to sign in with their existing accounts (e.g., Google account for Android devices, Apple ID for iOS devices) or create new accounts to access device-specific services and features.

2. **Account Creation:**

    - Mobile devices often require users to create or sign in with various accounts to access essential services and features. These accounts may include

        - Email accounts (e.g., Gmail, Outlook) for email communication

        - App store accounts (e.g., Google Play Store, Apple App Store) for downloading and installing applications

        - Cloud storage accounts (e.g., Google Drive, iCloud) for data backup and synchronization

    - Users should follow the on-screen prompts to create or sign in with their accounts, ensuring the proper synchronization of data and settings across devices.

3. **Network Configuration:**

    - Configuring network settings is essential for ensuring seamless connectivity and access to online services on mobile devices.

    - Users can configure Wi-Fi network settings by selecting their desired network from the available list and entering the appropriate credentials (e.g., SSID, password).

    - For mobile data connectivity, users may need to insert a SIM card (for cellular-enabled devices) and configure APN (Access Point Name) settings provided by their mobile network operator.

4. **Security Settings:**

    - Securing mobile devices is paramount to protect personal data and sensitive information from unauthorized access and cyber threats.
    - Users should enable device security features such as screen locks (e.g., PIN, pattern, fingerprint, face recognition) to prevent unauthorized access to their devices.
    - Additionally, users should configure security settings related to data encryption, app permissions, device administration, and remote device management (e.g., Find My iPhone, Find My Device).

By following these steps for setting up and configuring mobile devices, users can ensure a smooth and personalized experience while maximizing the functionality and security of their devices.

Mobile Device Connectivity

Mobile devices offer various connectivity options to facilitate communication, data transfer, and interaction with other devices. Understanding these connectivity options is crucial for optimizing device usage and fully leveraging their capabilities. While each of these has its associated benefits and potential fallbacks, users are often able to utilize multiple methods to ensure a streamless connection is maintained. Of course, we are not locked to a single method of connectivity, and these are often intertwined. It is still important to know the differences in connection methods and the associated details it creates.

1. **Wi-Fi:**
    - Wi-Fi connectivity allows mobile devices to connect to wireless local area networks (LANs) for Internet access and data transfer.
    - Users can connect their devices to Wi-Fi networks available in their vicinity by selecting the desired network from the list of available networks and entering the network password (if required).
    - Wi-Fi offers high-speed Internet access and is ideal for activities such as web browsing, streaming media, and downloading large files.
2. **Cellular Data:**
    - Cellular data connectivity enables mobile devices to connect to the Internet using cellular networks provided by mobile network operators.
    - Users can access cellular data services by inserting a SIM card into their devices and subscribing to a mobile data plan offered by their network operator.
    - Cellular data offers Internet access on the go, allowing users to stay connected even when Wi-Fi networks are unavailable.
3. **Bluetooth:**
    - Bluetooth technology enables short-range wireless communication between mobile devices and other Bluetooth-enabled devices, such as smartphones, tablets, headphones, and speakers.

- Users can pair their devices with Bluetooth accessories to transfer files, stream audio, and control compatible devices remotely.
- Bluetooth connections are typically established through the device's settings menu, where users can search for nearby Bluetooth devices and initiate pairing.

4. **Near Field Communication (NFC):**
   - NFC is a wireless communication technology that enables data exchange between mobile devices and NFC-enabled objects, such as payment terminals, smart tags, and posters.
   - Users can use NFC-enabled devices to make contactless payments, exchange digital business cards, and access information stored in NFC tags.
   - NFC functionality is often integrated into mobile devices' settings, allowing users to enable or disable NFC and configure NFC-related features.
5. **Mobile Hotspot:**
   - Mobile hotspot functionality allows mobile devices to share their cellular data connection with other devices, such as laptops, tablets, and gaming consoles.
   - Users can enable the mobile hotspot feature in their device settings, configure hotspot settings (e.g., network name, password), and connect other devices to the hotspot network.

- Mobile hotspots provide a convenient way to create a temporary Internet connection for devices that lack built-in cellular connectivity or Wi-Fi access.

By understanding and utilizing these connectivity options, users can enhance their mobile experience, stay connected, and take advantage of the diverse capabilities offered by their devices. This is what truly creates a seamless experience and allows us to maintain an extreme level of mobility, all without losing connection.

Mobile Device Applications

Mobile applications, commonly known as apps, play a central role in enhancing the functionality and versatility of mobile devices. Understanding the nuances of mobile applications, including app stores, installation methods, and app management, is essential for maximizing the utility of mobile devices. It is worth mentioning that different devices and operating systems utilize different app stores and methods of downloading applications. One feature that Android boasts about is the ability to download apps as a .apk file without the need to utilize the Play Store.

1. **Mobile Applications Overview:**

    - Mobile applications are software programs specifically designed to run on mobile devices, such as smartphones and tablets, to perform various tasks and activities.

    - Apps cater to a wide range of purposes, including productivity, entertainment, communication, social networking, gaming, utilities, and more.

- Users can access mobile applications through digital distribution platforms known as app stores, where they can browse, search, and download apps based on their preferences and requirements.

2. **App Stores:**
    - App stores serve as centralized platforms for discovering, acquiring, and managing mobile applications.
    - Major app stores include the Apple App Store for iOS devices, Google Play Store for Android devices, and Microsoft Store for Windows devices.
    - Each app store offers a vast catalog of apps categorized by genre, popularity, and relevance, allowing users to explore and discover new apps easily.

3. **Installation Methods:**
    - Mobile apps can be installed on devices through various methods, depending on the device's operating system and app distribution platform.
    - Users can download and install apps directly from the app store by searching for the desired app, selecting it, and initiating the installation process.
    - Additionally, users can install apps from third-party sources by enabling app sideloading in their device settings and downloading the app's APK file from external sources.

4. **App Management:**

   - Managing mobile apps involves tasks such as organizing apps, updating apps, and uninstalling unwanted apps to optimize device performance and storage space.
   - Users can organize their apps by categorizing them into folders, arranging them on home screens, and customizing app icons and layouts.
   - App updates are periodically released by developers to introduce new features, fix bugs, and enhance app performance and security. Users can manage app updates manually or enable automatic updates in their device settings.
   - Uninstalling apps removes them from the device, freeing up storage space and resources. Users can uninstall apps through the device's settings or directly from the app store.

By understanding mobile applications and their management, users can harness the full potential of their mobile devices, personalize their user experience, and access a vast array of services and functionalities tailored to their needs and preferences. Not only do they provide all the above benefits, but applications are also the primary source of mobile entertainment. Whether a user is playing a game or streaming a show, apps are what allows this to happen.

Mobile Device Security

Mobile device security is of paramount importance in today's digital landscape, where mobile devices contain vast amounts of sensitive information and are vulnerable to various security threats. Understanding and implementing effective security measures is crucial for protecting data, preserving privacy, and mitigating risks associated with mobile device usage. Security measures are a necessary consideration in each and every domain of the IT world and cannot be taken lightly.

1. **Introduction to Mobile Device Security:**
    - Mobile device security encompasses a wide range of principles, technologies, and practices aimed at safeguarding mobile devices from unauthorized access, data breaches, malware attacks, and other security threats.
    - Key security considerations for mobile devices include data encryption, authentication mechanisms, device management, application security, network security, and user awareness.
2. **Data Encryption:**
    - Data encryption involves encoding data into a format that can only be accessed or deciphered with the appropriate decryption key or credentials.
    - Mobile devices employ encryption techniques to protect data stored on the device, transmitted over networks, and accessed by applications.
    - Encryption algorithms, such as Advanced Encryption Standard (AES), are used to encrypt sensitive data, including user credentials, personal information, and confidential documents.

3. **Biometric Authentication:**

    - Biometric authentication utilizes unique physical or behavioral characteristics, such as fingerprints, facial features, or voice patterns, to verify the identity of users.
    - Mobile devices incorporate biometric authentication features, such as fingerprint scanners, facial recognition systems, and iris scanners, to enhance device security and streamline user authentication processes.
    - Biometric authentication offers a convenient and secure alternative to traditional authentication methods, such as passwords and PINs.

4. **Device Management:**

    - Mobile device management (MDM) solutions enable organizations to centrally manage and secure mobile devices deployed across their networks.
    - MDM platforms facilitate device provisioning, configuration, monitoring, and remote management tasks, ensuring compliance with security policies and regulatory requirements.
    - Mobile device management encompasses functionalities such as device inventory management, software updates, security policy enforcement, and remote wipe capabilities in case of loss or theft.

5. **Best Practices for Securing Mobile Devices:**
   - Implement strong passwords, PINs, or biometric authentication methods to prevent unauthorized access to devices.
   - Keep devices and operating systems up to date with the latest security patches and firmware updates to address known vulnerabilities.
   - Install and regularly update security software, such as antivirus and antimalware applications, to detect and remove malicious threats.
   - Enable device encryption to protect sensitive data stored on the device and utilize secure communication protocols for data transmission.
   - Exercise caution when downloading and installing apps from third-party sources, and review app permissions to minimize security risks.

Mobile Device Management (MDM)

Mobile Device Management (MDM) solutions play a crucial role in managing and securing mobile devices in enterprise environments, enabling organizations to effectively oversee their mobile device fleet, enforce security policies, and ensure regulatory compliance. This is effectively what allows an organization to control and account for their mobile device deployments. In addition, it plays a crucial role in assuring that the company standards and best practices are upheld, let alone the legal and ethical considerations. There are various deployment methods of

MDM, and we will cover those in detail in the following sections, but first let's break down what MDM details, its benefits, and the role it plays in our environment:

1. **Overview of Mobile Device Management Solutions:**
    - Mobile Device Management (MDM) solutions are software platforms designed to centrally manage and secure mobile devices, such as smartphones, tablets, and laptops, across an organization's network.
    - MDM solutions provide administrators with a unified interface for deploying, configuring, monitoring, and maintaining mobile devices, regardless of their operating systems or manufacturers.
    - These platforms offer a range of features and functionalities, including remote device management, policy enforcement, application deployment, data encryption, and compliance monitoring.
2. **Role of MDM in Enterprise Environments:**
    - In enterprise environments, MDM solutions serve as the cornerstone of mobile device security and management strategies, enabling organizations to maintain control over their mobile device ecosystem and protect sensitive data.
    - MDM platforms allow administrators to remotely configure device settings, enforce security policies, and distribute applications to ensure consistency and compliance across all managed devices.

- Through centralized management consoles, IT administrators can monitor device status, track device location, troubleshoot issues, and perform remote actions, such as locking or wiping devices in case of loss or theft.

3. **Key Features and Capabilities of MDM Solutions:**
    - **Remote Device Management:** MDM solutions enable administrators to remotely configure device settings, enforce security policies, and perform maintenance tasks without requiring physical access to the devices.
    - **Policy Enforcement:** MDM platforms allow organizations to define and enforce security policies, such as password requirements, encryption settings, app restrictions, and network access controls, to mitigate security risks and ensure compliance.
    - **Compliance Monitoring:** MDM solutions facilitate compliance monitoring by providing real-time insights into device configurations, security posture, and usage patterns, allowing organizations to identify and address potential security gaps or policy violations.
    - **Application Deployment:** MDM platforms streamline the deployment and management of enterprise applications by providing centralized app distribution, version control, and license management capabilities.

Mobile Device Management solutions empower organizations to effectively manage and secure their mobile device infrastructure, ensuring data protection, regulatory compliance, and operational efficiency in today's increasingly mobile-centric business environment.

Mobile Device Management Varieties

Now that we have a fair level of understanding towards its role and purpose, we can further break down mobile device management into the various deployment methods. Each of these has its own areas that may be more attractive to an organization, but again there is no true "Correct" answer, and it is entirely based on the overlying objectives of the entity at hand. You will often find that an organization may not adhere to any single style and alternatively incorporate a mash-up that better caters to their goals.

1. **Bring Your Own Device (BYOD) Management:**
    - BYOD management refers to the policies, procedures, and technologies implemented by organizations to securely manage and protect employee-owned devices used for work purposes.
    - BYOD management solutions allow organizations to establish security protocols, enforce compliance requirements, and manage corporate data on employee-owned devices while respecting user privacy.
    - Key features of BYOD management solutions include containerization, which segregates personal and corporate data on the device, secure access controls, remote wipe capabilities, and application whitelisting or blacklisting.

2. **Choose Your Own Device (CYOD) Management:**
    - CYOD management offers employees a selection of pre-approved devices from which they can choose for work-related tasks, providing a balance between employee choice and organizational control.
    - CYOD management solutions enable organizations to maintain security standards and regulatory compliance by restricting device options to those that meet predefined criteria, such as security features, operating system versions, and compatibility with enterprise applications.
    - With CYOD management, organizations can streamline device provisioning, configuration, and support processes while offering employees flexibility and autonomy in selecting devices that best suit their needs.
3. **Corporate-Owned, Personally Enabled (COPE) Management:**
    - COPE management involves providing employees with company-owned devices that allow for personal use outside of work hours, offering a blend of corporate control and user freedom.
    - COPE management solutions allow organizations to configure and manage company-owned devices with predefined security policies, applications, and data controls while allowing employees to customize their device settings and install personal applications.

- COPE management provides a balance between security and user experience, enabling organizations to protect sensitive corporate data while respecting employee privacy and preferences.

4. **Dedicated Device Management:**
    - Dedicated device management focuses on managing specialized devices, such as kiosks, point-of-sale terminals, and ruggedized equipment, deployed for specific business functions or industry use cases.
    - Dedicated device management solutions provide centralized control and monitoring capabilities for managing device configurations, updating firmware, troubleshooting issues, and ensuring uninterrupted operation of critical business processes.
    - These solutions are tailored to the unique requirements of dedicated devices, offering features such as remote management, application lockdown, peripheral control, and compliance reporting.

Each Mobile Device Management (MDM) solution type offers distinct advantages and considerations based on organizational needs, user preferences, and device usage scenarios. By selecting the appropriate MDM solution type, organizations can effectively manage and secure their mobile device ecosystem while empowering employees to work efficiently and securely. In doing so, this allows for security to be managed and ensures that compliance standards are met.

Regulatory Compliance Requirements

Mobile devices have become common tools in various industries, facilitating communication, collaboration, and productivity. However, with the widespread use of mobile devices comes the responsibility to comply with regulatory frameworks governing data privacy, security, and confidentiality. Organizations operating in sectors such as healthcare, finance, and telecommunications are subject to stringent regulations that mandate the protection of sensitive information handled on mobile devices.

For example, the General Data Protection Regulation (GDPR) imposes strict requirements for the processing and safeguarding of personal data, including data stored or accessed through mobile devices. Similarly, the Health Insurance Portability and Accountability Act (HIPAA) sets forth standards for the protection of electronic protected health information (ePHI) transmitted or stored on mobile devices used in healthcare settings. Failure to comply with these regulations can result in severe penalties, fines, legal liabilities, and reputational damage.

Mobile Device Usage Policies

To mitigate risks associated with mobile device usage and ensure compliance with regulatory requirements, organizations develop comprehensive mobile device usage policies tailored to their specific needs and industry regulations. These policies outline acceptable use guidelines, security controls, data protection measures, and employee responsibilities regarding the use of company-issued or personally owned mobile devices for work-related activities. Key components of mobile device usage policies include

- **Device Registration and Enrollment:** Procedures for registering and enrolling mobile devices in corporate networks or mobile device management (MDM) systems to enable centralized management, monitoring, and enforcement of security controls.
- **Password Requirements:** Specifications for creating strong, complex passwords or passphrases to authenticate device access and protect sensitive data from unauthorized access or disclosure.
- **Data Encryption Standards:** Requirements for encrypting data stored on mobile devices to prevent unauthorized access in the event of loss, theft, or unauthorized disclosure.
- **Application Usage Guidelines:** Guidelines for installing, updating, and using approved applications on mobile devices, including restrictions on downloading potentially malicious apps or accessing untrusted sources.
- **Network Access Controls:** Controls for securing network connections and access to corporate resources, including virtual private network (VPN) configurations, firewall rules, and network segmentation measures.
- **Incident Reporting Protocols:** Procedures for reporting security incidents, data breaches, lost or stolen devices, or suspicious activities involving mobile devices to designated IT personnel or security teams for investigation and response.

Risk Management Strategies

Effective risk management is essential for identifying, assessing, and mitigating risks associated with mobile device usage in organizational environments. Organizations implement risk management strategies to proactively identify vulnerabilities, assess potential threats, and prioritize risk mitigation efforts to safeguard sensitive information and ensure regulatory compliance. Let's go over some of the core components of these strategies:

- **Risk Identification:** Identification of potential risks and threats associated with mobile device usage, including unauthorized access, data breaches, malware infections, physical theft or loss, and social engineering attacks.
- **Vulnerability Assessment:** Regular assessment and testing of mobile device configurations, applications, and security controls to identify vulnerabilities, weaknesses, and misconfigurations that could be exploited by attackers.
- **Threat Modeling:** Development of threat models to analyze potential attack vectors, threat actors, and attack scenarios targeting mobile devices, applications, and data stored or transmitted on these devices.
- **Risk Prioritization:** Prioritization of identified risks based on their likelihood, impact, and severity to allocate resources effectively and focus on mitigating the most critical risks first.
- **Implementation of Controls:** Implementation of risk management controls, such as encryption, access controls, device management policies, security awareness training, and incident response procedures, to mitigate identified risks and enhance overall security posture.

Employee Training and Awareness

Employee training and awareness programs play a crucial role in educating staff about mobile device security risks, regulatory compliance requirements, and organizational policies and procedures. These programs aim to empower employees with the knowledge, skills, and awareness necessary to recognize and mitigate security threats, protect sensitive information, and comply with regulatory obligations. Regardless of how many times we cover this and similar topics, always keep in mind that this is one of, if not the most, crucial elements to consider ensuring security. Our users are our first line of defense and are in such need to be kept informed of proper training and awareness practices as they come available.

- **Security Awareness Training:** Training sessions, workshops, or online courses covering topics such as phishing awareness, social engineering tactics, password security, mobile device hygiene, and incident reporting procedures
- **Policy Acknowledgment:** Requirement for employees to review, acknowledge, and adhere to mobile device usage policies, data handling procedures, and security guidelines as part of their employment agreements or annual certifications
- **Ongoing Education:** Continuous education and reinforcement of security awareness through periodic training updates, security reminders, newsletters, and simulated phishing exercises to keep employees informed about evolving threats and best practices

- **Knowledge Assessment:** Assessment quizzes, surveys, or knowledge checks to evaluate employee understanding of mobile device security concepts, identify areas for improvement, and measure the effectiveness of training programs
- **Feedback Mechanisms:** Mechanisms for employees to provide feedback, report security concerns, or seek assistance from IT or security teams regarding mobile device security issues, policy clarifications, or training needs

Troubleshooting Mobile Device Issues

Mobile devices have become indispensable tools for communication, productivity, and entertainment, but they are not immune to technical issues that can disrupt their functionality. Effective troubleshooting techniques are essential for diagnosing and resolving common problems encountered with mobile devices. Normally, with these sections, I would look to include examples or details of the specific trouble issue at hand. However, in most of these cases, that is not a universal occurrence and can manifest in different ways.

1. **Device Freezing or Unresponsiveness:** This can occur when the device itself locks up and does not acknowledge user input. Often, the screen will be frozen to a still image or at times appear distorted.
    - **Restart the Device:** Performing a soft reset or rebooting the device can often resolve issues related to freezing or unresponsiveness caused by temporary software glitches or memory leaks.

- **Force Restart:** In cases of severe freezing or unresponsiveness, performing a force restart by holding down the power and volume buttons simultaneously for a few seconds may help restart the device.

- **Clear Cache and Data:** Clearing cache and temporary data accumulated by apps and the operating system can alleviate performance issues and resolve freezing problems.

2. **App Crashes or Errors:** These occur while an application is running and forcibly closes, sometimes resulting in error.

    - **Update Apps:** Ensure that all installed apps are up to date by checking for updates in the respective app stores. App updates often include bug fixes and performance improvements that can resolve crashes or errors.

    - **Clear App Cache and Data:** Clearing the cache and data of specific apps experiencing issues can help resolve app crashes or errors caused by corrupted cache files or misconfigured settings.

    - **Reinstall Problematic Apps:** If an app continues to crash or display errors, uninstalling and reinstalling the app may resolve underlying issues with the app's installation or configuration.

3. **Connectivity Issues:** This can range from a total inability to access the network, a slow or intermittent connection, to even Bluetooth peripheral connections.

- **Check Network Settings:** Verify that Wi-Fi, cellular data, and Bluetooth settings are properly configured and enabled. Ensure that airplane mode is turned off and that the device is within range of the network or Bluetooth device.
- **Restart Network Hardware:** Restarting routers, modems, or other network equipment can help resolve connectivity issues caused by temporary network disruptions or router malfunctions.
- **Forget and Reconnect to Networks:** For Wi-Fi connectivity issues, forgetting the problematic network and reconnecting to it with the correct credentials can often resolve connection problems.

4. **Battery Drainage or Charging Issues:** This will generally manifest with the battery draining at an accelerated level or when experiencing longer charging times. This is something of importance in that a bad battery can have severe consequences, including explosions.

    - **Check Battery Usage:** Review battery usage statistics in the device settings to identify apps or processes consuming excessive battery power. Close background apps and adjust settings to optimize battery life.
    - **Calibrate the Battery:** Calibrating the battery by fully charging and discharging the device can recalibrate battery performance indicators and improve battery accuracy.

- **Use Original Charging Accessories:** Ensure that the device is charged using original charging cables and adapters compatible with the device to prevent charging issues or damage to the battery.

5. **Hardware Failures:** These represent the most broad and diverse form of troubleshooting and can manifest in a near limitless way.

    - **Run Diagnostic Tests:** Some mobile devices offer built-in diagnostic tools or apps that can perform hardware tests to identify and diagnose hardware failures, such as faulty sensors, buttons, or display issues.

    - **Contact Manufacturer Support:** If troubleshooting steps fail to resolve hardware issues, contacting the device manufacturer's support or visiting an authorized service center for professional diagnosis and repair may be necessary.

By following these troubleshooting techniques and tips, users can effectively diagnose and resolve common issues encountered with mobile devices, ensuring optimal performance and reliability for their devices. Regular maintenance, software updates, and adherence to best practices can help prevent future problems and prolong the lifespan of mobile devices.

Emerging Mobile Technologies

As technology continues to evolve, new innovations in the mobile space are reshaping the way we interact with our devices and the world around us. As with all other domains, this is a rapidly evolving field and one that requires a practitioner to stay ahead of the curve with continuous learning.

With that in mind, here are insights into some of the most exciting emerging mobile technologies:

1. **Augmented Reality (AR):** Augmented reality overlays digital information onto the real-world environment, enhancing the user's perception and interaction with their surroundings. AR applications are transforming various industries, including gaming, education, healthcare, and retail. From immersive gaming experiences to interactive educational tools and virtual try-on features in e-commerce, AR is revolutionizing how we engage with mobile devices and the world.

2. **Virtual Reality (VR):** Virtual reality creates immersive, simulated environments that users can interact with using specialized VR headsets or mobile devices. VR technology offers exciting possibilities for entertainment, training, and virtual experiences. From immersive gaming experiences to virtual tours of real estate properties and virtual meetings, VR is expanding the boundaries of what is possible in mobile computing.

3. **Internet of Things (IoT) Integration:** The Internet of Things (IoT) involves connecting everyday objects to the Internet and enabling them to collect and exchange data. Mobile devices serve as central hubs for controlling and monitoring IoT devices, such as smart home appliances, wearable devices, and connected vehicles. IoT integration enables seamless connectivity and automation, enhancing convenience, efficiency, and productivity in various aspects of daily life.

4. **5G Technology:** The rollout of 5G networks promises to revolutionize mobile connectivity by delivering faster speeds, lower latency, and greater capacity. 5G technology opens new possibilities for mobile applications and services, such as high-definition streaming, real-time gaming, augmented reality, and autonomous vehicles. With increased network capabilities, 5G is poised to enable innovative mobile experiences and drive the growth of the mobile ecosystem.

5. **Edge Computing:** Edge computing involves processing data closer to the source of generation, reducing latency, and enhancing efficiency in data processing and analysis. Mobile devices equipped with edge computing capabilities can perform complex tasks locally, without relying solely on cloud-based services. Edge computing enables real-time processing of data from IoT devices, augmented reality applications, and other emerging technologies, enhancing responsiveness and enabling new mobile experiences.

These emerging mobile technologies represent the forefront of innovation in the mobile industry, offering exciting opportunities for developers, businesses, and consumers alike. By embracing these technologies, mobile devices are becoming more versatile, powerful, and integral to our daily lives, paving the way for a future of connected experiences and digital transformation.

Summary

In Chapter 6, we learned the various components, operating systems, connectivity options, security measures, and troubleshooting techniques of the mobile world. We began by thoroughly detailing the fundamental components of mobile devices, highlighting their importance in the functionality and operation of smartphones, tablets, and other portable gadgets. We then ventured into the domain of mobile operating systems, discussing the various platforms that power these devices and their unique features and capabilities.

Next, we continued with the setup and configuration of mobile devices, providing step-by-step guidance on initial device setup, account creation, network configuration, and security settings. We also reviewed mobile device connectivity, covering a wide range of connectivity options such as Wi-Fi, cellular data, Bluetooth, NFC, and mobile hotspots, along with their uses, limitations, and setup procedures. Security emerged as a critical theme in our discussion, as we emphasized the importance of implementing robust security measures to protect sensitive data and ensure the integrity of mobile devices. We explored various security principles, including data encryption, biometric authentication, and device management, along with best practices for securing mobile devices in enterprise environments.

Furthermore, we examined ***mobile device management (MDM)*** solutions and their role in managing and securing mobile devices in corporate settings. We discussed different MDM solution types, such as ***BYOD (Bring Your Own Device) and COPE (Corporate-Owned, Personally Enabled),*** along with their features, benefits, and implementation considerations. Our exploration concluded with an in-depth look at troubleshooting techniques for mobile devices, equipping readers with the knowledge and skills to diagnose and resolve common issues effectively.

As we transition to Chapter 7, we shift our focus from mobile devices to the realm of printing technology. In this chapter, we will explore the world of printers, covering their types, functions, peripherals, maintenance, troubleshooting, and security considerations. From inkjet and laser printers to dot matrix and thermal printers, we will review the diverse array of printing technologies and their applications in various industries.

CHAPTER 7

Printing Perfection

In this chapter, we continue our learning with printing technology, by understanding the requirements of various printers, their functionalities, maintenance requirements, troubleshooting techniques, and security protocols. These requirements are set forth by the CompTIA A+ certification exam and are logically followed in order to learn the material. This publication will serve to prepare you for the exam in both the practical and technical portions you will face.

From conventional inkjet and laser printers to specialized dot matrix and thermal printers, we delve into the variances of printing mechanisms to understand what provides such impeccable print quality. Our exploration begins with a detailed examination of printer types and their functionalities. We will compare different printing technologies, comparing their distinctive features, advantages, and limitations. In addition, we will learn the common printer peripherals and consumables, including paper, ink, toner, and maintenance kits, offering insightful advice on managing printer supplies and optimizing printing costs.

Maintenance will prove to be a large aspect of our discussion, as it is the best preventative measure for print failure. We provide actionable guidance on maintaining printers for peak performance and prolonged lifespan. This includes strategies for cleaning printheads, replacing ink cartridges, calibrating printers, and troubleshooting common issues like paper jams and print quality discrepancies. Properly maintaining printers

© Kodi A. Cochran 2024

K. A. Cochran, *CompTIA A+ Certification Companion*, Certification Study Companion Series,
https://doi.org/10.1007/979-8-8688-0867-8_7

will increase the lifetime of the equipment and simultaneously reduce downtime and unplanned maintenance events.

Security considerations take precedence as we highlight the significance of fortifying printers and safeguarding sensitive documents against potential security breaches. We breakdown encryption standards, authentication methods, and security protocols designed to fortify printers against unauthorized access and cyber threats, underscoring the imperative of robust security measures in the contemporary digital landscape. Printers may not appear to be the most critical aspects of our environment, but they are often seen as footholds for any potential attackers. If a printer is compromised, an attacker is more likely to breach the network and pivot to other more mission-critical endpoints. While they may not seem to pose a threat on their own, it's the surrounding infrastructure and environment we have to remember.

Furthermore, we scrutinize the environmental impact of printing and outline strategies for mitigating paper wastage, curbing energy consumption, and reducing carbon footprint through eco-friendly printing practices. From advocating paperless initiatives to embracing energy-efficient printing technologies, we advocate for sustainable printing practices to foster environmental stewardship. Resource waste and the impact printing has on the environment are rather significant. From the number of plastics used in creating these devices to the trees cut down to produce paper, this all has an impact on our natural environment. We, both as individuals and business entities, have a moral obligation to reduce our impact on our surroundings and better position our future generations.

Our exploration culminates with insights into emerging trends in printing technology, including 3D printing, mobile printing, and cloud-based printing solutions. We discern the transformative potential of these innovations in enhancing printing efficiency, accessibility, and versatility, paving the way for future advancements in the field of printing technology.

Understanding Printer Types

In the domain of printing, understanding the diversity of printer types is essential to making informed decisions that align with your specific needs and goals. This section provides a thorough overview of the various printer technologies available in the market, shedding light on their unique characteristics, advantages, and limitations. This may not be one of the most common or forefront topics you would think of when considering this field, but ask yourself a question. How many offices have you worked in that do not utilize this technology?

- **Inkjet Printers:** Inkjet printers utilize liquid ink cartridges to produce high-quality prints with vibrant colors and precise detail. Ideal for home and office use, inkjet printers excel in rendering photographs, graphics, and text documents with impressive clarity and richness. However, inkjet prints may be susceptible to smudging and fading over time, requiring careful handling and archival storage.

- **Laser Printers:** Laser printers employ toner cartridges and electrostatic technology to produce sharp, crisp prints at high speeds. Renowned for their efficiency and reliability, laser printers are well-suited for high-volume printing tasks in business environments. With superior text quality and faster print speeds compared to inkjet counterparts, laser printers are the preferred choice for professional documents, reports, and presentations.

- **Dot Matrix Printers:** Dot matrix printers utilize impact technology to create characters and images by striking an ink-soaked ribbon against a continuous feed of paper. Although less common in modern printing applications, dot matrix printers remain relevant in specialized industries such as banking, logistics, and manufacturing. Recognized for their durability and ability to produce multi-part forms, dot matrix printers offer a cost-effective solution for transactional printing needs.
- **Thermal Printers:** Thermal printers employ heat-sensitive paper and thermal printheads to generate images and text without the need for ink or toner. Widely used in retail, healthcare, and transportation sectors, thermal printers excel at producing receipts, labels, and barcode stickers with exceptional speed and clarity. While thermal prints are resistant to smudging and fading, they may be susceptible to heat and light exposure, necessitating careful handling and storage.

Comparison of Printer Technologies

When evaluating printer technologies, several factors come into play, including print quality, speed, cost-effectiveness, and suitability for specific applications. Inkjet printers offer superior color reproduction and photo printing capabilities but may incur higher operational costs due to ink cartridge replacements. In contrast, laser printers deliver fast, high-volume printing with sharp text and graphics but require initial investment in toner cartridges and maintenance kits. Dot matrix printers offer unmatched durability and multi-part form printing capabilities but may be limited in print quality and speed. Thermal printers excel in producing high-speed, high-resolution prints for specialized applications but may be restricted to thermal paper consumables.

By understanding the value of each printer type and their respective technologies, you can make informed decisions when selecting the most suitable printing solution for your personal or business needs. Whether prioritizing print quality, speed, or cost-effectiveness, there exists a printer technology tailored to meet your requirements and exceed your expectations.

Printer Components and Functions

Let's further break apart printers and grasp their inner mechanisms, including a comprehensive breakdown of printer components, and additionally highlighting their distinctive features across various printer types. This extensive coverage not only enhances our understanding of printer technology but also ensures compliance with the CompTIA A+ certification requirements.

1. **Inkjet Printers:**

    - **Printheads:** Inkjet printers rely on printheads to eject microscopic droplets of ink onto paper, creating text and images with precision. These printheads, typically integrated into ink cartridges or printhead assemblies, contain tiny nozzles that expel ink onto the paper's surface, resulting in vibrant and detailed prints.

    - **Ink Cartridges:** Inkjet printers utilize ink cartridges to store and dispense liquid ink onto paper. These cartridges, available in individual color cartridges or combined color cartridges, house reservoirs of ink tailored to specific color profiles. By selectively combining ink colors during printing, inkjet printers produce a wide range of hues and shades with impressive color accuracy.

- **Paper Feed Mechanism:** Inkjet printers employ paper feed mechanisms to transport paper through the printing process smoothly. These mechanisms, consisting of rollers and guides, ensure precise paper alignment and movement, minimizing the risk of paper jams and misfeeds during printing operations.

2. **Laser Printers:**

    - **Cartridges:** Laser printers utilize toner cartridges filled with powdered toner particles to create images on paper. Unlike liquid ink, toner particles adhere to paper through electrostatic attraction and heat fusion, resulting in durable and smudge-resistant prints. Toner cartridges contain reservoirs of toner powder, which are distributed onto paper using electrostatic charges and heat generated by the printer's fuser unit.

    - **Fuser Unit:** The fuser unit in laser printers plays a crucial role in permanently bonding toner particles to paper. This component consists of heated rollers that apply pressure and heat to the toner-coated paper, melting the toner particles and fusing them onto the paper's surface. As a result, laser printers produce high-quality prints with crisp text and graphics that resist smudging and fading.

- **Drum Unit:** Laser printers feature a drum unit responsible for transferring toner particles onto paper during the printing process. This photosensitive drum receives electrostatic charges from the printer's laser or LED (Light-Emitting Diode) assembly, attracting toner particles to form images on the drum's surface. Subsequently, the drum transfers the toner images onto paper, creating precise prints with exceptional detail and clarity.

3. **Dot Matrix Printers:**

- **Dot Matrix Printhead:** Dot matrix printers utilize a printhead containing a matrix of tiny pins to create characters and graphics on paper. These pins, arranged in vertical columns and controlled electronically, strike an ink-impregnated ribbon against the paper, imprinting dot patterns that form alphanumeric characters, symbols, and images.

- **Ribbon Cartridge:** Dot matrix printers rely on ribbon cartridges to supply ink to the printhead during printing operations. These cartridges contain ink-impregnated ribbons wound around spools, with the ink coating the ribbons transferred onto paper by the printhead's impact pins. Ribbon cartridges ensure consistent ink delivery and long-lasting print quality in dot matrix printing applications.

- **Paper Tractor Feeder:** Dot matrix printers feature paper tractor feeders to guide continuous paper forms through the printing process. These feeders consist of pairs of tractor wheels that grip the perforated edges of continuous paper, advancing it through the printer in a precise and controlled manner. By maintaining proper paper alignment and tension, paper tractor feeders facilitate the reliable printing of multipart forms and documents in dot matrix printers.

By exploring the unique components of inkjet, laser, and dot matrix printers, we gain a deeper understanding of their inner workings and functional capabilities. These distinctive features contribute to the diverse range of printing solutions available in today's digital landscape, catering to various printing needs and preferences across different industries and applications.

Printer Connectivity

Printers offer a multitude of connectivity options to accommodate diverse user needs and network environments. Understanding these connectivity options and their configuration processes is essential for seamless integration into both personal and professional settings. Different connections offer various utilities and ease of use features that may be more cohesive in your working environment.

- **USB Connectivity:** USB (Universal Serial Bus) remains one of the most common connectivity options for printers, providing a straightforward and reliable connection between the printer and a computer or other devices. Users can simply connect the printer to a computer using a USB cable, enabling direct communication and printing capabilities without the need for network infrastructure. To set up a printer via USB, users typically connect one end of the USB cable to the printer's USB port and the other end to an available USB port on the computer, followed by driver installation and configuration.

- **Ethernet Connectivity:** Ethernet connectivity offers networked printing capabilities, allowing printers to be connected to local area networks (LANs) via Ethernet cables. This wired connection enables shared printing among multiple users within the network, facilitating centralized printing management and control. To configure a printer for Ethernet connectivity, users connect the printer to an Ethernet port on their network router or switch using an Ethernet cable. Subsequently, users may need to configure network settings on the printer, such as IP address assignment and network protocol settings, to ensure proper communication within the network.
- **Wi-Fi Connectivity:** Wi-Fi connectivity enables wireless printing, allowing users to connect printers to Wi-Fi networks without the need for physical cables. This wireless connection offers greater flexibility and convenience, allowing users to print from various devices within the Wi-Fi network range. To set up a printer for Wi-Fi connectivity, users typically access the printer's settings menu to initiate the Wi-Fi setup process. During setup, users select the desired Wi-Fi network from the available networks list and enter the network's security key or passphrase, allowing the printer to establish a wireless connection to the network.

- **Bluetooth Connectivity:** Bluetooth connectivity enables direct communication between printers and Bluetooth-enabled devices, such as smartphones, tablets, and laptops, without the need for a Wi-Fi network or cables. This wireless connection offers a convenient printing solution for mobile devices, allowing users to print documents and photos directly from their smartphones or tablets. To configure a printer for Bluetooth connectivity, users must first ensure that both the printer and the target device have Bluetooth functionality enabled. Users then pair the printer with the device via Bluetooth settings, following the on-screen instructions to complete the pairing process and establish a wireless connection for printing.

By understanding the various connectivity options available for printers, users can select the most suitable connectivity method based on their specific requirements and network infrastructure. Whether opting for USB, Ethernet, Wi-Fi, or Bluetooth connectivity, configuring printers for network printing ensures seamless printing operations and enhanced productivity in both home and office environments.

Printer Setup and Configuration

This is not a daunting task but one that will likely be performed regularly by IT support professionals. Setting up and configuring printers involves several steps to ensure optimal performance and functionality; these will vary from manufacturer and type of printer, but most follow a common pattern. From installing printer drivers to fine-tuning print settings, proper setup and configuration are essential for achieving desired print results and maximizing efficiency. It is worth noting that the number one best practice is to always follow the installation guide, but to cover the general steps, let's take a closer look at what all this entails in the real world:

1. **Installing Printer Drivers:**
    - Before using a printer, users must install the necessary printer drivers on their computers or devices. Printer drivers facilitate communication between the operating system and the printer, enabling the computer to send print jobs to the printer accurately.
    - Printer drivers can typically be downloaded from the manufacturer's website or installed using the installation CD provided with the printer. Users should ensure they download the correct drivers compatible with their operating system (e.g., Windows, macOS, Linux).
    - Once downloaded, users can run the driver installation program and follow the on-screen instructions to complete the installation process. After installation, the printer should be recognized by the operating system, allowing users to select it as a printing device.
2. **Configuring Print Settings:**
    - After installing printer drivers, users can configure print settings to customize their printing experience and meet specific requirements. Print settings may include options for paper size, orientation, quality, and layout.

- Users can access print settings through the print dialog box that appears when printing a document or directly through the printer's settings menu. Depending on the printer model and software, users can adjust various parameters to optimize print output and efficiency.
- Common print settings include selecting the desired paper size and type, adjusting print quality settings (e.g., draft, standard, high), choosing color or grayscale printing, and specifying the number of copies to print.

3. **Managing Printer Queues:**

- Printer queues refer to the list of print jobs waiting to be processed by the printer. Managing printer queues allows users to prioritize, cancel, or monitor print jobs effectively.
- Users can access the printer queue by opening the printer properties or settings on their computer. From the printer queue window, users can view the status of print jobs, pause or resume printing, and cancel individual or multiple print jobs as needed.
- In multi-user environments or networked printers, administrators may have additional options for managing printer queues, such as setting print job priorities, restricting access, and monitoring print activity.

4. **Optimizing Print Quality:**

    - To achieve optimal print quality, users can fine-tune print settings to match the desired output and printing requirements. This may involve adjusting resolution, color settings, and paper types to ensure clear, vibrant, and accurate prints.
    - Users can experiment with different print settings to find the ideal configuration for their specific printing needs. For example, selecting a higher print resolution may result in sharper images and text, while adjusting color settings can enhance color accuracy and saturation.
    - Additionally, users should ensure they use high-quality paper appropriate for the intended print job, as paper quality can significantly impact print results.

By following these guidelines for printer setup and configuration, users can streamline their printing workflow, optimize print quality, and achieve efficient printing operations tailored to their preferences and requirements. Just to reiterate the above, it is always in your best interest to follow the user manual as there will be variance depending on the brand and model.

Printer Maintenance and Troubleshooting

Proper maintenance and timely troubleshooting are essential for ensuring the smooth operation and longevity of printers. By adhering to best practices and employing effective troubleshooting techniques, users can address common printer issues and keep their devices in optimal condition. Proper maintenance can prevent a lot of the long-term problems that one will face with regular printer usage, especially in an office environment. Ensuring that printers are well taken care of will not only increase the lifespan of the device but also reduce the unscheduled downtime for trouble-related issues. Both maintenance and troubleshooting go hand in hand to ensure the longevity of the device.

Printer Maintenance Best Practices

1. **Cleaning Printheads:** Over time, printheads may accumulate dust, debris, or dried ink, leading to print quality issues such as streaks or smudges. Regularly cleaning printheads can help maintain optimal print quality. Users can typically access printheads through the printer's settings menu or maintenance panel. Follow manufacturer instructions to perform printhead cleaning procedures using recommended cleaning solutions or tools.

2. **Replacing Ink Cartridges:** When ink levels are low or depleted, users should replace ink cartridges promptly to avoid interruptions in printing. Most printers provide notifications or indicators when ink levels are low. Follow manufacturer guidelines to safely replace ink cartridges and ensure proper installation. Additionally, store unused ink cartridges properly to prevent drying or damage.

3. **Calibrating Printers:** Printer calibration ensures accurate alignment and color consistency in printed output. Users can calibrate printers using built-in calibration tools or software provided by

the manufacturer. Calibration procedures may involve adjusting color settings, print alignment, and density levels to achieve optimal print results. Regular calibration can help maintain print accuracy and consistency over time.

Printer Troubleshooting Techniques

1. **Paper Jams:** Paper jams are a common issue that can occur due to misaligned paper, debris in the paper path, or worn paper feed rollers. To resolve paper jams, users should first power off the printer and carefully remove any jammed paper using designated access points or trays. Clear any obstructions and ensure the paper path is clean before resuming printing.
2. **Print Quality Problems:** Print quality issues such as blurry or faded prints may arise due to various factors, including clogged printheads, low ink levels, or incorrect print settings. Users can troubleshoot print quality problems by performing printhead cleaning, replacing depleted ink cartridges, adjusting print settings, and using high-quality paper. Refer to printer documentation or online resources for specific troubleshooting steps based on the observed print quality issues.
3. **Connectivity Issues:** Connectivity issues can prevent printers from communicating with computers or networks, resulting in print job errors or delays. Troubleshoot connectivity issues

by ensuring proper cable connections, restarting the printer and connected devices, and verifying network settings. Users can also update printer drivers or firmware to resolve compatibility issues with the operating system or network environment.

By following these maintenance best practices and troubleshooting techniques, users can effectively address common printer issues, maintain optimal print quality, and prolong the lifespan of their printers. Regular maintenance and proactive troubleshooting can help minimize downtime and ensure reliable printing operations.

Printer Peripherals and Consumables

Printer peripherals and consumables play a necessary role in ensuring efficient printing operations and maintaining print quality. In fact, without the consumables, a printer would be unable to function. Understanding these components and adopting effective management practices can help users optimize printing processes and minimize costs. Here's an overview of printer peripherals and consumables, along with tips for effective management:

Printer Accessories

- **Paper:** Paper is the primary medium for printing documents, photos, and other materials. Various types of paper are available, including standard bond paper, photo paper, and specialty paper. Users should select the appropriate paper type and size based on the intended use and print requirements. Proper paper handling, storage, and loading are essential to prevent paper jams and ensure consistent print quality.

- **Ink and Toner Cartridges:** Ink and toner cartridges contain the printing materials necessary for producing text and images on paper. Ink cartridges are typically used in inkjet printers, while toner cartridges are used in laser printers. Users should use genuine or high-quality compatible cartridges recommended by the printer manufacturer to ensure optimal print quality and device performance. Proper storage and handling of cartridges can help extend their lifespan and prevent print quality issues.
- **Maintenance Kits:** Maintenance kits include various components and supplies needed for routine printer maintenance and upkeep. These kits may include cleaning materials, replacement parts, and maintenance tools required to clean printheads, rollers, and other printer components. Regular maintenance using maintenance kits can help prevent equipment failures, reduce downtime, and prolong the lifespan of printers.

Tips for Managing Printer Supplies

- **Inventory Management:** Maintain an inventory of printer supplies, including paper, ink, toner, and maintenance kits, to ensure availability when needed. Regularly monitor supply levels and reorder items as necessary to avoid stockouts or delays in printing tasks.
- **Cost Optimization:** Explore cost-saving measures to minimize printing expenses, such as purchasing supplies in bulk, leveraging discounts or promotions,

and selecting compatible or remanufactured cartridges from reputable suppliers. Additionally, consider implementing print management solutions or policies to control print volumes and reduce unnecessary printing.

- **Quality Assurance:** Prioritize print quality by using high-quality paper and genuine printer supplies recommended by the manufacturer. Avoid using low-quality or incompatible consumables, as they may compromise print quality, damage printer components, or void warranty coverage. Conduct regular print quality tests and maintenance checks to identify and address issues promptly.

By understanding the role of printer peripherals and consumables and implementing effective management practices, users can ensure smooth printing operations, maintain print quality, and minimize printing costs over time. Proactive management of printer supplies is essential for optimizing printing processes and maximizing the value of printing investments.

Printer Security Considerations

Printers, like other network-connected devices, are susceptible to various security risks that can compromise sensitive information and expose organizations to potential threats. Understanding these risks and implementing robust security measures are essential for safeguarding printers and protecting sensitive documents. Keep in mind that the primary goal is ensuring the safety and security of your entire infrastructure and is not limited to the printer itself. Some organizations may not have sensitive documents routed through the printer, but all organizations have sensitive components. If a printer is compromised, it is significantly easier for an attacker to pivot to a more mission-critical device. With that in mind, these components are just as necessary to properly secure. Here's an overview of printer security considerations, along with best practices for securing printers and mitigating security risks:

Overview of Printer Security Risks

- **Unauthorized Access:** Hackers and unauthorized users may attempt to gain access to printers to steal sensitive information, execute malicious attacks, or disrupt printing operations.
- **Data Breaches:** Printers may store copies of printed documents, which can contain confidential or sensitive information. Inadequate security measures may result in data breaches if unauthorized users' access or intercept printed documents.
- **Malware Attacks:** Printers are susceptible to malware infections, including viruses, ransomware, and other malicious software. Malware attacks can exploit vulnerabilities in printer firmware or software to compromise device security and compromise data integrity.
- **Network Vulnerabilities:** Printers connected to the network can serve as potential entry points for cyber attackers to infiltrate the network and launch attacks on other devices or systems.

Best Practices for Printer Security

- **User Authentication:** Implement user authentication mechanisms, such as PIN codes, passwords, or biometric authentication, to control access to printers and ensure that only authorized users can initiate print jobs or access printer settings.
- **Encryption:** Enable encryption protocols, such as Secure Sockets Layer (SSL) or Transport Layer Security (TLS), to encrypt print data transmitted between devices and printers over the network. Encryption helps protect data confidentiality and prevent unauthorized interception or eavesdropping.
- **Access Controls:** Configure access controls to restrict printer access based on user roles, departments, or privileges. Define and enforce access policies to limit the functions and features accessible to different user groups and prevent unauthorized usage or configuration changes.
- **Firmware Updates:** Regularly update printer firmware and software to patch known vulnerabilities, address security flaws, and improve device security. Monitor manufacturer updates and security advisories to stay informed about emerging threats and security patches.
- **Network Segmentation:** Implement network segmentation to isolate printers from other network devices and create separate network zones or VLANs for printers. This helps contain security breaches and limit the impact of potential attacks on other network resources.

- **Security Audits:** Conduct regular security audits and vulnerability assessments to identify potential security weaknesses, assess compliance with security policies, and address gaps in printer security controls.

By adopting these best practices and implementing comprehensive security measures, organizations can enhance printer security, mitigate security risks, and protect sensitive information from unauthorized access or exploitation. Proactive security measures are essential for maintaining the confidentiality, integrity, and availability of printer resources and safeguarding organizational assets against cyber threats.

Environmental Impact of Printing

Printing activities have a significant environmental footprint, contributing to paper waste, energy consumption, and carbon emissions. Understanding the environmental impact of printing and adopting sustainable printing practices are essential for minimizing ecological damage and promoting environmental conservation. Let's break apart what impact regular printer usage has upon our natural environment:

1. **Paper Waste:**

    - Printing often results in the generation of paper waste, including discarded documents, misprints, and obsolete printouts. Paper waste contributes to deforestation, habitat destruction, and landfill accumulation, posing environmental challenges.

    - To reduce paper waste, organizations can implement paperless initiatives, such as digital document management systems, electronic workflows, and online collaboration tools. By embracing digital alternatives to paper-based processes, organizations can minimize paper consumption and reduce the volume of paper waste generated.

2. **Energy Consumption:**

    - Printing devices, such as printers and multifunction devices, consume energy during operation, including printing, scanning, copying, and standby modes. Energy consumption contributes to greenhouse gas emissions, air pollution, and resource depletion, exacerbating climate change and environmental degradation.

    - To reduce energy consumption, organizations can implement energy-efficient printing practices, such as configuring printers to enter low-power or sleep modes when not in use, scheduling automatic shutdowns during non-business hours, and investing in ENERGY STAR certified printing equipment. Additionally, organizations can consolidate printing resources, deploy centralized print servers, and optimize printer fleet management to minimize energy usage and improve energy efficiency.

3. **Carbon Footprint:**

    - Printing activities contribute to the carbon footprint of organizations, as energy consumption and paper production processes release carbon dioxide (CO2) and other greenhouse gases into the atmosphere. Carbon emissions from printing operations contribute to global warming, climate change, and environmental degradation, affecting ecosystems, biodiversity, and human health.

- To reduce carbon emissions, organizations can adopt eco-friendly printing practices, such as using recycled paper, eco-friendly ink cartridges, and sustainable printing materials. Additionally, organizations can implement carbon offset programs, renewable energy initiatives, and environmental sustainability policies to mitigate the environmental impact of printing and promote eco-conscious behavior.

By implementing these strategies and promoting environmental stewardship, organizations can reduce the environmental impact of printing activities, conserve natural resources, and contribute to a sustainable future. Embracing eco-friendly printing practices not only reduces ecological harm but also fosters corporate responsibility, enhances brand reputation, and demonstrates a commitment to environmental sustainability. Every one of us should take accountability and do our part in maintaining the environment and preventing further harm.

Emerging Trends in Printing Technology

As printing technology continues to evolve, several emerging trends are shaping the future of the printing industry. These trends encompass innovative solutions that leverage advancements in technology to address diverse needs and drive new possibilities in printing. These are still not the most common but are becoming increasingly popular and more advanced with time.

1. **3D Printing:**
    - 3D printing, also known as additive manufacturing, is revolutionizing traditional manufacturing processes by enabling the creation of three-dimensional objects layer by layer from digital designs.
    - Emerging applications of 3D printing span various industries, including aerospace, automotive, healthcare, architecture, and consumer goods. From rapid prototyping and customized product manufacturing to medical device fabrication and architectural modeling, 3D printing offers unparalleled flexibility and versatility.
    - Future developments in 3D printing technology may include advancements in materials science, increased printing speed and resolution, and the integration of artificial intelligence (AI) and machine learning algorithms for optimized printing processes.
2. **Mobile Printing:**
    - With the proliferation of mobile devices such as smartphones and tablets, mobile printing has become increasingly popular, allowing users to print documents and images directly from their mobile devices.
    - Mobile printing solutions encompass wireless printing technologies, mobile applications, and cloud-based printing services that enable seamless printing from mobile devices to compatible printers.

- Future trends in mobile printing may involve enhanced mobile printing capabilities, improved compatibility across devices and platforms, and integration with emerging technologies such as augmented reality (AR) and virtual reality (VR) for interactive printing experiences.

3. **Cloud-Based Printing Solutions:**

    - Cloud-based printing solutions leverage cloud computing technology to provide scalable, accessible, and secure printing services from anywhere, at any time.
    - These solutions enable users to store documents in the cloud, access printing resources remotely, and initiate print jobs from web-enabled devices, enhancing productivity and flexibility.
    - Future developments in cloud-based printing may include enhanced collaboration features, advanced document management capabilities, and integration with Internet of Things (IoT) devices for automated printing workflows.

Discussion of Potential Applications and Future Developments

The potential applications of emerging printing technologies are vast and varied, spanning multiple industries and sectors. From personalized healthcare solutions and sustainable manufacturing practices to immersive entertainment experiences and educational innovations, printing technology continues to push the boundaries of what's possible.

Looking ahead, future developments in printing technology are expected to focus on enhancing efficiency, improving quality, and expanding the scope of applications. Advancements in materials science, digital design software, and automation technologies will drive innovation and unlock new opportunities in areas such as bioprinting, nanotechnology, and digital fabrication. As printing technology evolves, it will play a central role in shaping the future of production, design, and communication, driving innovation, empowering creativity, and fueling economic growth in the digital age.

By embracing emerging trends and exploring new possibilities, organizations and individuals can harness the transformative potential of printing technology to drive positive change and create a better future for all.

Summary and Conclusion

In this chapter, we covered the requirements of printing technology, exploring the various types of printers, their components, functions, and maintenance requirements. We discussed the importance of understanding printers in modern computing environments and highlighted the key considerations for optimizing printing processes and minimizing environmental impact. From inkjet and laser printers to emerging trends such as 3D printing and mobile printing, we reviewed printing technology and its potential applications across industries. Understanding printers is essential for IT professionals and individuals alike, as printers play a crucial role in facilitating communication, documentation, and creative expression. By mastering the fundamentals of printing technology, users can effectively utilize printing resources, troubleshoot common issues, and implement best practices for efficient and sustainable printing operations.

As we conclude this chapter, we encourage readers to further explore the world of printing technology and its evolving capabilities. Whether in professional settings or personal endeavors, a deeper understanding of printers can lead to enhanced productivity, cost savings, and environmental stewardship. By staying informed about the latest developments in printing technology and embracing innovative solutions, individuals can leverage printing technology to drive positive outcomes and contribute to a more efficient and sustainable future.

With a solid understanding of printing technology under our belts, we are now turning our eyes toward hardware components. In Chapter 8, we will learn all about computer hardware, exploring key components such as RAM, storage devices, motherboards, and power supply units.

CHAPTER 8

Hardware Handbook: Exploring Essential Components

Welcome to Chapter 8 of our comprehensive guide. In this chapter, we continue into the heart of computer hardware, where we will learn the very components that power our digital world. Computer hardware forms the backbone of modern computing systems, providing the necessary processing power, storage capacity, and connectivity to support a wide range of applications and tasks. From the central processing unit (CPU) to the power supply unit (PSU), each component plays a critical role in ensuring the smooth operation of computing devices.

Throughout this chapter, we will learn the fundamental building blocks of hardware, offering insights into their functions, installation procedures, and troubleshooting techniques. Whether you're a seasoned IT professional or an aspiring enthusiast, this chapter will equip you with the knowledge and skills needed to understand, maintain, and optimize hardware components effectively. From the basics of component anatomy to advanced troubleshooting strategies, this chapter will serve as your indispensable guide to mastering essential hardware components in the digital age. Without further ado, let's dive into the world of hardware and unlock the secrets of computing power and performance.

© Kodi A. Cochran 2024

K. A. Cochran, *CompTIA A+ Certification Companion*, Certification Study Companion Series,
https://doi.org/10.1007/979-8-8688-0867-8_8

Understanding RAM

Random Access Memory (RAM) is a crucial component of any computing system, serving as temporary storage for data and instructions that the CPU needs to access quickly. In this section, we'll review the various aspects of RAM, including its types, installation procedures, and troubleshooting techniques. This has briefly been covered previously in our chapter to cover laptops; however, we will now perform a deep dive and elaborate upon some of those previously mentioned concepts.

Types of RAM

RAM technology has evolved over the years, with different generations offering improvements in speed, efficiency, and capacity. The most common types of RAM include DDR, DDR2, DDR3, DDR4, and DDR5. Each type has its own set of characteristics, such as data transfer rates, voltage requirements, and physical dimensions. Understanding the differences between these types is essential for selecting compatible RAM modules for your system. As we have discussed in prior sections, there are also different form factors of RAM, and we will further cover that in another section.

1. **DDR (Double Data Rate Synchronous Dynamic Random Access Memory)**:

    - **Purpose**: DDR was introduced as an improvement over SDRAM (Synchronous Dynamic Random Access Memory) to increase data transfer rates.

    - **Historical Improvements**: DDR was the first generation of DDR memory, offering double the data transfer rates of SDRAM by transferring data on both the rising and falling edges of the clock signal.

- **Uses**: DDR memory was commonly used in desktop computers and early laptops.

2. **DDR2 (Double Data Rate 2 Synchronous Dynamic Random Access Memory)**:

   - **Purpose**: DDR2 aimed to further increase data transfer rates and reduce power consumption compared to DDR.
   - **Historical Improvements**: DDR2 introduced improvements such as higher clock speeds, prefetch buffers, and on-die termination to enhance performance and efficiency.
   - **Uses**: DDR2 memory became standard in mid-range and high-end desktops, workstations, and servers.

3. **DDR3 (Double Data Rate 3 Synchronous Dynamic Random Access Memory)**:

   - **Purpose**: DDR3 continued the trend of increasing data transfer rates and reducing power consumption compared to DDR2.
   - **Historical Improvements**: DDR3 further improved data transfer rates, reduced voltage requirements, and introduced higher capacities compared to DDR2.
   - **Uses**: DDR3 memory became mainstream in consumer desktops, laptops, and servers due to its improved performance and efficiency.

4. **DDR4 (Double Data Rate 4 Synchronous Dynamic Random Access Memory)**:

    - **Purpose**: DDR4 was developed to provide even higher data transfer rates, lower power consumption, and increased capacities compared to DDR3.
    - **Historical Improvements**: DDR4 introduced advancements such as higher data transfer rates, improved power efficiency, and increased memory density compared to DDR3.
    - **Uses**: DDR4 memory is currently the standard for modern computing systems, including desktops, laptops, servers, and high-performance computing (HPC) environments.

5. **DDR5 (Double Data Rate 5 Synchronous Dynamic Random Access Memory)**:

    - **Purpose**: DDR5 represents the next evolution in DDR memory technology, aiming to further increase data transfer rates and efficiency.
    - **Historical Improvements**: DDR5 is expected to offer significant improvements in data transfer rates, energy efficiency, and capacity compared to DDR4.
    - **Uses**: DDR5 memory is anticipated to become the standard for future computing systems, offering enhanced performance and capabilities for emerging technologies such as artificial intelligence (AI), machine learning, and 5G networking.

Each generation of DDR memory builds upon the advancements of its predecessors, offering improved performance, efficiency, and capacity to meet the growing demands of modern computing applications. Understanding the differences between these types of RAMs is essential for selecting the right memory solution for your specific requirements. This is another spot of note for those aspiring to take the CompTIA A+ certification.

Installation Procedures for RAM Modules

Installing RAM modules is a relatively straightforward process, but it requires careful attention to ensure compatibility and proper installation. In this section, we'll provide step-by-step instructions for installing RAM modules in desktop and laptop computers. This includes locating the RAM slots on the motherboard, inserting the modules correctly, and securing them in place. We'll also cover best practices for handling RAM modules to prevent damage from electrostatic discharge (ESD).

1. **Prepare the Workspace:**
    - Power off your computer and disconnect all cables.
    - Place your computer on a flat, stable surface with ample lighting.
2. **Identify the RAM Slots:**
    - Open the case of your computer. The RAM slots are typically located near the CPU and are long, rectangular slots on the motherboard.
3. **Remove Existing RAM (If Applicable):**
    - If there are existing RAM modules in the slots, press down on the tabs at either end of the module to release it.
    - Gently pull the module out of the slot.

4. **Prepare New RAM Modules:**

    - If you're installing multiple RAM modules, ensure they are of the same type (e.g., DDR4) and capacity.
    - Handle the RAM modules carefully by the edges to avoid damaging the sensitive components.
    - If there are 4 slots, motherboards will often color coordinate slot 1 with 3 and 2 with 4 in order to show where identical RAM sticks should be placed.

5. **Align the Notch:**

    - Check the notch on the RAM module to ensure it matches the key in the RAM slot. Most RAM modules have a notch off-center to prevent incorrect installation.
    - Align the notch on the RAM module with the key in the RAM slot.

6. **Insert the RAM Module:**

    - Hold the RAM module at a slight angle, with the connector pins facing downward.
    - Gently insert the RAM module into the slot, applying even pressure until the module clicks into place. The amount of pressure needed can often be more than expected; be sure to evenly distribute the pressure and progress slowly until you feel the click.
    - Ensure that the tabs on either end of the slot click into place, securing the RAM module.

7. **Repeat for Additional Modules (If Applicable):**
    - If you're installing multiple RAM modules, repeat the process for each module, ensuring they are properly seated in their respective slots.
8. **Close the Computer Case:**
    - Once all RAM modules are installed, close the case of your computer and secure it with screws or latches.
9. **Power on the Computer:**
    - Reconnect all cables and peripherals to your computer.
    - Power on your computer and wait for it to boot up.
    - Check the system properties or BIOS to verify that the new RAM is detected and properly recognized.

Common Issues Related to RAM and Troubleshooting Techniques

Despite its importance, RAM can sometimes experience issues that affect system performance and stability. Common problems include insufficient memory errors, system crashes, and application freezes. In this section, we'll explore the most common issues related to RAM and provide troubleshooting techniques to diagnose and resolve them effectively. This includes running diagnostic tests, checking for compatibility issues, and updating device drivers. With components, there are many similar symptoms that can be a multitude of things, but by knowing the more common issues, we are better prepared to eliminate likely causes.

Computer Fails to Boot

- **Troubleshooting Steps:**
  - Ensure that the RAM modules are properly seated in their slots. Remove and reinsert them if necessary.
  - Check for compatibility issues between the RAM modules and the motherboard. Consult the motherboard manual for supporting RAM configurations.
  - Test each RAM module individually by booting the computer with one module at a time. This can help identify faulty modules.
  - If the computer still fails to boot, try resetting the CMOS (Complementary Metal-Oxide-Semiconductor) settings by removing the CMOS battery for two or three minutes and then reinstalling it.

Blue Screen Errors (BSOD)

- **Troubleshooting Steps:**
  - Run a memory diagnostic test using built-in Windows tools like Windows Memory Diagnostic or third-party software like Memtest86. This can help identify faulty RAM modules.
  - Check for overheating issues, as excessive heat can cause RAM errors. Ensure proper airflow and cooling inside the computer case.

- Update device drivers and BIOS firmware to the latest versions, as outdated software can sometimes cause memory-related issues.

System Freezes or Crashes

- **Troubleshooting Steps:**
  - Check for software conflicts or memory leaks in running applications. Close unnecessary programs and monitor system resource usage.
  - Verify that the RAM modules are compatible with the motherboard and operating system. Refer to the manufacturer's specifications and compatibility lists.
  - Test the RAM modules in another computer, if possible, to determine if the issue is related to the RAM or other hardware components.

Memory Errors or Corruptions

- **Troubleshooting Steps:**
  - Run a memory diagnostic test as mentioned earlier to identify any errors or corruptions in the RAM modules.
  - Check for physical damage or corrosion on the RAM modules. Clean the connectors with a soft, dry cloth if necessary.
  - Ensure that the RAM modules receive adequate power from the motherboard. Check the motherboard's power connections and voltage settings.

Incompatibility with Overclocking

- **Troubleshooting Steps:**
    - Disable any overclocking settings in the BIOS or UEFI firmware and revert to default clock speeds. Overclocking can sometimes cause instability and errors, especially with RAM.
    - Test the RAM modules at their default clock speeds to determine if the issue persists. If stability improves, gradually increase clock speeds while monitoring for stability issues.

Storage Devices Overview

Storage devices play a crucial role in computing, providing a means to store and retrieve data. There are several types of storage devices available, each with its own set of characteristics and capabilities. Though in today's age it is not common for a hard disk drive to be chosen over a solid-state drive in modern technology. One of the primary use cases that you would see an HDD would be in either a legacy deployment or as a storage solution that does not require a timely retrieval. Solid state enables a significant increase in both speed and storage size, while eliminating the risk of most part failure and contributing to less maintenance.

1. **Hard Disk Drives (HDDs):**
    - HDDs utilize spinning magnetic disks to store data.
    - They are known for their large storage capacities and relatively low cost per gigabyte.
    - However, HDDs are generally slower than other types of storage due to mechanical components and moving parts.

- They are suitable for applications where large amounts of data need to be stored economically, such as mass storage and archival purposes.

2. **Solid State Drives (SSDs):**
    - SSDs use flash memory to store data, resulting in much faster read and write speeds compared to HDDs.
    - They are more durable and reliable than HDDs since they have no moving parts.
    - SSDs are generally more expensive per gigabyte than HDDs but offer better performance and energy efficiency.
    - They are ideal for applications requiring fast data access, such as operating system boot drives, gaming, and high-performance computing.
3. **NVMe Drives:**
    - NVMe (Non-Volatile Memory Express) drives are a type of SSD that utilizes the PCIe (Peripheral Component Interconnect Express) interface for even faster data transfer speeds.
    - They offer significantly lower latency and higher bandwidth compared to traditional SSDs connected via SATA.
    - NVMe drives are often used in high-performance computing environments, such as gaming rigs, workstations, and data centers, where speed is paramount.

Installation Methods for Various Storage Devices

1. **HDDs and SSDs:**

   I. Physically install the drive into an available drive bay in the computer case.

   II. Connect the drive to the motherboard using appropriate cables (SATA cables for HDDs and SSDs).

   III. Secure the drive in place using screws or drive mounting brackets provided with the computer case.

2. **NVMe Drives:**

   I. Insert the NVMe drive into an available M.2 slot on the motherboard.

   II. Secure the drive in place with the retention screw provided with the motherboard.

   III. Some motherboards may require additional thermal pads or heat sinks for cooling NVMe drives, especially high-performance models.

Introduction to RAID (Redundant Array of Independent Disks) and Its Configurations

RAID is a data storage virtualization technology that combines multiple physical disk drives into a single logical unit for the purpose of data redundancy, performance improvement, or both. There are several RAID configurations available, each offering different levels of redundancy and performance. This is a method that can protect against the loss of data and, in some cases, ensure compliance standards are met. RAID arrays are best deployed based on the business needs of the organization, and each has its own benefits they bring to the table; as such, it is best to have a thorough understanding of the various configurations.

1. **RAID 0 (Striping):**
    - Distributes data evenly across multiple drives (minimum two) to improve performance.
    - Provides no data redundancy, meaning a single drive failure can result in data loss.
    - Suitable for applications requiring high performance and large storage capacity but with lower importance on data protection.
2. **RAID 1 (Mirroring):**
    - Mirrors data across multiple drives (minimum two) to provide redundancy.
    - Offers improved data reliability and fault tolerance, as data is duplicated on each drive.
    - Suitable for applications requiring high data availability and reliability, such as critical business systems and databases.
3. **RAID 5 (Striping with Parity):**
    - Distributes data and parity information across multiple drives (minimum three) for both performance and redundancy.
    - Provides fault tolerance and data protection against a single drive failure.
    - Offers a balance between performance, storage efficiency, and data protection.

4. **RAID 10 (Mirrored Stripes):**
    - Combines RAID 1 mirroring and RAID 0 striping to provide both redundancy and performance.
    - Requires a minimum of four drives, with data mirrored between pairs of drives and then striped across mirrored pairs.
    - Offers high performance and fault tolerance, making it suitable for demanding applications such as databases and virtualization.

By understanding the differences between various types of storage devices and RAID configurations, you can make informed decisions when selecting and configuring storage solutions for your computing needs. There will likely be several questions referencing RAID arrays on the certification exam, so please keep that in mind and take the time to fully understand this concept.

Motherboards and Processors

Let's explore the essential components and functions of motherboards, as well as different CPU types and their installation procedures. From there, we will continue with compatibility considerations between motherboards and CPUs. These are commonly seen as the brain of a computer or the central nervous system and, in function, work very similar. Nearly all components of a computer will either integrate or route through the motherboard, making this one of the most integral components of any system.

Motherboards:

1. **Functions and Components:**
    - The motherboard serves as the main circuit board in a computer system, providing connectivity and communication between various hardware components.
    - Key components include the CPU socket, RAM slots, expansion slots (such as PCIe), storage connectors (SATA, M.2), power connectors, and peripheral ports (USB, Ethernet, audio).
    - Other components like the chipset, BIOS/UEFI firmware, and onboard controllers (for audio, networking, and storage) are integral to the motherboard's functionality.

CPU (Central Processing Unit):

2. **Types and Installation Procedures:**
    - CPUs come in various types, including Intel and AMD processors, each with different architectures, core counts, clock speeds, and socket types.
    - Installation typically involves aligning the CPU with the socket on the motherboard, ensuring proper orientation, and securing it in place with the retention mechanism.
    - Thermal paste application and attaching the CPU cooler are additional steps in the installation process to ensure proper heat dissipation.

3. **Compatibility Considerations:**
    - Motherboards and CPUs must be compatible in terms of socket type, chipset support, and power requirements.
    - Socket compatibility is crucial, as different CPUs require specific socket types (e.g., LGA 1200 for Intel's 10th and 11th Gen CPUs, AM4 for AMD Ryzen processors).
    - Chipset support dictates features and capabilities, such as overclocking, memory speed, and PCIe lanes. Ensuring compatibility between the motherboard chipset and CPU is essential for optimal performance.
    - Power requirements, including CPU power delivery and thermal design, should match the motherboard's capabilities to prevent instability and overheating issues.

By understanding the functions and components of motherboards, as well as CPU types and compatibility considerations, users can effectively select and install components for a reliable and high-performance computing system.

Power Supply Units (PSUs)

A Power Supply Unit (PSU) is a vital component of a computer system, responsible for converting AC power from a wall outlet into DC power suitable for powering the internal components of the computer. Understanding PSU concepts, installation procedures, and troubleshooting techniques is essential for building and maintaining a reliable computer system. I did want to make note that on the A+ examination, there is typical mention of modular vs. traditional PSUs. What this is referencing is that in earlier years, the power supply unit would have a "Braided" cable, where all the various connectors would be held together. Now, the standard is for a modular power supply unit, where there are various plug-ins to both aid in cable management as well as usability.

1. **Overview of PSU Concepts:**
    - **Wattage:** Wattage indicates the maximum power output capacity of the PSU, measured in watts (W). Higher-wattage PSUs can support more power-hungry components.
    - **Efficiency Ratings:** PSU efficiency refers to how effectively it converts AC power into DC power. Efficiency ratings, such as 80 Plus Bronze, Silver, Gold, Platinum, and Titanium, indicate the PSU's energy efficiency under various load conditions.
    - **Connectors:** PSUs come with various connectors to supply power to different components, including the motherboard, CPU, graphics card, storage drives, and peripherals. Common connectors include 24-pin ATX, 8-pin EPS, SATA, PCIe, and Molex connectors.
2. **Installation Steps for PSUs:**
    - **Choose the Right PSU:** Select a PSU with sufficient wattage and the necessary connectors to power all components in the system.
    - **Prepare the Case:** Remove the side panel of the computer case and locate the PSU mounting area.

- **Mount the PSU:** Align the PSU with the mounting screw holes in the case and secure it in place using screws provided with the case.
- **Connect Cables:** Connect the necessary cables from the PSU to the motherboard, CPU, graphics card, storage drives, and other components. Ensure proper cable routing and organization for optimal airflow and cable management.
- **Test the PSU:** After installation, perform a quick test to ensure the PSU powers on properly by connecting it to a power source and switching on the power supply.

3. **Troubleshooting Common PSU Issues:**
    - **Power Failure:** If the computer fails to power on or experiences intermittent shutdowns, the PSU may be faulty. Check power connections and perform a PSU voltage test using a multimeter to verify proper voltage output.
    - **Overheating:** Overheating can occur if the PSU's cooling fan fails or if airflow within the case is obstructed. Ensure proper ventilation and monitor PSU temperatures using hardware monitoring tools. Replace the PSU or add additional case fans if necessary.

By familiarizing yourself with PSU concepts, installation procedures, and troubleshooting techniques, you can ensure a stable and reliable power supply for your computer system. In doing so, you will minimize the risk of hardware failures and system downtime.

Troubleshooting Hardware Components

Troubleshooting hardware components is a crucial skill for IT professionals, allowing them to identify and resolve issues that may arise with computer systems. By following systematic troubleshooting steps and employing effective techniques, hardware problems can be diagnosed and resolved efficiently, minimizing downtime, and ensuring optimal system performance.

1. **Comprehensive Overview of Troubleshooting Techniques:**
    - **Systematic Approach:** Adopt a systematic approach to troubleshooting hardware issues, starting with identifying the symptoms, gathering information, and analyzing potential causes before implementing solutions.
    - **Diagnostic Tools:** Utilize diagnostic tools, such as hardware diagnostic software and built-in system diagnostics, to identify faulty hardware components and pinpoint the root cause of the problem.
    - **Hardware Testing:** Perform hardware tests, including memory tests, CPU stress tests, and disk checks, to assess the integrity and performance of individual components.
    - **Visual Inspection:** Conduct a visual inspection of hardware components, checking for physical damage, loose connections, and signs of overheating or corrosion.
    - **Isolation Testing:** Isolate hardware components by disconnecting or replacing them one at a time to identify the specific component causing the issue.

2. **Identifying and Diagnosing Hardware Problems:**

    - **Common Hardware Issues:** Familiarize yourself with common hardware problems, such as memory errors, CPU overheating, disk failures, and peripheral malfunctions, to expedite diagnosis and resolution.

    - **Symptom Analysis:** Analyze symptoms reported by users or observed during system operation to narrow down potential causes of hardware problems.

    - **Diagnostic Procedures:** Follow established diagnostic procedures for troubleshooting specific hardware components, referring to manufacturer documentation and industry best practices.

    - **Documentation:** Maintain detailed documentation of troubleshooting steps taken, including hardware tests performed, diagnostic results, and solutions implemented, to facilitate future troubleshooting efforts and knowledge sharing.

By mastering troubleshooting techniques and developing a systematic approach to diagnosing hardware problems, IT professionals can effectively address hardware issues in computer systems, ensuring reliable performance and minimizing disruptions to user productivity. This is of significant benefit to those looking to join the field of Information Technology and will surely aid in daily tasks.

Summary and Conclusion

In this chapter, we learned the essential components of computer hardware, providing a comprehensive understanding of RAM, storage devices, power supply units (PSUs), and troubleshooting techniques for hardware components. We began by exploring the various types of RAM, including DDR, DDR2, DDR3, and DDR4, discussing their characteristics, installation procedures, and common issues. Next, we examined different types of storage devices, such as HDDs, SSDs, and NVMe drives, highlighting their differences in functionality, performance, and installation methods. Additionally, we introduced RAID (Redundant Array of Independent Disks) and its configurations, emphasizing its role in data redundancy and performance enhancement.

We then shifted our focus to power supply units (PSUs), providing an overview of PSU concepts, installation steps, and troubleshooting common PSU issues like power failure and overheating. From there, we viewed popular troubleshooting techniques for hardware components, stressing the importance of a systematic approach to diagnosing and resolving hardware problems. Understanding hardware fundamentals is paramount for IT professionals to effectively maintain, troubleshoot, and optimize computer systems. By mastering the concepts and techniques covered in this chapter, professionals can ensure reliable system performance, minimize downtime, and enhance user productivity. We encourage further exploration and practical application of hardware knowledge to stay abreast of evolving technologies and industry trends.

Transitioning from the world of hardware, we now continue our learning with operating systems (OS). Operating systems serve as the backbone of computing, providing a platform for executing applications, managing resources, and facilitating user interactions. In Chapter 9, we will cover the domain of operating systems, exploring their functionalities, configurations, and management. From Windows and macOS to Linux and Unix-based systems, we will review all the requirements of operating systems and equip you with the knowledge and skills to navigate and harness their power effectively.

CHAPTER 9

Operating Systems: The Brains Behind the Screen

Operating systems (OS) form the cornerstone of modern computing, serving as a crucial interface between hardware components and software applications. Essentially, an operating system manages system resources, facilitates communication between hardware and software, and provides users with a platform to interact with their devices. Throughout the evolution of computing, operating systems have undergone significant development, adapting to technological advancements, and changing user demands. From the early days of mainframe computers to the modern presence of smartphones and IoT devices, operating systems have played a pivotal role in shaping the digital landscape. Though there are various operating systems to choose from, each having its pros and cons, all fit to serve a unified purpose. That is to allow an individual to "speak" with a computer through peripherals such as keyboards and mice.

In this chapter, we will continue our learning into the domain of operating systems, delving into their fundamental concepts, historical progression, and diverse ecosystems. We will compare major OS families, including the dominant desktop platforms such as Windows, macOS, and Linux, as well as specialized operating systems tailored for mobile

© Kodi A. Cochran 2024

K. A. Cochran, *CompTIA A+ Certification Companion*, Certification Study Companion Series,
https://doi.org/10.1007/979-8-8688-0867-8_9

devices like Android and iOS. Through this exploration, we aim to provide a holistic understanding of operating systems and their impact on computing environments. By the end of this chapter, we will have covered all requirements of the CompTIA A+ certification exam, and the reader will be adequately prepared for testing on this portion.

Historical Timeline of Operating System Development

When trying to understand where we are today in technology, it is always worthwhile to look to the past and see how far we have come. With that in mind, we will begin our learning process by reviewing a brief historical timeline about operating systems, their developments, and significant milestones. While reviewing this portion, try and imagine what all has transpired to get from one step to the next.

1. **1950–1960s: Early Operating Systems**
   - The birth of operating systems can be traced back to the era of mainframe computers in the 1950s and 1960s.
   - One of the earliest operating systems, the General Motors Research Operating System (GM-NAA I/O), was developed by General Motors for IBM mainframes in 1956.
   - Other notable operating systems of this period include the Batch Processing Monitor (BPM) and the Compatible Time-Sharing System (CTSS).

2. **1970s: Rise of Time-Sharing and Unix**
    - The 1970s saw the emergence of time-sharing systems, allowing multiple users to access a computer simultaneously.
    - Unix, developed by AT&T Bell Labs in the late 1960s and early 1970s, became a pioneering operating system known for its portability, multitasking capabilities, and hierarchical file system.
    - In 1970, IBM introduced the Virtual Machine/370 (VM/370) operating system, enabling multiple virtual machines to run on a single mainframe.
3. **1980s: Personal Computing and GUIs**
    - The 1980s witnessed the rise of personal computing, marked by the introduction of microcomputers and desktop operating systems.
    - Microsoft's MS-DOS (Microsoft Disk Operating System) became one of the most widely used operating systems for IBM PC-compatible computers.
    - Apple released the Macintosh in 1984, featuring the graphical user interface (GUI) and the Macintosh Operating System (Mac OS).
    - Microsoft Windows made its debut in 1985 with Windows 1.0, offering a graphical shell for MS-DOS.
4. **1990s: Windows Dominance and the Internet Era**
    - Microsoft Windows cemented its dominance in the operating system market during the 1990s, with the release of Windows 3.0, Windows 95, Windows 98, and Windows NT.

- Linux, an open-source Unix-like operating system, gained popularity among developers and enthusiasts, fueled by the GNU Project and the Free Software Foundation.
- The emergence of the Internet led to the development of network-centric operating systems and platforms, such as Windows NT Server, Novell NetWare, and various Unix variants optimized for networking.

5. **2000–2010s: Mobile and Cloud Computing**
    - The 2000s witnessed the convergence of mobile computing and the Internet, leading to the rise of mobile operating systems like Symbian, BlackBerry OS, iOS, and Android.
    - Apple revolutionized the smartphone industry with the introduction of the iPhone and iOS in 2007.
    - Google's Android operating system emerged as a dominant force in the mobile market, offering an open-source platform for smartphones and tablets.
    - Cloud computing became increasingly prominent, driving the development of cloud-based operating systems and platforms such as Amazon Web Services (AWS), Microsoft Azure, and Google Cloud Platform.
6. **Present and Future: Continued Innovation and Integration**
    - Operating systems continue to evolve to meet the demands of modern computing, incorporating features such as virtualization, containerization, artificial intelligence, and edge computing.

- Hybrid and multi-cloud environments are becoming more prevalent, requiring operating systems that can seamlessly integrate with diverse infrastructure and services.
- The future of operating systems is expected to focus on enhancing security, privacy, and interoperability, while also embracing emerging technologies such as quantum computing and decentralized systems.

Throughout its history, the evolution of operating systems has been driven by advancements in hardware, software, and user needs, shaping the way we interact with computers and devices in an ever-changing digital landscape. We have already come a very long way over the years, and it would be nearly impossible to predict how far this technology will advance.

Comparing Major Operating Systems

In a similar fashion to mobile devices and brand preferences, when considering computers, one will always at some point compare brands. With this said, operating systems have unique use purposes and the most common to date is Windows. That is not to say that it is superior to the others, but it is well established and generally seen as easy to use. Let's continue and compare the major players of this field:

1. **Windows:**
    - Developed by Microsoft, Windows is one of the most widely used operating systems for personal computers.

- Known for its user-friendly graphical interface, compatibility with a wide range of hardware and software, and extensive support for productivity applications.
- Offers various editions tailored for different user needs, including Windows 10 Home, Windows 10 Pro, and Windows 10 Enterprise.
- Regular updates and patches are released by Microsoft to improve security, performance, and functionality.
- Widely used in business, education, and home environments, with a large ecosystem of third-party developers and software vendors.

2. **macOS:**
    - Developed by Apple Inc., macOS is the operating system used exclusively on Apple's Macintosh computers.
    - Known for its sleek and intuitive user interface, seamless integration with other Apple devices and services, and robust security features.
    - Offers features such as Time Machine for automated backups, Spotlight for quick file searches, and iCloud for cloud storage and synchronization.
    - macOS updates are typically released annually, introducing new features, performance enhancements, and security improvements.

- Popular among creative professionals, developers, and individuals seeking premium computing experience.

3. **Linux:**
    - Linux is an open-source operating system kernel developed by Linus Torvalds and released under the GNU General Public License.
    - Known for its flexibility, stability, and scalability, Linux powers a wide range of computing devices, from servers and mainframes to embedded systems and smartphones.
    - Offers numerous distributions (distros) tailored for different use cases and user preferences, such as Ubuntu, Fedora, CentOS, and Debian.
    - Features a command-line interface (CLI) as well as graphical desktop environments like GNOME, KDE, and Xfce.
    - Popular among developers, system administrators, and enthusiasts due to its customization options, community support, and free availability.
4. **Unix:**
    - Unix is a family of multitasking, multiuser operating systems originally developed by AT&T Bell Labs in the late 1960s.
    - Known for its stability, security, and support for networking and multiprocessing, Unix has influenced the design of many modern operating systems.

- Variants of Unix include BSD (Berkeley Software Distribution), Solaris, HP-UX, AIX, and macOS (which is based on BSD).
- Often used in enterprise environments, scientific research, and high-performance computing due to its robustness and scalability.
- Provides a rich set of command-line utilities and programming tools for system administration and software development.

5. **Mobile Operating Systems (Android, iOS):**
    - Android, developed by Google, is an open-source operating system based on the Linux kernel, primarily used in smartphones and tablets.
    - Known for its customizable interface, extensive app ecosystem (via Google Play Store), and integration with Google services.
    - iOS, developed by Apple Inc., is a proprietary operating system exclusively used on Apple's iPhone, iPad, and iPod Touch devices.
    - Known for its seamless user experience, tight integration with Apple's ecosystem, and emphasis on privacy and security.
    - Both Android and iOS offer regular updates with new features, performance improvements, and security patches to enhance the user experience and address vulnerabilities.

Operating System Fundamentals

Now that we understand the history of modern operating systems, as well as the differences between the various OS type implementations, we will further our understanding of the key components held within. By having a stronger understanding of the components surrounding an operating system, we are better prepared to understand how they function as a whole. With that in mind, let's break this down into easy to follow categories:

1. **Core Components and Architecture:**
    - **Kernel:** The core component of an operating system that manages system resources, such as memory, CPU, and I/O devices, and provides essential services to other software.
    - **Shell:** The interface between the user and the operating system, allowing users to interact with the system through commands or scripts.
    - **File System:** The mechanism used by the operating system to organize and store data on storage devices, providing a hierarchical structure for files and directories.
2. **Types of User Interfaces:**
    - **Command-Line Interface (CLI):** A text-based interface that allows users to interact with the operating system by typing commands and receiving text-based feedback.
    - **Graphical User Interface (GUI):** A visual interface that uses graphical elements such as windows, icons, menus, and buttons to enable users to interact with the system using a mouse or touchpad.

3. **Basic File System Concepts:**
    - **Directories:** Containers used to organize files hierarchically, forming a directory tree structure.
    - **Files:** Units of data stored on a storage device, identified by a unique name, and organized within directories.
    - **Metadata:** Additional information associated with files, such as file size, creation date, modification date, and file permissions.
    - **File Permissions:** Access control settings that determine which users or groups can read, write, or execute a file, providing security and privacy control.

Installing and Upgrading Operating Systems

Now that we have a solid foundational understanding of operating systems and their use cases, let's investigate what it entails to install and/or upgrade them. This is a process that you will inevitably face at some point within the field, and in addition, it is a learning requirement for the CompTIA A+ certification exam. Let's continue by breaking down the steps and considerations to be made while addressing this topic. To note that in real-world residential scenarios, most operating systems will either queue for an update or automatically apply it as released. In enterprise environments, particularly those with sensitive business functions, it is better to try and test updates prior to releasing them to the production environment.

1. **Pre-installation Considerations:**
   - **Hardware Compatibility:** Ensuring that the hardware components of the computer meet the requirements specified by the operating system vendor
   - **System Requirements:** Reviewing the minimum and recommended system specifications for the operating system to ensure optimal performance
   - **Partitioning:** Planning and configuring disk partitions to allocate storage space for the operating system installation, data storage, and system files
2. **Installation Methods:**
   - **Clean Install:** Installing the operating system on a blank or formatted hard drive, erasing all existing data and configurations
   - **Upgrade:** Upgrading an existing operating system to a newer version while preserving user settings, applications, and data
   - **Dual Boot:** Installing multiple operating systems on a single computer, allowing users to choose which OS to boot into during startup
   - **Virtualization:** Running the operating system as a virtual machine on a host operating system, providing isolation and flexibility for testing or running multiple OSes simultaneously

3. **Post-installation Tasks:**
    - **Device Driver Installation:** Installing drivers for hardware components that are not natively supported by the operating system to ensure proper functionality
    - **System Updates:** Applying software updates, patches, and security fixes released by the operating system vendor to enhance stability, performance, and security
    - **Activation:** Activating the operating system by entering a valid product key or license information to validate the installation and authenticate the user's license
    - **Customization:** Configuring system settings, preferences, and user accounts to personalize the operating system environment according to user preferences and requirements

Operating System Configuration

Understanding the purpose and benefits of configuring an operating system is essential for IT professionals, as it enables them to tailor the system to meet specific user needs, enhance performance, and ensure security. In the context of the CompTIA A+ exam, familiarity with operating system configuration is crucial for demonstrating competency in managing and maintaining computer systems. More than just passing the exam and achieving the certification, it is the knowledge that is of benefit to most Information Technology practitioners.

Another contributing factor to all configurations in technology is security. It is always best practice to thoroughly review and configure all critical components of a device to ensure that security needs are properly met, including the operating system of the device as many attributes are configured at this level. Whether you are a seasoned veteran or seeking to enter the field, this is a section heavily recommended.

Customizing System Settings

Customizing system settings allows users to personalize their computing experience and optimize system performance. It is worth noting that personalization settings aren't merely just for user preference. This is also the feature that allows accessibility options and provides a more inclusive experience for all to enjoy. This is significantly more important than one might assume at first glance and should be thoroughly considered. Here's a step-by-step process for customizing system settings:

1. **Display Preferences:** Adjust screen resolution, brightness, and color settings to suit user preferences.
2. **Language Settings:** Select the preferred language for the user interface and input methods.
3. **Accessibility Options:** Enable accessibility features such as screen readers, magnifiers, and keyboard shortcuts for users with disabilities.
4. **Power Management:** Configure power-saving settings to optimize battery life on laptops or conserve energy on desktop computers.

Managing User Accounts and Access Control

Effective user account management and access control are critical for maintaining system security and privacy. This will be covered later in more extensive detail, but we will review it here as well, due to a number of these features residing at the OS level. User accounts and permissions are a tremendous factor when considering security and cannot be taken lightly by any means. Here's how to manage user accounts and access control:

1. **Importance:** User account management allows administrators to create, modify, and delete user accounts, assign appropriate permissions, and enforce security policies.

2. **User Types:** Define user account types, such as standard user, administrator, and guest accounts, each with specific privileges and restrictions.

3. **Permissions:** Set permissions for files, folders, and system resources to control user access and prevent unauthorized actions.

4. **Authentication Methods:** Implement authentication mechanisms such as passwords, PINs, biometrics, or multi-factor authentication to verify user identity and prevent unauthorized access.

Configuring Network Settings

Configuring network settings is essential for establishing and maintaining network connectivity. This is the very element that allows us to relate to the digital world and ensures our privacy within it. More than that though, it is what allows us to be secure in both our personal and professional life, while accessing the Internet. Network settings and configurations are often overlooked and underappreciated, but it is a significant factor of security and topic of the CompTIA A+ certification exam requirements. Here's how to configure network settings:

1. **IP Addressing:** Assign static or dynamic IP addresses to network interfaces to enable communication with other devices on the network.

2. **DNS Configuration:** Specify DNS server addresses to resolve domain names to IP addresses and facilitate Internet access.

3. **Network Protocols:** Enable or disable network protocols such as TCP/IP, IPv4, and IPv6, and configure protocol settings for optimal network performance.

4. **Network Shares:** Create and manage shared folders or drives to allow users to access files and resources over the network securely.

By mastering operating system configuration, IT professionals can effectively manage computer systems, enhance user productivity, and ensure system security and stability. By further ensuring that the network settings and user accounts and permissions are correct, both our local and online security needs are better accounted for.

Managing Files and Directories

Understanding the file system hierarchy is crucial for efficiently organizing and accessing data on a computer. The file system organizes data into a hierarchical structure consisting of folders, files, and subdirectories. Not only are these items likely to be on the exam, but it is something you will encounter in your professional career. Two of the most common considerations to know are the following:

1. **Directory Structure:** The file system hierarchy is organized into directories, which can contain files and subdirectories. The root directory, denoted by "/," is the top-level directory from which all other directories and files stem.

2. **Pathnames:** Pathnames are used to specify the location of a file or directory within the file system hierarchy. Absolute pathnames start from the root directory, while relative pathnames start from the current working directory.

File Attributes and Permissions

These are what dictate how files and directories are accessed and managed by users and processes. Permitting is the very means that provision access to items by a user. By understanding this foundational element, you will be better prepared to understand how files are accessed, secured, and managed. Some of the more important attributes and permissions include

1. **Read, Write, and Execute Permissions:** These permissions control the actions users can perform on files and directories. The read permission allows viewing the contents of a file or listing the contents of a directory. The write permission allows modifying or deleting a file, as well as creating, renaming, or deleting files within a directory. The execute permission allows executing a file as a program or script or accessing files within a directory.

2. **Ownership:** Each file and directory are associated with an owner and a group. The owner has full control over the file or directory, including modifying permissions and changing ownership. The group consists of users with similar access rights.

3. **ACLs (Access Control Lists):** ACLs provide a more granular level of access control by allowing administrators to define custom access permissions for specific users or groups on individual files and directories.

File Management

This section will review in-field tasks that involve manipulating files and directories to organize data and perform various operations. These are very general tasks that one will see in an entry-level position but may also be included in the A+ examination. These should be fairly well known by all readers, but to ensure we are covering all topics of the exam. Some common file management tasks include

1. **Creating Files and Directories:** Users can create new files and directories using commands or graphical file managers.
2. **Copying and Moving Files:** Files can be copied to duplicate them or moved to relocate them within the file system hierarchy. The "cp" command is used for copying files, while the "mv" command is used for moving files.
3. **Renaming and Deleting Files:** Files can be renamed to change their names or deleted to remove them from the file system. The "mv" command can be used to rename files, while the "rm" command is used to delete files.

By understanding file system hierarchy, file attributes and permissions, and common file management tasks, users can effectively organize and manage their data on a computer system. Not only is this a requirement of nearly all positions within IT, but it is guaranteed to pop up at least once on the exam.

Operating System Maintenance and Troubleshooting

Performing routine system maintenance tasks is essential for ensuring the stability and performance of an operating system. Routine maintenance and monitoring ensure system uptime and performance metrics are maintained. This is a necessity to follow and is one of the most critical factors in technical support. Now that we understand the building blocks that create an operating system, we can learn the troubleshooting techniques and maintenance tasks, such as

1. **Disk Cleanup:** Disk cleanup removes temporary files, system caches, and other unnecessary data from the disk to free up storage space and improve system performance.

2. **Defragmentation:** Defragmentation rearranges fragmented files on the disk to optimize disk read/write performance. This process reduces file fragmentation and improves disk access speeds.

3. **Disk Integrity Checks:** Disk integrity checks scan the disk for errors and bad sectors, ensuring data integrity and preventing data loss due to disk failures.

Common OS Issues and Support

Now that we have covered some of the general maintenance and ongoing tasks, we are going to look at the most common OS issues. Diagnosing and resolving common OS issues is a crucial skill for troubleshooting system problems and maintaining system reliability. At times, these can be difficult to diagnose as the symptoms may be similar to other issues, but knowing the most common issues allows us to eliminate potential causes. Common OS issues include

1. **Boot Failure:** Boot failure occurs when the operating system fails to load properly during the startup process. Possible causes include corrupted system files, hardware failures, and misconfigured boot settings.

2. **System Crashes:** System crashes, also known as system freezes or blue screen errors (BSOD), occur when the operating system encounters a critical error that prevents it from functioning properly. These errors can be caused by hardware issues, incompatible drivers, or software conflicts.

3. **Application Errors:** Application errors occur when software programs encounter issues that prevent them from running correctly. These errors can be caused by software bugs, compatibility issues, or insufficient system resources.

4. **Performance Degradation:** Performance degradation refers to a gradual decline in system performance over time. This can be caused by various factors, including software bloat, disk fragmentation, and resource-intensive background processes.

Common Troubleshooting Tools and Utilities

Having the right tool for the job is always a significant support in our daily lives. This is no less true in the technical world, and there are numerous utilities and tools we can utilize for support. Troubleshooting tools and utilities are essential for diagnosing and resolving OS issues effectively. Common troubleshooting tools include

1. **Task Manager:** Task Manager is a system utility that provides real-time information about system processes, resource usage, and application performance. It allows users to monitor and manage running processes, terminate unresponsive applications, and identify resource-intensive tasks.

2. **Event Viewer:** Event Viewer is a system tool that logs system events, errors, and warnings. It helps users diagnose and troubleshoot system issues by providing detailed information about system events and error messages.

3. **System File Checker (SFC):** System File Checker is a command-line utility that scans and repairs corrupted system files. It verifies the integrity of system files and replaces missing or damaged files with cached copies from the Windows installation media.

4. **Safe Mode:** Safe Mode is a diagnostic mode of Windows that starts the operating system with minimal drivers and services. It allows users to troubleshoot system problems by isolating software conflicts and driver issues.

Security and Privacy in Operating Systems

Operating systems (OS) play a critical role in ensuring the security and privacy of computer systems. Understanding OS security features and implementing best practices is essential for safeguarding sensitive data and protecting against various cyber threats. While this has been previously mentioned in other sections, this will act as an overview and further highlight the topic. Here are the key aspects of security and privacy in operating systems:

1. **Overview of OS Security Features:** Operating systems come with built-in security features designed to protect against malware, unauthorized access, and other security threats. These features may include

    - **Built-in Firewalls:** Firewalls monitor and control incoming and outgoing network traffic to prevent unauthorized access and protect against network-based attacks.
    - **Antivirus Software:** Antivirus software detects, removes, and prevents the spread of malicious software (malware), such as viruses, worms, and Trojans, on the system.
    - **Encryption:** Encryption is used to secure sensitive data by converting it into a coded format that can only be deciphered with the correct encryption key.
    - **User Authentication Methods:** User authentication methods, such as passwords, biometrics (e.g., fingerprint or facial recognition), and multi-factor authentication (MFA), verify the identity of users before granting access to the system.

2. **Protecting Privacy:** In addition to security measures, operating systems offer features to protect user privacy and control the collection and use of personal data. Users can enhance their privacy by

    - **Configuring Privacy Settings:** Operating systems provide settings to control data sharing, location tracking, and other privacy-related features. Users should review and customize these settings according to their preferences.
    - **Managing Cookies:** Cookies are small text files stored by websites on a user's device to track browsing activity. Users can manage cookie settings in their web browsers to control which cookies are accepted and how long they are retained.
    - **Preventing Unauthorized Access to Personal Data:** Users should take steps to prevent unauthorized access to their personal data by enabling password protection, encrypting sensitive files, and avoiding sharing sensitive information with unknown or untrusted sources.

3. **Best Practices for Securing Operating Systems:** To maintain a secure and privacy-aware computing environment, users should follow best practices, including

    - **Regular Updates:** Keeping the operating system and installed software up to date with the latest security patches and updates helps address known vulnerabilities and protect against emerging threats.

- **Strong Passwords:** Using complex and unique passwords for user accounts and regularly updating them can help prevent unauthorized access to the system.
- **Data Backup Strategies:** Implementing regular data backup procedures ensures that critical data can be restored in the event of data loss due to hardware failure, malware infection, or other unforeseen circumstances.

By understanding and implementing these security and privacy measures, users can enhance the protection of their operating systems and mitigate the risks associated with cyber threats and privacy breaches. This will not only protect the organization but also ensure that data is maintained, confidential, and available for use as intended.

Advanced Operating System Concepts

Operating systems encompass advanced concepts and technologies that extend beyond basic functionality. Covering these concepts provides deeper insights into system management, resource utilization, and enhanced user experiences. It is likely that there will be questions regarding these items on the certification exam, so it is highly recommended to thoroughly understand the differences among these items. Here are some advanced operating system concepts to explore:

1. **Virtualization Technologies:** Virtualization enables the creation and management of virtual machines (VMs) and containers, allowing multiple operating systems to run concurrently on a single physical machine. Key components include

- **Virtual Machines (VMs):** VMs simulate hardware functionality, enabling the execution of multiple operating systems and applications on a single physical host.
- **Hypervisors:** Hypervisors manage and allocate hardware resources to VMs, facilitating efficient resource utilization and isolation between virtualized environments.
- **Containerization:** Containerization platforms like Docker provide lightweight, portable, and isolated environments for deploying and running applications, streamlining development, and deployment processes.

2. **Remote Access and Administration Tools:** Remote access and administration tools enable users to manage systems and resources from remote locations. Common tools and protocols include

    - **Remote Desktop Protocol (RDP):** RDP allows users to connect to and control remote Windows-based systems, facilitating remote administration and support tasks.
    - **Secure Shell (SSH):** SSH provides secure remote access to Unix-based systems, enabling encrypted communication and remote command execution over a network.

- **Remote Management Consoles:** Remote management consoles provide centralized management and monitoring capabilities for distributed systems, allowing administrators to configure, troubleshoot, and maintain systems remotely.

3. **Command-Line Interface (CLI) Basics:** Command-line interfaces offer powerful capabilities for system management and automation. Understanding CLI basics involves

   - **Navigating Directories:** Using commands like cd (change directory) to navigate the file system hierarchy and explore directory structures.
   - **Executing Commands:** Running commands to perform various tasks, such as file manipulation, process management, and system configuration.
   - **Scripting with Shell Scripts:** Writing shell scripts using scripting languages like Bash (Unix/Linux) or PowerShell (Windows) to automate repetitive tasks, customize system behavior, and streamline administrative workflows.

Summary and Conclusion

In this chapter, we have learned the essential aspects of operating systems (OS), ranging from foundational concepts to advanced techniques. We began by defining the role of an OS in computing and explored the historical evolution of major OS families, including Windows, macOS, Linux, Unix, and mobile operating systems like Android and iOS. Our experience through operating systems continued with an in-depth examination of core components and architecture, user interfaces, file system concepts, and user account management. We then switched gears to the installation and upgrading processes, emphasizing pre-installation considerations, installation methods, and post-installation tasks.

Operating system configuration was another topic, where we discussed customizing system settings, managing user accounts, configuring network settings, and optimizing security and privacy features. Additionally, we viewed advanced concepts such as virtualization technologies, remote access tools, and command-line interface basics, providing insights into modern system management practices. Throughout the chapter, we underscored the significance of operating system knowledge for IT professionals across various roles, including system administrators, help desk technicians, and network administrators. Operating systems serve as the foundation of computing environments, and proficiency in OS management is essential for ensuring system reliability, security, and performance.

As we conclude this chapter, we encourage further exploration and skill development in operating systems through hands-on practice, certification courses, and continued learning opportunities. By mastering operating system fundamentals and embracing advanced concepts, IT professionals can enhance their capabilities and contribute effectively to the dynamic world of Information Technology.

We now transition to Chapter 10 and change our focus to software and support, essential components of the computing landscape. While operating systems form the backbone of computing environments, software applications and support services play a pivotal role in enhancing functionality, productivity, and user experience. In this next chapter, we will explore various types of applications, deployment methods, and support strategies. From productivity suites to specialized tools, software encompasses a broad spectrum of solutions designed to meet the diverse needs of users and organizations. Additionally, we will examine the importance of effective support services in ensuring the smooth operation of software applications, troubleshooting issues, and aiding users.

CHAPTER 10

Software and Support

As we begin to learn about the various types of software implementations and the support thereof, we first will need to understand some of the basics of software. This is likely a topic that readers will have at least a fair level of knowledge of; however, we still want to ensure that we are checking off the requirements of the CompTIA A+ certification exam.

Software Types

1. **System Software:** This category includes operating systems, device drivers, and utilities that enable the hardware to function properly. Examples of system software are Microsoft Windows, macOS, Linux, and BIOS firmware.
2. **Application Software:** Application software refers to programs designed to perform specific tasks or functions for end-users. This category encompasses a wide range of software, including word processors, spreadsheets, web browsers, email clients, and multimedia players.
3. **Utility Software:** Utility software serves to enhance or optimize the performance of a computer system. It includes antivirus programs, disk cleanup tools, backup software, and system optimization utilities.

© Kodi A. Cochran 2024

K. A. Cochran, *CompTIA A+ Certification Companion*, Certification Study Companion Series,
https://doi.org/10.1007/979-8-8688-0867-8_10

Licensing

Now that we have covered the different forms of software implementations, we can further our understanding by reviewing the different forms of licensing software utilizes. It is something that is important, especially about maintaining compliance, but I can assure you, licensing is something to thoroughly understand and consider. Developers of software and applications will utilize different methods for ongoing licensing, and it is not necessarily universal. However, they all will fit into one of the below licensing model categories:

1. **Proprietary Software:** Proprietary software is owned and distributed by a single entity or company. Users must purchase a license to use the software, and the source code is typically not available for modification or redistribution. Examples include Microsoft Office, Adobe Photoshop, and Oracle Database.

2. **Open-Source Software:** Open-source software is freely available to use, modify, and distribute. The source code is openly accessible, allowing developers to collaborate and improve the software. Examples of open-source software include Linux, Apache web server, Mozilla Firefox, and LibreOffice.

3. **Freeware:** Freeware is software that is distributed for free, with no cost to the user. However, the source code is usually not available, and users may not have permission to modify or redistribute the software. Examples of freeware include Skype, Spotify, and Adobe Acrobat Reader.

4. **Shareware:** Shareware is distributed as trialware, allowing users to try the software before purchasing a license. After a trial period, users are typically required to pay for continued use or additional features. Examples of shareware include WinRAR, WinZip, and some antivirus programs.

Understanding the differences between these licensing models is crucial for both software developers and end-users, as it impacts usage rights, distribution, and legal obligations. This cannot be taken lightly as the legal penalties if misused can be severe and inflict financial repercussions. For example, licensing for an application's personal usage could not be utilized in place of an enterprise account. Having the appropriate license for the application and entity type is necessary to ensure compliance standards are met.

Importance of Updates

Regular software updates and patches are essential for maintaining the security and performance of computer systems. Updates often include fixes for security vulnerabilities, bug fixes, performance improvements, and new features. Failure to install updates promptly can leave systems vulnerable to cyber threats such as malware, viruses, and hacking attacks. Therefore, it's imperative for users to regularly check for updates from software vendors and apply them as soon as they become available to ensure the integrity and security of their systems.

Zero-day attacks occur when a vulnerability has yet to be released to the general public and there is no known fix. On the other hand, a vulnerability is present when there is any instance of software, application, or firmware that is not kept up to date on patching. With that said, it is highly beneficial to try and test patches as they are released to ensure they will function in your production environment, as this will reduce the risk of known vulnerabilities within your infrastructure.

Software Installation and Deployment

This section seeks to thoroughly explain the process and management of software installations and the requirements of their ongoing maintenance. There are a vast number of considerations to make in this regard, but we are going to ensure to meet the various requirements set forth by CompTIA for the purpose of the A+ certification exam. In a lot of smaller environments, it is typically fully automated for patches to be rolled out throughout the organization as they are released. In areas that are more sensitive, it is pretty common to see patches manually pushed to endpoints on an as-needed basis once adequate testing has been conducted. Regardless of the method utilized or the environment in question, there are several methods that can assist this process.

Methods for Installing Software

Software installation is a necessity in the field of IT, serving as a foundational aspect of system setup and maintenance. The A+ certification mandates proficiency in software installation methods, recognizing their critical role in ensuring the functionality and security of computing environments. By understanding and implementing diverse installation approaches, IT professionals can effectively deploy software solutions tailored to organizational needs while adhering to industry best practices.

- **Manual Installation:** Users procure installation files, either from physical media or digital downloads. They then execute the installer, following prompts to customize settings and finalize the installation process.

- **Automated Deployment:** In enterprise environments, automated deployment is prevalent. IT administrators leverage scripts or configuration files to automate software rollout across multiple devices concurrently. This method enhances consistency and efficiency.
- **Software Distribution Tools:** Enterprises employ centralized software distribution tools to streamline deployment tasks. These platforms automate processes such as patch management and license tracking, optimizing management in large-scale deployments.

Considerations for Software Compatibility

Software compatibility assessments are fundamental to the A+ curriculum, reflecting the need for IT professionals to discern and mitigate potential conflicts that may arise during deployment. By evaluating hardware requirements, operating system support, and version compatibility, candidates demonstrate their ability to safeguard system integrity and optimize software performance. This section equips learners with the essential skills to navigate compatibility challenges, aligning with the A+ objective of proficiency in system configuration and troubleshooting. There are three main considerations to keep in mind when evaluating the compatibility of software with an endpoint:

- **Hardware Requirements:** Assess whether the system meets the software's minimum hardware prerequisites. Insufficient resources may lead to performance issues or installation failures.
- **Operating System Support:** Validate compatibility with the device's operating system and its specific version. Deploying on an unsupported OS can result in functionality issues or system instability.

- **Version Compatibility:** Ensure compatibility with other installed software and system components. Incompatibilities can trigger conflicts, impeding the software's functionality.

Troubleshooting Software Installation

Proficiency in troubleshooting software installation issues is a cornerstone of the A+ certification, underscoring the importance of diagnosing and resolving deployment challenges effectively. This section empowers candidates with the requisite knowledge and methodologies to address common pitfalls encountered during software installation. By mastering techniques for resolving dependency errors, installation failures, and compatibility conflicts, IT professionals demonstrate their readiness to troubleshoot diverse software deployment scenarios, fulfilling the A+ competency in problem-solving and system maintenance. Not only that, but this is a routine task that will be encountered often among individuals working within IT.

- **Dependency Errors:** Certain software relies on specific libraries or frameworks. Failure to meet these dependencies can trigger installation errors, necessitating resolution through dependency installation or configuration adjustments.
- **Installation Failures:** Corrupted installation files or system configurations may lead to installation failures. Troubleshooting involves diagnosing and addressing the underlying issues, such as file integrity checks or system compatibility assessments.

- **Compatibility Conflicts:** Incompatibilities with existing software or system configurations can precipitate conflicts during installation. Resolving such conflicts may entail modifying settings, updating system components, or employing compatibility modes.

Software Configuration and Customization

This section reviews the process of configuring and customizing software to suit individual and organizational needs. Understanding software configuration and customization is crucial for IT professionals, aligning with the requirements outlined in the CompTIA A+ certification exam. By mastering this skill set, individuals can optimize software performance, enhance user experience, and ensure seamless integration within computing environments. This is something that is recommended for all of those within the field to learn as every user is different and with that in mind, personal preferences can be significantly different from one to another. There are also considerations to be made regarding accessibility concerns to ensure that users are properly accommodated.

Configuring Software Settings and Preferences

Configuring software settings and preferences involves tailoring applications to meet specific user requirements and operational objectives. This includes customizing user preferences, application settings, and various configuration options to align with organizational standards and user preferences. By familiarizing themselves with software settings menus and configuration panels, IT professionals can efficiently adjust parameters such as security settings, notification preferences, and data management options to optimize software functionality and usability.

The actual configuration of software can vary greatly depending on the software at hand. Often it can be found within the settings or preferences, normally located by a "Gear" icon or a "?". Typically speaking, there should be some form of help drop-down, information on the official site, or even forums that could better assist an individual with customizing settings for a particular installation. For further guidance, it is best to review the materials provided as a reference to various settings and/or configurations. After all, nobody knows the software like the creators!

Personalizing User Interfaces

Personalizing user interfaces enhances user engagement and productivity by allowing individuals to customize their computing experience according to personal preferences and workflow requirements. All people are different, and preferences can range from color schemes to more technical considerations like organization or workflow processes. To meet these needs, the modification of visual elements such as themes, skins, and user-defined shortcuts can create a personalized interface that reflects individual preferences and enhances usability. By empowering users to tailor their interface to their liking, organizations can improve user satisfaction, efficiency, and overall productivity. This, in turn, will create a higher level of productivity and quality of work for the employees, in addition to improving the employee morale levels.

Customizing Software Behavior

Customizing software behavior involves fine-tuning the way applications interact with users and handling various tasks to streamline workflow and improve efficiency. This includes configuring default file associations, keyboard shortcuts, and startup options to automate repetitive tasks, streamline workflows, and optimize productivity. By customizing software behavior to align with specific user requirements and operational workflows, IT professionals can enhance user efficiency, minimize errors, and maximize the utility of software applications within organizational settings.

By equipping individuals with the knowledge and skills to configure and customize software effectively, this section addresses key competencies outlined in the CompTIA A+ certification exam. Thus, preparing learners to meet the diverse challenges of modern computing environments. Everyone is different and has differing needs, preferences, and requirements, and this portion will empower the reader to better facilitate the requests of those users.

Software Maintenance and Updates

This section explores the critical aspects of software maintenance and updates, emphasizing their importance in ensuring the reliability, security, and performance of software applications. Understanding software maintenance and update procedures is essential for IT professionals. By mastering these processes, individuals can effectively manage software lifecycles, mitigate security risks, and optimize software performance within organizational environments. Not only are these items important to know for those working within the field or seeking entry, but they are also in line with CompTIA's A+ certification examinations current requirements.

Importance of Software Maintenance

Software maintenance encompasses a range of activities aimed at preserving and enhancing the functionality and performance of software applications over time. It involves addressing issues such as bug fixes, performance optimizations, and feature enhancements to ensure that software remains efficient, reliable, and compatible with evolving user needs and technological advancements. By prioritizing software maintenance, organizations can minimize downtime, improve user experience, and extend the longevity of software investments.

Performing Software Updates and Upgrades

Software updates and upgrades are integral to maintaining the security, stability, and functionality of software applications. Updates typically include patches, bug fixes, and security enhancements released by software vendors to address vulnerabilities and improve performance. This section explores various methods for performing software updates, including manual updates, automatic updates, and version migration. By staying abreast of the latest updates and upgrades, IT professionals can proactively address security vulnerabilities, enhance system stability, and ensure compatibility with emerging technologies. Here we will go over the different versions of performing updates in a finer detail:

1. **Manual Updates**: In manual updates, users initiate the update process themselves by downloading and installing updates from the software vendor's website or through the software's built-in update mechanism. This method gives users control over when and how updates are installed, allowing them to review release notes and choose which updates to apply.
2. **Automatic Updates**: Automatic updates involve the software periodically checking for updates in the background and automatically downloading and installing them without user intervention. This approach ensures that systems are continuously updated with the latest patches and security fixes,

reducing the risk of vulnerabilities. However, it may also lead to unexpected changes or disruptions if updates are installed at inconvenient times.

3. **Centralized Update Management**: In organizations with multiple devices, centralized update management systems can be used to streamline the update process. These systems allow IT administrators to deploy updates across a network of devices from a central console. This ensures consistency in updates and enables administrators to schedule updates during off-peak hours to minimize disruptions to productivity.

4. **Patch Management Tools**: Patch management tools automate the process of identifying, downloading, and deploying software patches and updates across an organization's IT infrastructure. These tools provide visibility into the patch status of all devices, allowing administrators to prioritize critical updates and ensure compliance with security policies and regulations.

5. **Containerized Updates**: Containerization technologies such as Docker enable applications to be packaged with their dependencies into lightweight, portable containers. Updates to containerized applications can be easily managed by replacing the existing container with an updated version, minimizing downtime, and ensuring consistency across different environments.

6. **Rolling Updates**: Rolling updates involve gradually updating software components across a distributed system without interrupting service. This approach ensures that updates are applied incrementally, allowing for continuous availability and reducing the risk of downtime associated with large-scale updates.
7. **Version Migration**: Version migration involves transitioning from one major version of software to another, typically to take advantage of new features, performance improvements, or security enhancements. This process may require careful planning, testing, and coordination to ensure a smooth transition and minimize disruption to users.

Managing Software Licenses and Subscriptions

Effective management of software licenses and subscriptions is essential for ensuring compliance with licensing agreements and optimizing software usage within organizational environments. This involves tasks such as license renewal, activation, and monitoring to track usage and maintain compliance with vendor requirements. By implementing robust license management practices, organizations can minimize legal risks, prevent unauthorized software usage, and optimize software procurement and utilization. Maintaining licensing is often a part of asset management and inventory control and is often delegated to the IT personnel to administer.

- **Volume Licensing:** Volume licensing programs enable organizations to procure software licenses in bulk, often at discounted rates. IT professionals must understand the intricacies of volume licensing agreements and compliance requirements to manage licenses effectively and avoid legal ramifications.

- **License Management Tools:** License management tools provide centralized visibility and control over software licenses, activations, and usage metrics. These tools help organizations track license entitlements, monitor compliance, and optimize license allocation across the enterprise.
- **License Servers:** Some software applications require license servers to manage concurrent license usage effectively. License servers authenticate user access and ensure compliance with license restrictions, preventing unauthorized usage and optimizing license utilization.

Software Support and Troubleshooting

In this section, we will learn more about software support and troubleshooting, addressing the unique challenges encountered by IT professionals in managing software issues within organizational environments. Proficiency in software support and troubleshooting is essential for ensuring the reliability, functionality, and performance of software applications. By mastering these techniques, individuals can effectively diagnose and resolve software-related issues, minimizing downtime and optimizing productivity across diverse computing environments.

Accessing Software Support Resources

One of the first steps in troubleshooting software issues is to leverage available support resources provided by software vendors. These resources include online documentation, user manuals, knowledge bases, and community forums, which offer valuable insights, troubleshooting tips, and solutions to common software problems. IT professionals can utilize these resources to gain a deeper understanding of software functionality, identify potential issues, and access step-by-step guides for resolving software-related issues effectively. There is no limit to the amount of available information to us in this day and age, allowing us to research particular issues on the spot in real time.

Troubleshooting Common Software Issues

IT professionals encounter a wide range of software issues in their daily operations, ranging from application crashes and error messages to performance slowdowns and compatibility issues. This section provides comprehensive guidance on diagnosing and resolving common software problems, addressing key issues such as

- **Application Crashes:** When software applications unexpectedly terminate or crash, it can disrupt productivity and impact the user experience. Troubleshooting application crashes involves analyzing error messages, identifying potential causes such as software conflicts or hardware issues, and implementing appropriate solutions such as reinstalling the application, updating drivers, or performing system repairs.
- **Error Messages:** Error messages are indicators of underlying issues within software applications, operating systems, or hardware components. IT professionals must interpret error messages accurately, diagnose the root cause of the problem, and implement corrective actions such as applying software patches, configuring settings, or reinstalling drivers to resolve the issue effectively.

- **Performance Slowdowns:** Performance slowdowns can occur due to various factors, including resource constraints, software conflicts, or malware infections. Troubleshooting performance issues involves analyzing system resource usage, identifying resource-intensive processes or applications, and optimizing system settings to improve performance. Additionally, IT professionals can utilize diagnostic tools and utilities to monitor system performance, identify bottlenecks, and implement performance optimization strategies.

Utilizing Diagnostic Tools and Utilities

Diagnostic tools and utilities play a crucial role in troubleshooting software issues, providing IT professionals with insights into system behavior, resource utilization, and performance metrics. Common diagnostic tools include system logs, task managers, performance monitors, and troubleshooting wizards, which enable IT professionals to identify and address software-related issues efficiently. By leveraging these tools, IT professionals can diagnose system errors, analyze system performance, and implement corrective actions to resolve software issues and optimize system functionality. Let's review some of the most common tools:

1. **System Logs**: System logs are records generated by the operating system and applications that provide information about system events, errors, and warnings. These logs are invaluable for diagnosing software issues, as they can help identify the root cause of errors, track system performance over time, and troubleshoot issues such as crashes or failures.

System logs are typically stored in files or databases and can be accessed using utilities like Event Viewer in Windows or syslog in Unix-based systems.

2. **Task Manager (Windows)/Activity Monitor (macOS)**: Task Manager on Windows and Activity Monitor on macOS are system utilities that provide real-time information about running processes, CPU usage, memory usage, disk activity, and network activity. These tools allow users to identify resource-intensive processes, monitor system performance, and terminate or prioritize tasks to improve system responsiveness. Task Manager and Activity Monitor are essential for diagnosing performance issues, troubleshooting application crashes, and managing system resources effectively.

3. **Performance Monitors**: Performance monitoring tools such as PerfMon (Windows) and sar (Unix-based systems) allow users to track and analyze system performance metrics over time. These tools provide detailed insights into CPU usage, memory utilization, disk I/O, network traffic, and other performance indicators, helping users identify bottlenecks, optimize system configuration, and anticipate resource requirements. Performance monitors are essential for proactive performance management, capacity planning, and troubleshooting performance-related issues in software applications.

4. **Troubleshooting Wizards**: Troubleshooting wizards are interactive guides or automated tools that assist users in diagnosing and resolving common software issues. These wizards walk users through a series of diagnostic steps, perform automated tests, and suggest solutions based on the symptoms reported. Troubleshooting wizards are often integrated into operating systems, applications, and support portals, providing users with a user-friendly and systematic approach to problem-solving. Examples include Windows Troubleshooters, macOS Diagnostics, and diagnostic tools provided by software vendors for specific applications or services.

5. **Diagnostic Utilities**: Diagnostic utilities are specialized tools designed to diagnose specific types of software issues or system components. These utilities may perform tasks such as hardware diagnostics, disk integrity checks, network connectivity tests, and malware scans. Diagnostic utilities can help identify hardware failures, software conflicts, configuration errors, and security threats, enabling users to take corrective action to resolve issues effectively. Examples include CHKDSK (Windows), fsck (Unix-based systems), ipconfig (Windows), ping (Unix-based systems), and antivirus software with built-in scanning and cleaning capabilities.

Software Security Best Practices

Now that we have a finer level of understanding towards software, applications, and security, let's look at some of the best practices pertaining to this domain. These may be like prior sections but are being individually highlighted in order to meet the requirements of the CompTIA A+ examination. Security is of importance across the board in this field, as any crack in our defense renders all other preparations useless. Please review each of these topics and correlate it to the context of this chapter:

1. **Overview of Software Security Threats**: Software security threats encompass a wide range of malicious activities aimed at compromising the confidentiality, integrity, and availability of software systems. Common threats include

    - **Malware**: Malicious software designed to infiltrate, damage, or gain unauthorized access to computer systems. Examples include viruses, worms, trojans, and spyware.
    - **Ransomware**: Malware that encrypts files or locks users out of their systems, demanding payment for decryption or restoration of access.
    - **Phishing**: Social engineering attacks that trick users into revealing sensitive information such as passwords, credit card numbers, or personal data by impersonating trusted entities.
    - **Social Engineering Attacks**: Manipulative techniques used to deceive individuals or organizations into divulging confidential information, providing access to restricted resources, or performing unauthorized actions.

2. **Implementing Security Measures**:
    - **Antivirus Software**: Antivirus software detects, prevents, and removes malware infections from computer systems by scanning files, emails, and web traffic for malicious code.
    - **Firewalls**: Firewalls monitor and control incoming and outgoing network traffic based on predefined security rules, protecting against unauthorized access and network-based attacks.
    - **Intrusion Detection Systems (IDS)**: IDS monitors network traffic for suspicious activity or signs of security breaches, alerting administrators to potential threats or attacks in real-time.
    - **Encryption**: Encryption scrambles data to prevent unauthorized access, ensuring confidentiality and integrity during transmission and storage. Techniques such as SSL/TLS encryption for web traffic and file encryption for sensitive data help safeguard against eavesdropping and data breaches.
3. **Secure Software Development Practices**:
    - **Secure Coding Guidelines**: Establishing coding standards and best practices to mitigate common security vulnerabilities such as buffer overflows, injection attacks, and insecure cryptographic implementations.
    - **Vulnerability Assessments**: Regularly assessing software applications for known vulnerabilities using automated scanning tools, penetration testing, and code analysis techniques.

- **Code Reviews**: Conducting thorough reviews of software code by peers or security experts to identify and remediate security weaknesses, logic flaws, and coding errors early in the development lifecycle.

By implementing these software security best practices, organizations can mitigate the risk of security breaches, protect sensitive data, and ensure the integrity and reliability of their software systems. Not only is this crucial to any organization's operational environment, but it is a requirement for those seeking the certification. Security is one of the most fundamental concepts through each of the domains in IT.

Software Compatibility and Interoperability

In this section, we explore the critical aspects of software compatibility and interoperability, essential for ensuring seamless integration and functionality across diverse software environments. Compatibility refers to the ability of software components to work together harmoniously, while interoperability involves the interaction and exchange of data between different software platforms. By understanding these concepts and implementing effective strategies, individuals can mitigate compatibility challenges and optimize software interoperability in organizational settings. This is of further importance for those seeking to take the CompTIA A+ certification exam, as these are required topics and often of mention.

Ensuring Compatibility Between Software Components

Software applications often rely on a multitude of external components, including libraries, frameworks, and runtime environments, to function effectively. These components provide essential functionality and support various features of the application. However, ensuring compatibility between these software components is paramount to avoid conflicts, maintain system stability, and guarantee seamless operation. IT professionals must carefully verify compatibility requirements and dependencies when deploying new software or updates, considering the following aspects:

1. **Library and Framework Compatibility**: Libraries and frameworks are integral parts of software development, providing reusable code modules and predefined functionalities. Before integrating a new library or framework into an application, IT professionals must ensure compatibility with the existing codebase and dependencies. This involves checking for version compatibility, API changes, and potential conflicts with other libraries or frameworks used in the application.

2. **Runtime Environment Compatibility**: The runtime environment, including programming languages, runtime libraries, and virtual machines, plays a crucial role in executing software applications. IT professionals need to ensure compatibility between the application code and the runtime environment to prevent runtime errors, crashes, or performance issues. This may involve verifying language versions, runtime library dependencies, and compatibility with underlying operating systems or hardware architectures.

3. **Dependency Management**: Modern software applications often rely on numerous third-party dependencies, such as package managers, modules, or plugins, to extend functionality or streamline development. Effective dependency management involves tracking dependencies, managing version updates, and resolving conflicts between conflicting versions or dependencies. IT professionals must employ robust dependency management practices to ensure the stability and security of software applications.

4. **Testing and Validation**: Thorough testing and validation are essential steps in ensuring compatibility between software components. IT professionals should conduct comprehensive compatibility testing, including integration testing, regression testing, and platform-specific testing, to identify and address any compatibility issues or inconsistencies. This may involve testing the application across different environments, platforms, and configurations to validate compatibility with various setups and scenarios.

By verifying compatibility requirements and dependencies, IT professionals can mitigate the risk of compatibility issues and streamline deployment processes. This will ensure the seamless operation of software applications across diverse environments and configurations and reduce conflict among applications.

Interoperability Between Different Software Platforms

Interoperability plays a crucial role in modern computing environments, enabling the exchange of data and functionality between diverse software platforms, systems, and applications. It ensures seamless collaboration, integration, and communication across different environments, enhancing productivity, efficiency, and user experience. Key considerations for facilitating interoperability include

1. **File Format Compatibility**: File format compatibility ensures that data can be exchanged and interpreted correctly between different software applications. IT professionals must consider the compatibility of file formats such as documents, images, videos, and spreadsheets when integrating software solutions. This involves supporting standard file formats and implementing conversion mechanisms to facilitate interoperability between disparate systems.

2. **Data Exchange Protocols**: Data exchange protocols define the rules and standards for exchanging data between systems and applications. IT professionals must select appropriate protocols, such as HTTP, SOAP, REST, or GraphQL, based on the specific requirements of the integration project. This involves considering factors such as data volume, security, performance, and real-time communication needs to ensure efficient and reliable data exchange.

3. **Integration Application Programming Interfaces (APIs)**: Integration APIs provide standardized interfaces for accessing and interacting with software services, systems, and data sources. IT professionals must leverage integration APIs to facilitate interoperability between different software platforms and enable seamless data exchange and functionality sharing. This involves implementing API endpoints, authentication mechanisms, error handling, and data transformation logic to support interoperability requirements.

4. **Standards Compliance**: Compliance with industry standards and specifications is essential for ensuring interoperability between software solutions. IT professionals must adhere to established standards, such as XML, JSON, OData, or OpenAPI, to promote compatibility and interoperability across heterogeneous systems and technologies. This involves following best practices, guidelines, and specifications defined by industry consortia, standards bodies, or regulatory authorities.

5. **Data Mapping and Transformation**: Data mapping and transformation enable the conversion of data formats, structures, and semantics to facilitate interoperability between disparate systems. IT professionals must implement data mapping and transformation logic to reconcile differences in data representations, schemas, and semantics when integrating software solutions. This involves defining mapping rules, transformations, and validation checks to ensure accurate and consistent data exchange.

By addressing these interoperability considerations, IT professionals can design, implement, and maintain software solutions that seamlessly collaborate and integrate with diverse platforms, systems, and environments. This promotes interoperability, scalability, and flexibility, enabling organizations to leverage the full potential of their software investments and achieve their business objectives effectively.

Addressing Compatibility Issues

Despite proactive measures, compatibility issues may still arise due to software updates, configuration changes, or platform updates. Please keep in mind that some compatibility issues may not be so easily overcome and require a change to the infrastructure or a different application entirely. To address compatibility issues effectively, IT professionals can leverage various strategies, including

- **Software Patches and Updates:** Software vendors frequently release patches and updates to address compatibility issues and enhance functionality. IT professionals must stay informed about available updates and apply them promptly to resolve compatibility issues and mitigate potential security risks.
- **Compatibility Modes:** Some operating systems and software applications offer compatibility modes, allowing users to emulate the behavior of earlier versions to maintain compatibility with legacy software or hardware. IT professionals can enable compatibility modes as a temporary workaround for compatibility issues while exploring permanent solutions.

By emphasizing the importance of software compatibility and interoperability, this section addresses key competencies outlined in the CompTIA A+ certification exam, empowering individuals to effectively manage compatibility challenges and optimize software interoperability in organizational settings. Having this knowledge will also prepare those seeking entry to the workforce to have a better understanding of real-world issues they will face.

Software Deployment Strategies

Effective software deployment encompasses the process of installing, configuring, and maintaining applications across various computing environments in a systematic and efficient manner. It plays a crucial role in ensuring that software solutions are deployed correctly, adhere to organizational policies, and comply with regulatory requirements. Key aspects of effective software deployment include

1. **Streamlined Processes**: By implementing best practices and standardized procedures, organizations can streamline software deployment processes, reducing manual intervention and minimizing errors. This enables IT teams to deploy applications more efficiently and consistently across different environments, saving time and resources.
2. **Optimized Resource Utilization**: Effective software deployment allows organizations to optimize resource utilization by ensuring that software applications are deployed only where needed and in the appropriate configuration. This helps minimize resource wastage and maximize the efficiency of computing resources, leading to cost savings and improved performance.

3. **Enhanced Organizational Productivity**: By automating repetitive tasks and standardizing deployment processes, effective software deployment enhances organizational productivity. IT teams can focus on strategic initiatives and value-added tasks rather than spending time on routine deployment activities, resulting in increased efficiency and agility.

4. **Mitigation of Security Risks**: Effective software deployment plays a crucial role in mitigating security risks by addressing vulnerabilities, applying patches, and enforcing security policies during the deployment process. By ensuring that software applications are up-to-date and configured securely, organizations can reduce the risk of cyber-attacks, data breaches, and compliance violations.

5. **Adherence to Compliance Requirements**: Effective software deployment helps organizations adhere to regulatory requirements and industry standards by ensuring that software applications are deployed in accordance with relevant policies and regulations. This includes implementing access controls, encryption, and audit trails to protect sensitive data and ensure compliance with data protection laws.

6. **Continuous Improvement**: By monitoring and evaluating software deployment processes, organizations can identify areas for improvement and implement corrective actions to enhance efficiency and effectiveness. This involves gathering feedback from stakeholders, analyzing deployment

metrics, and refining deployment procedures to optimize performance and achieve better outcomes over time.

7. **Continuous Deployment:** As items continue to be updated over time, this allows for updates to be released as time goes. This is part of an iterative process that addresses version control and patch management by routinely deploying updates as time progresses.

Overall, effective software deployment is essential for maintaining the integrity, security, and performance of software applications in diverse computing environments. By implementing best practices, organizations can streamline deployment processes, optimize resource utilization, and enhance organizational productivity while mitigating security risks and ensuring compliance with regulatory requirements.

Deploying Software in Enterprise Environments

Enterprise environments often require centralized software deployment mechanisms to ensure consistency and compliance across many devices. This cannot be iterated enough; always ensure that software is adequately vetted and tested prior to deploying in any production environment. There are many different strategies and management methods; some of the most common deployment strategies include

- **Centralized Deployment:** IT administrators utilize centralized deployment tools or management platforms to distribute software packages to end-user devices. This approach enables administrators to control software versions, configurations, and updates centrally, ensuring uniformity and compliance with organizational standards.

- **Group Policies:** Group Policy Objects (GPOs) enable administrators to enforce software installation and configuration settings across groups of devices within Active Directory domains. By defining software deployment policies centrally, administrators can ensure consistent software deployment and configuration management.
- **Software Deployment Platforms:** Enterprise-grade software deployment platforms offer comprehensive features for automating software distribution, patch management, and license tracking. These platforms streamline deployment tasks, optimize resource utilization, and facilitate compliance with software licensing agreements and regulatory requirements.

Software Lifecycle Management

Software lifecycle management encompasses the processes and activities involved in managing software from acquisition to retirement. It ensures that software assets are effectively utilized, maintained, and retired in alignment with organizational goals and objectives. Some assets will last longer than others and require differing maintenance needs, but all will follow the same lifecycle process. The software lifecycle consists of several key stages:

1. **Software Acquisition**: This stage involves procuring software licenses through vendor agreements or procurement processes. Organizations must carefully evaluate licensing terms and conditions to ensure compliance and avoid potential legal and financial risks. By acquiring software

licenses strategically, organizations can optimize their software investments and maximize value for money.

2. **Software Deployment**: IT professionals deploy software packages to end-user devices, ensuring that they are configured correctly and compatible with existing infrastructure and configurations. Effective software deployment practices involve thorough testing, user training, and change management to minimize disruptions and ensure a smooth transition. By deploying software efficiently, organizations can enhance productivity, streamline business processes, and improve user satisfaction.

3. **Software Maintenance**: Regular maintenance activities, such as applying patches, updates, and security fixes, are essential for keeping software secure, stable, and up-to-date. Software vendors release updates to address vulnerabilities, improve performance, and introduce new features, requiring organizations to implement a proactive maintenance strategy. By staying current with software updates, organizations can mitigate security risks, optimize performance, and extend the lifespan of their software investments.

4. **Software Retirement**: End-of-life (EOL) and end-of-support (EOS) announcements signal the need to retire outdated or unsupported software. Organizations must transition to alternative solutions or upgrade to newer versions to maintain compliance and security. Properly retiring software

involves data migration, license decommissioning, and communication with stakeholders to ensure a smooth transition. By retiring software in a timely manner, organizations can minimize security vulnerabilities, reduce maintenance costs, and align with industry best practices.

By emphasizing the importance of software deployment strategies, license management, and software lifecycle management, this section addresses the core competencies outlined in the CompTIA A+ certification exam. Through practical examples and case studies, learners gain valuable insights into streamlining software deployment processes, optimizing license management, and ensuring compliance with software licensing agreements and regulatory requirements in enterprise environments. Effective software lifecycle management enables organizations to maximize the value of their software investments, minimize risks, and achieve their business objectives efficiently.

Summary and Conclusion

In this chapter, we explored the contents of software management and support, addressing essential concepts and practices crucial for IT professionals. Throughout the chapter, we learned the different aspects of software, including installation, configuration, maintenance, troubleshooting, security, and deployment strategies. By covering these topics, we aimed to equip readers with the knowledge and skills necessary to effectively manage software assets and support end-users in diverse computing environments.

Key takeaways from this chapter include the recognition of software as a critical component of modern IT infrastructure, playing a pivotal role in ensuring the reliability, security, and performance of computer systems. We emphasized the importance of software management and support for

IT professionals, highlighting their responsibility in maintaining software integrity, addressing user needs, and safeguarding organizational assets. Furthermore, we underscored the significance of continuous learning and professional development in software management. IT professionals are encouraged to pursue certification programs, training courses, and practical experience to stay abreast of emerging technologies, best practices, and industry trends. By investing in ongoing education and skill enhancement, professionals can enhance their capabilities, advance their careers, and contribute effectively to organizational success.

As we conclude this chapter, we invite readers to reflect on the knowledge and insights gained, recognizing the importance of software management and support in the ever-evolving landscape of IT. Whether troubleshooting software issues, deploying new applications, or ensuring compliance with licensing agreements, IT professionals play a vital role in driving innovation, efficiency, and productivity in organizations worldwide.

Having explored the topics of software management and support, we now turn our attention to an equally critical aspect of Information Technology, security. In Chapter 11, we will address the crucial topic of cybersecurity, learning fundamental concepts, best practices, and emerging trends essential for safeguarding digital assets and mitigating threats. From understanding the principles of information security to implementing robust defense mechanisms, we will equip readers with the knowledge and skills necessary to navigate the evolving cybersecurity landscape effectively.

CHAPTER 11

Sufficient Security

In an age where digitalization connects nearly every aspect of our lives, cybersecurity stands at the frontline to protect our digital assets from malicious actors. This chapter opens the world of cybersecurity, an essential discipline in the field of IT that encompasses a broad spectrum of principles, practices, and technologies aimed at safeguarding sensitive information and mitigating cyber threats. At its core, cybersecurity is about ensuring the CIA triad, which is confidentiality, integrity, and availability of information in digital systems. These three values form the foundational support of all other domains within the field. Rest assured; the CIA triad will be covered very thoroughly throughout this chapter. In addition to the CIA triad, this chapter covers a range of principles, including risk management, access control, encryption, and incident response, all aimed at fortifying defenses against cyber threats.

The importance of cybersecurity cannot be overstated. As organizations increasingly rely on digital technologies to conduct business, the risk of cyber-attacks looms large. Cybersecurity measures are essential for protecting critical infrastructure, safeguarding financial transactions, preserving privacy, and maintaining public trust in digital services. Between e-commerce, social media, and online interactions, there is a tremendous amount of monetary value, as well as sensitive data, that resides among the Internet. Cyber-attacks have cost more than just financial strain to individuals; some have even lost their lives to these incidents.

© Kodi A. Cochran 2024

K. A. Cochran, *CompTIA A+ Certification Companion*, Certification Study Companion Series,
https://doi.org/10.1007/979-8-8688-0867-8_11

The history of cybersecurity is intertwined with the evolution of computing technology and its adoption into our personal space. From the early days of mainframe computers to the interconnected networks of today, cybersecurity has evolved in response to emerging threats and vulnerabilities. Understanding this history provides valuable insights into the evolution of cyber threats and the corresponding strategies for defense. As time progresses and technology advances, this will become an even higher concern for those living in the modern world. Our once "digital" safety has now moved to our daily lives and personal well-being.

As we progress through this chapter, we will explore the foundational principles, emerging trends, and best practices that underpin effective cybersecurity strategies.

Understanding Threat Landscape

This section aims to provide a comprehensive exploration of common cybersecurity threats, the actors driving them, and the evolving trends shaping the cybersecurity landscape. The importance of understanding this material cannot be stressed enough as it not only is a requirement of the CompTIA A+ certification, but if mishandled can have significant real-world consequences. This portion of our reading is what directly addresses the security of people going about their daily lives and must be taken seriously. As our defenses become more intricate and detailed, so does the opposition and it effectively creates an enormous-scale game of cat and mouse.

Common Cybersecurity Threats

The most likely threat in the field of IT is generally that of an "Insider Threat," whether or not the individual was intentionally malicious or not. Human error accounts for the vast majority of incidents that we face annually. Other cyber threats manifest in diverse forms, each posing unique risks to digital security. Malicious software, or malware, represents a prevalent threat, encompassing various types such as worms, trojans, backdoors, and rootkits. Here we will learn of all common threats, not just malware, but the people that are behind them as social engineers:

- **Worms:** Worms are a type of self-replicating malware designed to spread across networks rapidly. They exploit vulnerabilities in software or network protocols to propagate without user intervention. Once a system is infected, the worm can independently scan the network for other vulnerable systems to infect, leading to exponential spread. Worms can cause significant disruptions to network infrastructure and compromise the confidentiality, integrity, and availability of data.

- **Trojans:** Malicious programs that masquerade as legitimate software to deceive users into executing them. Unlike viruses or worms, Trojans do not self-replicate. Instead, they rely on social engineering tactics to trick users into downloading and executing them. Once activated, Trojans can perform a variety of malicious actions, such as stealing sensitive information, installing backdoors, or facilitating further malware infections. They often exploit trust relationships between users and software vendors to evade detection and gain unauthorized access to systems.

- **Backdoors:** Provide methods of bypassing authentication or security controls to gain unauthorized access to compromised systems. They are typically installed by attackers to maintain persistent access to a compromised system even after initial access has been secured. Backdoors may be installed through various means, such as exploiting software vulnerabilities, leveraging weak or default passwords, or using social engineering tactics. Once installed, backdoors enable attackers to execute commands, exfiltrate data, or launch further attacks without detection.

- **Rootkits:** Stealthy malware designed to conceal their presence and provide persistent access to compromised systems. They typically operate at the lowest levels of the operating system, known as the kernel, allowing them to intercept and manipulate system calls to evade detection by traditional security mechanisms. Rootkits often include components that hide their files, processes, network connections, and registry entries from antivirus software and system administrators. They are commonly used by attackers to maintain control over compromised systems and execute malicious activities without detection.
- **Phishing:** A form of social engineering attack that uses deceptive tactics to trick individuals into divulging sensitive information, such as login credentials, financial details, or personal information. Attackers often impersonate trusted entities, such as banks, social media platforms, or government agencies, and send fraudulent emails or messages with links to fake websites or forms. Phishing attacks exploit human psychology and trust relationships to manipulate victims into disclosing confidential information, which can then be used for identity theft, financial fraud, or other malicious purposes.

- **Spear Phishing:** Targeted form of phishing attack that tailors messages to specific individuals or organizations. Unlike generic phishing emails, which are sent to a wide audience, spear phishing emails are carefully crafted to appear legitimate and relevant to the recipient. Attackers research their targets to gather personal information or exploit current events or relationships to increase the likelihood of success. Spear phishing attacks often target high-value individuals or organizations, such as executives, employees, or government officials, and may be used to steal sensitive information or gain unauthorized access to corporate networks.
- **Whaling:** A specialized form of spear phishing attack that targets high-profile individuals or executives within organizations. Also known as CEO fraud or business email compromise (BEC), whaling attacks aim to deceive senior executives into taking actions that compromise security or transfer funds to attackers. These attacks often involve impersonating company executives or trusted business partners and requesting sensitive information, wire transfers, or other fraudulent activities. Whaling attacks exploit the authority and trust associated with executive positions to bypass traditional security measures and defraud organizations of significant financial or sensitive data.
- **Smishing:** A form of phishing attack conducted via SMS or text messages. Attackers send fraudulent text messages containing links to fake websites or forms, encouraging recipients to disclose sensitive information or download malicious software. Smishing

attacks exploit the widespread use of mobile devices and the sense of urgency associated with text messages to trick victims into clicking on malicious links or providing personal information. These attacks may also leverage social engineering tactics, such as posing as legitimate businesses or financial institutions, to increase their effectiveness.

- **Vishing:** Another form of phishing attack conducted via voice calls or VoIP technology. Attackers use automated voice messages or live callers to impersonate trusted entities, such as banks, government agencies, or tech support services, and deceive victims into divulging sensitive information or performing actions that compromise security. Vishing attacks often employ scare tactics, urgency, or incentives to manipulate victims into complying with their demands, such as providing account credentials, verifying personal information, or transferring funds. These attacks exploit the human tendency to trust auditory cues and authoritative voices, making them particularly effective against unsuspecting individuals.
- **Ransomware:** Type of malware that encrypts files or locks systems, demanding ransom payments for their release. Attackers typically use social engineering tactics, such as phishing emails or malicious attachments, to infect victims' systems with ransomware. Once activated, the ransomware encrypts the victim's files using strong encryption algorithms, rendering them inaccessible. Attackers then demand payment, usually in cryptocurrency, in exchange for the decryption key needed to unlock the files or restore

access to the system. Ransomware attacks can have devastating consequences, causing data loss, financial damage, and operational disruptions for individuals and organizations alike.

- **Social Engineering:** A broad category of cyber-attacks that exploit human psychology and manipulation to deceive individuals into divulging confidential information or performing actions that compromise security. These attacks rely on psychological manipulation, deception, and persuasion techniques to exploit human trust, curiosity, or fear. Social engineering attacks can take various forms, such as phishing, pretexting, baiting, or tailgating, and may target individuals, organizations, or even entire societies. They exploit inherent human vulnerabilities and cognitive biases to bypass technical security controls and gain unauthorized access to sensitive information or systems.

I would highly suggest making these into flash cards and thoroughly studying them. Where these are the most commonly faced threats, it is likely that you will see a number of them on the CompTIA A+ exam and even future CompTIA exams like the Security+. These are also key elements of the field and a need to know for any seeking entry into the workforce.

Threat Actors and Motivations

Similar to any other crime or act, cyber-attacks all have a human element with their own goals and ideas in mind. These can greatly range from someone who is newer to the field and learning the various processes of pre-made tools, all the way to a nation-state that is highly funded and skilled, or it could even just be an internal employee, whether intending to cause damage or not. The most common incident is actually the last scenario; a newer employee learning the ropes or an established employee with the grudge is generally the most likely to do significant damage to an organization.

- **Script Kiddies:** These are inexperienced individuals who use pre-packaged tools to launch attacks, often for fun or notoriety. While their actions may seem harmless, they can still cause disruptions and vulnerabilities in digital systems.
- **Hacktivists:** Hacktivists leverage hacking techniques to promote social or political causes. Their actions are driven by ideology, aiming to raise awareness or enact change through digital means.
- **Criminal Hackers:** Criminal hackers seek financial gain through cybercrime activities such as stealing sensitive data, conducting fraud, or extorting individuals and organizations for monetary rewards.
- **Nation-States:** Nation-state actors engage in cyber espionage, sabotage, or warfare to further strategic objectives, including gathering intelligence, disrupting adversaries' operations, or exerting influence on global affairs.
- **Insiders:** Perhaps the most underestimated threat, insiders pose significant risks due to their access to sensitive systems and data. Whether unintentional or malicious, insiders can exploit their privileges for personal gain or sabotage, making them formidable adversaries.

By examining the various cybersecurity threats and understanding the motivations driving threat actors, organizations and individuals can better assess their risks, implement effective security measures, and mitigate the impact of cyber-attacks. Recognizing the diversity of threat actors allows for targeted defenses and proactive measures to safeguard against evolving cyber threats. Having a sensible understanding of the "why" behind a matter will better prepare us for any potential attack.

Principles of Secure Computing

Within cybersecurity, the adherence to fundamental principles is essential for ensuring the integrity, confidentiality, and availability of digital assets. This section views the three core principles of secure computing, encapsulated by the CIA triad: confidentiality, integrity, and availability. Particularly in considering the process of security, the CIA triad is an extremely common theme and can be applied to nearly every scenario. Any potential incident or event that could happen would affect one of the three categories of the CIA triad.

Confidentiality: Emphasizes the protection of sensitive information from unauthorized access or disclosure. It ensures that only authorized individuals or systems can access and view sensitive data, preventing unauthorized disclosure or exposure. Confidentiality measures may include encryption, access controls, and data classification to safeguard sensitive information from unauthorized access, interception, or disclosure.

Integrity: Ensures the accuracy, reliability, and consistency of data throughout its lifecycle. It focuses on preventing unauthorized or malicious alterations to data, ensuring that information remains trustworthy and unaltered. Integrity controls, such as checksums, digital signatures, and access controls, verify the authenticity and integrity of data, detecting and preventing unauthorized modifications, deletions, or tampering attempts.

Availability: Guarantees that information and resources are accessible and usable when needed by authorized users. It emphasizes the reliability, responsiveness, and continuous availability of systems and services, enabling users to access critical resources without disruption. Availability measures, such as redundancy, failover mechanisms, and disaster recovery plans, mitigate the impact of disruptions, ensuring uninterrupted access to essential services and data.

By adhering to the principles of confidentiality, integrity, and availability, organizations can establish a robust security posture that protects against a wide range of cyber threats and vulnerabilities. These principles serve as the foundation for designing, implementing, and maintaining effective security controls and measures, ensuring the resilience and security of digital assets in today's evolving threat landscape. Learning these values early will allow you to more effectively understand the protective measures to consider when implementing a new solution or reviewing an organization's infrastructure.

No matter your knowledge level of the Information Technology field, the CIA triad is a key element when progressing into cybersecurity, or alternatively when attempting the CompTIA A+ Certification exam.

Security Controls

Security controls are measures, mechanisms, or procedures implemented to reduce the risk of unauthorized access, data breaches, or cybersecurity incidents. These come in different forms and change the environment accordingly. They encompass a wide range of technical, administrative, and physical safeguards designed to protect information assets, systems, and networks from security threats. These are the means to further assist our IT practitioners with their daily tasks and ongoing support. Proper implementation of security controls can make a world of difference.

With keeping security at the forefront of our minds, let's further this conversation by imaging defense in depth. If an organization were to only use physical controls, how would that prevent an attacker from remoting in or exploiting a vulnerability? Using different methods of controls with differing implementations will allow for an overall more robust defense against would-be threats.

Physical Controls

Physical controls are measures taken to protect the physical environment where information systems and data are stored or accessed. These controls are designed to prevent unauthorized physical access, damage, or interference with IT assets. Examples include

- **Locks and Access Control Systems:** Secure doors and gates with locks, keycards, or biometric access controls.
- **Surveillance Cameras:** Monitor and record activity in and around sensitive areas.
- **Security Guards:** Personnel who monitor access points and ensure only authorized individuals gain entry.
- **Environmental Controls:** Systems to manage temperature, humidity, and power supply to prevent damage to IT equipment.

Logical Controls

Logical controls, also known as technical controls, are measures implemented through hardware and software to protect information systems and manage user access. Examples include

- **Firewalls:** Filter and control incoming and outgoing network traffic based on predetermined security rules.

- **Encryption:** Protect data in transit and at rest by converting it into a coded format that can only be read by authorized parties.
- **Antivirus and Anti-malware Software:** Detect and prevent malicious software from compromising systems.
- **Access Control Lists (ACLs):** Define which users or system processes are granted access to resources and what operations they can perform.

Administrative Controls

Administrative controls are policies, procedures, and practices designed to manage the overall security program within an organization. They help ensure that security measures are consistently applied and that employees understand their roles and responsibilities. Examples include

- **Security Policies:** Formal documents outlining the organization's approach to security and defining acceptable use of resources
- **Training and Awareness Programs:** Educate employees about security best practices and how to recognize and respond to security threats
- **Incident Response Plans:** Procedures for identifying, responding to, and recovering from security incidents
- **Audits and Assessments:** Regular reviews and evaluations of security measures to ensure compliance with policies and identify areas for improvement

Organizational Controls

Organizational controls focus on the structure and governance of the security program within the organization. These controls ensure that security is integrated into the organization's culture and operations. Examples include

- **Risk Management Frameworks:** Methodologies for identifying, assessing, and managing security risks
- **Governance Committees:** Groups responsible for overseeing the security program and making strategic decisions
- **Segregation of Duties:** Ensuring that no single individual has control over all aspects of a critical process to prevent fraud and errors
- **Third-Party Management:** Policies and procedures for assessing and managing the security practices of vendors and partners

Security Control Implementation

Proper implementation of security controls involves

- **Risk Assessment:** Identifying and evaluating risks to determine which controls are necessary.
- **Control Selection:** Choosing the appropriate controls based on the risk assessment and organizational requirements.
- **Deployment:** Implementing the selected controls in a manner that integrates with existing processes and systems.

- **Monitoring and Maintenance:** Continuously monitoring the effectiveness of controls and adjusting as needed to address evolving threats.

Types of Security Controls

Now that we have reviewed the various forms of controls, we can look towards the goals these controls seek to address. Some are in place to try to prevent an attack entirely, while others exist simply to deter an attacker from trying. Each has its own place in the field, and none are better than the others; in fact, it is once again best to utilize multiple controls for the best overall defense.

1. **Preventive Controls:** Aim to stop security incidents before they occur by thwarting unauthorized access or malicious activities. Examples include firewalls, access controls, encryption, and intrusion prevention systems (IPS). These controls serve as barriers or deterrents, preventing unauthorized access or exploitation of vulnerabilities.

2. **Detective Controls:** Designed to identify and detect security incidents or unauthorized activities promptly. They include security monitoring tools, intrusion detection systems (IDS), security information and event management (SIEM) solutions, and log analysis tools. Detective controls provide visibility into security events and anomalies, enabling timely detection and response to potential threats.

3. **Corrective Controls:** Implemented to mitigate the impact of security incidents or breaches after they occur. They include incident response procedures, data recovery mechanisms, system restoration processes, and vulnerability patching. Corrective controls aim to minimize the damage caused by security incidents and restore affected systems or data to a secure state.

4. **Compensating Controls:** Alternative measures implemented to address security requirements when primary controls are not feasible or effective. They provide additional safeguards or mitigating measures to reduce risks to an acceptable level. Compensating controls may include manual processes, alternative security mechanisms, or additional security layers.

Role of Security Controls in Risk Mitigation

Security controls play a critical role in mitigating cybersecurity risks by reducing the likelihood and impact of security incidents. They help organizations identify and address vulnerabilities, protect sensitive data, and ensure the confidentiality, integrity, and availability of information assets. By implementing a layered defense strategy with a combination of preventive, detective, and corrective controls, organizations can effectively manage risks and enhance their overall security posture. These are in place to aid us along the way and should be embraced.

Challenges and Considerations

While security controls are vital for safeguarding against cyber threats, organizations encounter numerous hurdles in their deployment and management. These challenges span resource limitations, regulatory compliance mandates, dynamic threat landscapes, and the intricate nature of technology ecosystems. Addressing these obstacles requires a multifaceted approach that prioritizes risk management and resilience. A rule of thumb is that the more secure an environment is, the more "red-tape" and barriers exist along the way. Based on the organizational risk appetite, a happy medium must be found between security and ease of use for both to succeed.

1. **Resource Constraints**: Many organizations grapple with limited budgets, manpower shortages, and time constraints when implementing security controls. Balancing the allocation of resources against the need for robust defenses can be a daunting task, particularly for small to medium-sized enterprises (SMEs) with finite resources.

2. **Compliance Requirements**: Compliance with industry regulations and data protection laws adds another layer of complexity to security control implementation. Organizations must navigate a maze of legal and regulatory frameworks, ensuring that their security measures align with specific mandates while protecting sensitive data and customer privacy.

3. **Evolving Threat Landscapes**: The cybersecurity threat landscape is in a constant state of flux, with threat actors continually devising new tactics and exploiting emerging vulnerabilities. Staying ahead

of these evolving threats requires organizations to adopt proactive security measures, threat intelligence capabilities, and continuous monitoring practices.

4. **Complex Technology Environments**: Modern IT infrastructures are increasingly complex, incorporating a mix of on-premises systems, cloud services, mobile devices, and IoT endpoints. Managing security controls across this diverse ecosystem presents significant challenges, requiring integration, interoperability, and centralized management solutions.

Considering these challenges, organizations must adopt a risk-based approach to security, focusing on identifying and prioritizing critical assets and vulnerabilities. By conducting comprehensive risk assessments, organizations can allocate resources effectively, address the most pressing security threats, and tailor their security controls to mitigate specific risks. Moreover, organizations should embrace a culture of continuous improvement, regularly evaluating and enhancing their security controls to adapt to emerging threats and evolving business needs. This iterative approach enables organizations to maintain resilience in the face of evolving cybersecurity challenges and ensure the protection of their valuable assets and sensitive data.

Defense-in-Depth

Imagine your organization's IT infrastructure as a medieval castle, and cyber threats as would-be invaders seeking to breach its defenses. In this analogy, defense-in-depth acts as the fortress's layered defenses, designed to repel attackers and safeguard valuable assets. Now this may not sound like the most realistic scenario to consider, but it in fact is the most similar to a secured network. The more barriers you have between you and an attacker, the less likely they are to stick through until they succeed.

1. **Moat as the Outer Perimeter**: At the outermost layer of defense, we have the moat, representing perimeter security measures such as firewalls, intrusion detection systems (IDS), and network segmentation. These defenses create a barrier between the outside world and your organization's network, deterring unauthorized access and blocking known threats from entering.

2. **Stone Wall as the Middle Layer**: Beyond the moat lies the sturdy stone wall, symbolizing endpoint protection solutions such as antivirus software, endpoint detection and response (EDR), and mobile device management (MDM). These defenses fortify individual devices and endpoints within your network, guarding against malware, ransomware, and other forms of cyber-attacks.

3. **Inner Keep as the Last Line of Defense**: Finally, at the heart of the castle stands the inner keep, representing internal controls and measures such as access controls, encryption, and data loss prevention (DLP) solutions. These safeguards protect your organization's most sensitive data and critical assets, ensuring that even if outer defenses are breached, attackers face formidable obstacles to reaching their ultimate objectives.

By layering these defenses, akin to adding successive layers to our cyber castle, organizations can significantly bolster their security posture and resilience against cyber threats. Even if attackers manage to breach one layer of defense, they are met with additional barriers and obstacles at each subsequent layer, increasing the likelihood of detection and containment before significant harm can occur. Just as a well-fortified castle instills fear in potential invaders, a robust defense-in-depth strategy instills confidence in your organization's ability to withstand cyber threats and protect its valuable resources.

Key Components of Defense-in-Depth

Now that we know the reasoning behind providing a layered defense, we can further our understanding by reviewing the core elements that compose it. In this section, we will view the components that build our castle from the ground up. With each component, another layer of defense is added. Now that we have visualized what this means, we can look into it more practically. Barriers can be placed anywhere among an organization, but they are some crucial bottlenecks that are ideally made to establish these security layers.

1. **Perimeter Security:** The outermost layer of defense, perimeter security controls protect the boundary between an organization's internal network and external environments. These controls include firewalls, intrusion prevention systems (IPS), network segmentation, and access controls to prevent unauthorized access and block malicious traffic from entering the network.

2. **Network Security:** Network security controls focus on securing internal network traffic and communications between devices and systems. This layer includes network monitoring, encryption, virtual private networks (VPNs), and secure protocols to protect data in transit and prevent unauthorized interception or tampering.

3. **Endpoint Security:** Endpoint security controls protect individual devices and endpoints, such as computers, servers, mobile devices, and IoT devices. These controls include antivirus software, endpoint detection and response (EDR), device encryption, patch management, and application whitelisting to detect, prevent, and remediate security threats at the endpoint level.

4. **Application Security:** Application security controls focus on securing software applications and web services against cyber threats and vulnerabilities. This layer includes secure coding practices, web application firewalls (WAFs), runtime application self-protection (RASP), and vulnerability scanning to identify and mitigate security flaws in applications and prevent exploitation by attackers.

5. **Data Security:** Data security controls protect sensitive data and information assets from unauthorized access, disclosure, or manipulation. These controls include data encryption, access controls, data loss prevention (DLP), data masking, and secure data storage to ensure the confidentiality, integrity, and availability of critical data throughout its lifecycle.

Layered Security Strategies

Layered security strategies complement defense-in-depth principles by incorporating multiple security layers and controls to address specific risks and vulnerabilities. These strategies involve the strategic deployment of security measures across different levels of the IT infrastructure, from the network perimeter to individual endpoints and applications. By combining complementary security technologies and controls, layered security strategies provide comprehensive protection against evolving cyber threats and help organizations maintain a strong security posture.

Benefits of Defense-in-Depth and Layered Security

- **Increased Resilience:** Defense-in-depth and layered security strategies enhance an organization's resilience to cyber-attacks by reducing the likelihood of successful breaches and minimizing the impact of security incidents.
- **Comprehensive Protection:** By deploying multiple layers of security controls, organizations can protect against a wide range of threats and vulnerabilities, including malware, phishing, insider threats, and advanced persistent threats (APTs).
- **Adaptability and Flexibility:** These strategies allow organizations to adapt to changing threat landscapes and emerging security challenges by implementing a flexible and scalable security architecture that can evolve over time.
- **Regulatory Compliance:** Defense-in-depth and layered security approaches align with regulatory requirements and industry best practices, enabling organizations to meet compliance obligations and demonstrate due diligence in protecting sensitive information and data privacy.

Defense-in-depth and layered security strategies are essential components of a robust cybersecurity framework, providing organizations with the necessary tools and measures to effectively protect their digital assets and mitigate cyber risks. By adopting a proactive and multi-layered approach to security, organizations can enhance their resilience to cyber threats and maintain a strong security posture in today's complex and dynamic threat landscape.

Network Security Fundamentals

Network security is a critical aspect of cybersecurity, focusing on protecting the integrity, confidentiality, and availability of data transmitted across computer networks. This section provides an overview of key network security concepts and technologies, including firewalls, intrusion detection systems (IDS), intrusion prevention systems (IPS), and virtual private networks (VPN). By furthering our understanding of these topics, we position ourselves to best assist those we support in our daily duties.

1. **Firewalls:** Essential network security devices that monitor and control incoming and outgoing network traffic based on predetermined security rules. They act as a barrier between trusted internal networks and untrusted external networks, such as the Internet, by inspecting packets and blocking or allowing them based on predefined criteria. There are several types of firewalls, including:

    - **Packet Filtering Firewalls:** Examine packet headers and filter traffic based on IP addresses, port numbers, and other protocol fields.

- **Stateful Inspection Firewalls:** Maintain state information for active connections and make filtering decisions based on the context of the traffic flow.
- **Proxy Firewalls:** Act as intermediaries between clients and servers, inspecting and filtering traffic at the application layer.

2. **Intrusion Detection Systems (IDS):** Network security tools designed to detect and respond to suspicious or malicious activities on a network. IDS analyzes network traffic and system logs to identify potential security threats, such as unauthorized access attempts, malware infections, or unusual network behavior. There are two main types of IDS:
    - **Network-Based IDS (NIDS):** Monitors network traffic in real-time, analyzing packets for signs of malicious activity or policy violations.
    - **Host-Based IDS (HIDS):** Monitors individual host systems, including servers, workstations, and endpoints, for signs of unauthorized access or suspicious activity.
3. **Intrusion Prevention Systems (IPS):** Builds upon the capabilities of IDS by not only detecting but also actively blocking or mitigating detected threats in real-time. IPS can automatically respond to security incidents by dropping malicious packets, blocking network traffic, or alerting security administrators. By combining detection and prevention capabilities, IPS helps organizations proactively defend against cyber threats and protect network assets.

4. **Virtual Private Networks (VPN):** Enable secure communication over public networks, such as the Internet, by creating encrypted tunnels between remote users or branch offices and a central network infrastructure. VPNs ensure confidentiality and privacy by encrypting data traffic and authenticating users through authentication protocols, such as IPSec (Internet Protocol Security) or SSL/TLS (Secure Sockets Layer/Transport Layer Security). VPNs are commonly used to provide remote access to corporate networks, secure data transmission between geographically dispersed locations, and protect sensitive information from interception or eavesdropping.

Understanding these network security fundamentals is essential for building a strong defense against cyber threats and ensuring the security and integrity of network infrastructure. By implementing robust network security measures, organizations can safeguard their digital assets, mitigate risks, and maintain trust and confidence in their network operations. Not only can these improve our quality of work within the field, but by understanding these various items, we are more prepared to meet the CompTIA A+ examination's requirements.

Network Segmentation and Its Role in Improving Security Posture

Network segmentation is a security strategy that involves dividing a computer network into smaller, isolated segments or subnetworks. Each segment, also known as a network zone or VLAN (Virtual Local Area Network), operates independently and has its own set of security policies and access controls. With segmentation, if a particular zone is breached, the other separate zones are safe for the time being. Not only does this provide a strong layer of defense, but it also can improve the quality of service within an organization's environment. This section provides an overview of network segmentation and its significant role in enhancing the overall security posture of an organization.

1. **Definition and Purpose:** Network segmentation aims to restrict the lateral movement of threats within a network by compartmentalizing resources and limiting communication between network segments. By dividing the network into smaller, more manageable segments, organizations can contain security incidents, minimize the impact of potential breaches, and reduce the attack surface exposed to malicious actors.

2. **Improved Security Isolation:** Network segmentation enhances security isolation by segregating critical assets, sensitive data, and high-risk systems into separate network zones. By isolating resources based on their function, sensitivity, or risk level, organizations can enforce stricter access controls and implement targeted security measures to protect valuable assets from unauthorized access or compromise.

3. **Granular Access Control:** Segmented networks enable organizations to implement granular access control policies tailored to the specific requirements of each network segment. By defining access rules based on user roles, device types, or network locations, organizations can enforce the principle

of least privilege and ensure that users and devices only have access to the resources necessary for their legitimate business functions.

4. **Containment of Threats:** In the event of a security incident or compromise, network segmentation helps contain the spread of threats and limit the scope of potential damage. By confining malicious activity to a single network segment, organizations can prevent threats from propagating to other parts of the network and minimize the impact on critical systems and services.

5. **Compliance Requirements:** Network segmentation is often mandated by industry regulations and compliance standards, such as PCI DSS (Payment Card Industry Data Security Standard) or HIPAA (Health Insurance Portability and Accountability Act), which require organizations to implement strong access controls and protect sensitive data from unauthorized access or disclosure. By adhering to these requirements, organizations can demonstrate compliance with regulatory obligations and industry best practices.

6. **Scalability and Flexibility:** Modern network segmentation solutions offer scalability and flexibility to accommodate evolving business requirements and dynamic IT environments. Virtualization technologies, software-defined networking (SDN), and cloud-based solutions enable organizations to dynamically adjust network segmentation policies, scale network resources up or down as needed, and adapt to changing security threats and operational demands.

Network Protocols and Encryption Standards

Secure network protocols and encryption standards are essential components of robust cybersecurity strategies. This section reviews the significance of secure network protocols and encryption standards, highlighting their role in safeguarding data integrity, confidentiality, and authenticity across communication channels. Network protocols are fundamental to ensuring the confidentiality, integrity, and authenticity of data transmitted over computer networks. These protocols establish standardized rules and procedures for data exchange between networked devices, facilitating secure communication while mitigating the risk of interception, eavesdropping, or tampering by malicious actors.

Common Secure Network Protocols

The following are only the most common network security protocols that are outlined by the requirements of the certification exam. This by no means provides a full and thorough coverage of all applicable protocols but will more than cover the most used and likely to be found on the exam. It is my personal recommendation for those seeking entry into the field or interested in higher certifications in the future to do additional research on various network protocols. Particularly those looking towards the Network+ or Security+ will find this topic popping up frequently.

- **Transport Layer Security (TLS) and Secure Sockets Layer (SSL):** TLS and SSL protocols encrypt data transmitted between web browsers and servers, providing a secure communication channel for online transactions, sensitive information exchange, and web browsing. These protocols authenticate the identities of communicating parties and establish encrypted connections to protect data confidentiality and integrity.

- **Internet Protocol Security (IPsec):** IPsec provides network-layer security by encrypting and authenticating IP packets exchanged between network devices. IPsec can be used to establish virtual private networks (VPNs), secure communication between remote offices, and protect data transmitted over untrusted networks, such as the Internet.
- **Secure Shell (SSH):** SSH is a cryptographic network protocol that enables secure remote access and command execution on networked devices. SSH encrypts communication sessions between clients and servers, preventing unauthorized interception or tampering of sensitive data, login credentials, and administrative commands.
- **Virtual Private Network (VPN) Protocols:** VPN protocols such as OpenVPN, L2TP/IPsec, and IKEv2/IPsec establish encrypted tunnels between remote users and corporate networks, enabling secure remote access and data transmission over public networks. VPNs protect sensitive information from eavesdropping and interception by encrypting data traffic between endpoints.

Encryption Standards and Algorithms

Encryption standards and algorithms play a pivotal role in securing data at rest and in transit by converting plaintext data into ciphertext using mathematical algorithms and cryptographic keys. There are both symmetric and asymmetric standards for encryption and ciphers that utilize a stream method or block. For the purposes of this publication, we will not be reviewing those as deeply. This is not a comprehensive breakdown of all encryption standards and algorithms, and it is highly recommended to perform individual research on the history, application, and range of others in the event of future certifications. To meet the purpose of this publication, we are only going to cover the most common standards as recommended by the CompTIA A+ guidelines. Common encryption standards include

- **Advanced Encryption Standard (AES):** AES is a widely adopted symmetric encryption algorithm used to protect sensitive data in transit and at rest. AES offers strong encryption capabilities and is employed in various security protocols and applications, including TLS, IPsec, and disk encryption.
- **RSA (Rivest-Shamir-Adleman) Encryption:** RSA is an asymmetric encryption algorithm used for key exchange, digital signatures, and public-key encryption. RSA relies on the mathematical properties of prime numbers to secure communication channels and verify the authenticity of digital certificates.
- **Elliptic Curve Cryptography (ECC):** ECC is a cryptographic algorithm based on elliptic curves, offering strong security with shorter key lengths compared to traditional encryption algorithms. ECC is used in SSL/TLS certificates, digital signatures, and secure messaging applications.
- **Diffie-Hellman Key Exchange:** Diffie-Hellman is a key exchange protocol that allows two parties to establish a shared secret key over an insecure communication channel. Diffie-Hellman key exchange is used in conjunction with symmetric encryption algorithms to establish secure communication channels in SSL/TLS, IPsec, and VPN protocols.

Endpoint Security

Endpoint security plays a pivotal role in safeguarding devices such as computers, smartphones, and tablets from cybersecurity threats. This section explores various endpoint security solutions and strategies aimed at protecting endpoints from malware, unauthorized access, and data breaches. Here we will look at the deployments that are most commonly used on a daily basis among our users and how to maintain adequate security measures. In this section, we will review the different forms of security that can be used to protect a particular endpoint, regardless of the type of control or implementation that it would fall under:

- **Antivirus Software:** Antivirus software detects, prevents, and removes malware infections on endpoints by scanning files, monitoring system activity, and blocking malicious processes. These solutions use signature-based detection, heuristic analysis, and behavioral monitoring to identify and mitigate threats.
- **Endpoint Detection and Response (EDR):** EDR solutions provide advanced threat detection and incident response capabilities on endpoints by continuously monitoring system activity, analyzing behavior patterns, and detecting suspicious activities indicative of cyber threats. EDR platforms offer real-time threat visibility, automated response actions, and forensic analysis capabilities to enhance endpoint security posture.
- **Mobile Device Management (MDM):** MDM solutions enable organizations to manage and secure mobile devices, such as smartphones and tablets, by enforcing security policies, controlling device settings, and

remotely monitoring device activity. MDM platforms facilitate device enrollment, application management, data encryption, and remote wipe capabilities to protect sensitive information and mitigate mobile security risks.

Strategies for Securing Endpoints

There are numerous different strategies to utilize when considering the proper security of endpoints is met. Though there are significant differences between the approach of this topic, some of the most common and known methods incorporate the following:

- **Patch Management:** Regularly updating software and firmware on endpoints to address security vulnerabilities, software bugs, and performance issues. Organizations should implement automated patch management processes to ensure timely deployment of security patches and software updates across all endpoints.
- **Device Encryption:** Safeguards sensitive data stored on endpoints by encrypting data at rest, preventing unauthorized access in case of device theft or loss. Full-disk encryption and file-level encryption solutions protect data integrity and confidentiality, ensuring compliance with data protection regulations and industry standards.
- **Application Whitelisting:** Restricts the execution of unauthorized or unapproved software on endpoints by allowing only trusted applications to run. Organizations define a list of approved applications and software

publishers, preventing malware, ransomware, and unauthorized programs from compromising endpoint security. Application whitelisting enhances security posture by reducing the attack surface and minimizing the risk of malware infections.

Data Security and Privacy

Data security and privacy are both constant topics in today's digital world where sensitive information is constantly at risk of unauthorized access, theft, or misuse. This not only poses potential legal issues, let alone ethical ones, but it can cause major financial or reputational backlash. Whether viewing data privacy from an individual or organizational perspective, there is a lot at risk, causing a tremendous amount of concern. This section provides an overview of key data security principles and strategies aimed at protecting confidential data and preserving privacy.

1. **Data Security Principles:**
    - **Data Classification:** Data classification involves categorizing data based on its sensitivity, importance, and regulatory requirements. Organizations classify data into categories such as public, internal use only, confidential, and restricted access, enabling them to apply appropriate security controls and access restrictions based on data sensitivity.
    - **Encryption:** Encryption is a fundamental data security technique that transforms plaintext data into ciphertext, rendering it unreadable to unauthorized individuals or malicious actors. By encrypting data at rest and in transit using strong

cryptographic algorithms and encryption keys, organizations can safeguard sensitive information from interception, unauthorized access, and data breaches.

- **Data Loss Prevention (DLP):** Data loss prevention (DLP) solutions help organizations monitor, detect, and prevent unauthorized data exfiltration, leakage, or loss. DLP technologies employ content inspection, contextual analysis, and policy enforcement mechanisms to identify and mitigate data security risks across endpoints, networks, and cloud environments.

2. **Data Privacy Measures:**

- **Regulatory Compliance:** Compliance with data protection regulations, such as the General Data Protection Regulation (GDPR) and the California Consumer Privacy Act (CCPA), is essential for ensuring data privacy and avoiding regulatory penalties. Organizations must adhere to legal requirements related to data collection, processing, storage, and sharing, implementing privacy-by-design principles and transparent data handling practices.

- **Privacy Policies and Notices:** Privacy policies and notices inform individuals about how organizations collect, use, disclose, and protect their personal information. Organizations should provide clear and concise privacy statements that outline data processing practices, data retention policies, and individual rights regarding data access, correction, and deletion.

- **Data Minimization:** Data minimization involves limiting the collection, storage, and retention of personal data to the minimum necessary for achieving specific business purposes. By reducing the scope of data processing and minimizing data exposure, organizations can mitigate privacy risks and enhance data protection.

3. **Data Security Best Practices:**

- **Access Control:** Implement robust access control mechanisms to enforce the principle of least privilege and restrict unauthorized access to sensitive data. Role-based access control (RBAC), multi-factor authentication (MFA), and privileged access management (PAM) help prevent unauthorized data access and privilege escalation.
- **Data Backup and Recovery:** Maintain regular backups of critical data and establish disaster recovery procedures to ensure data availability and resilience in the event of data loss, corruption, or ransomware attacks. Backup encryption and secure offsite storage protect backup data from unauthorized access and tampering.
- **Employee Training and Awareness:** Provide comprehensive cybersecurity awareness training to employees, educating them about data security best practices, privacy policies, and the importance of safeguarding sensitive information. By promoting a culture of security awareness and accountability, organizations can empower employees to recognize and report security incidents and data privacy concerns.

Incident Response and Disaster Recovery

Organizations must be prepared to respond swiftly and effectively to security incidents and mitigate their impact on business operations. This is not to say to rush into action; however, the odds of a positive outcome in an incident or disaster are significantly increased with adequate preparation. This section provides an overview of incident response frameworks and disaster recovery strategies aimed at minimizing downtime, data loss, and reputational damage in the event of security breaches or catastrophic events.

1. **Incident Response Frameworks:**

    - **Preparation:** Incident response begins with proactive measures to prepare for potential security incidents. This phase involves establishing incident response policies, procedures, and roles within the organization. It also includes conducting risk assessments, defining incident severity levels, and developing incident response plans tailored to various scenarios.

    - **Detection:** The detection phase focuses on identifying and analyzing indicators of compromise (IOCs) and security events that may indicate a potential security incident. Organizations deploy security monitoring tools, intrusion detection systems (IDS), and security information and event management (SIEM) solutions to detect anomalous behavior, unauthorized access attempts, or suspicious network activity.

    - **Containment:** Upon detecting a security incident, the containment phase aims to prevent the further spread of the threat and minimize its impact on the organization's systems and data. Incident responders isolate affected systems, disable compromised accounts or services, and implement temporary controls to limit the attacker's ability to escalate privileges or access additional resources.

- **Eradication:** In the eradication phase, incident responders focus on removing the root cause of the security incident and restoring affected systems to a secure state. This may involve identifying and patching vulnerabilities, removing malware or unauthorized access points, and restoring data from backups to eliminate residual threats.

- **Recovery:** The recovery phase involves restoring normal operations and services after a security incident. Incident responders leverage disaster recovery plans, backup data, and system snapshots to recover affected systems and data. They also conduct post-incident reviews and lessons learned sessions to identify areas for improvement and strengthen future incident response efforts.

2. **Disaster Recovery Strategies:**

    - **Business Continuity Planning:** Business continuity planning involves developing strategies and procedures to ensure the continued operation of critical business functions in the event of disruptions or disasters. Organizations identify key resources, establish recovery time objectives (RTOs) and recovery point objectives (RPOs), and implement redundant systems and failover mechanisms to minimize downtime and data loss.

- **Backup and Restore:** Backup and restore procedures are essential components of disaster recovery planning. Organizations regularly back up critical data and systems to secure offsite locations or cloud-based storage solutions. They also conduct periodic data recovery tests and validate backup integrity to ensure data availability and resilience in the event of data loss or corruption.
- **Incident Response Coordination:** Incident response and disaster recovery efforts are closely coordinated to ensure a cohesive and effective response to security incidents and catastrophic events. Incident response teams collaborate with disaster recovery teams to assess the impact of incidents, prioritize recovery efforts, and restore business operations in a timely manner.

By adopting incident response frameworks and disaster recovery strategies, organizations can effectively mitigate the impact of security incidents, minimize downtime, and ensure the resilience and continuity of critical business operations. Proactive preparation, rapid detection, and decisive response are essential elements of effective incident response and disaster recovery practices in today's dynamic threat landscape.

Importance of Disaster Recovery Planning and Business Continuity

When we are properly prepared for an emergency, we are more likely to reduce the negative effects felt as a whole. This not only will reduce stress levels of all of those involved, but it can potentially save a tremendous sum of money or even circumvent a total loss. Planning for an event that has not yet happened may seem silly to some, but it is by no means a topic to take lightly.

Mitigating Downtime: Disruptions such as natural disasters, cyber-attacks, hardware failures, or human errors can lead to significant downtime, resulting in lost revenue, productivity, and customer trust. Disaster recovery planning and business continuity strategies aim to minimize these disruptions and facilitate rapid recovery.

Ensuring Data Integrity: In the event of data loss or corruption, organizations risk irreparable damage to their reputation and financial stability. Disaster recovery planning includes measures to back up critical data, implement redundant systems, and restore operations to a secure state.

Regulatory Compliance: Many industries are subject to regulatory requirements mandating the implementation of disaster recovery and business continuity measures. Compliance with regulations such as the Health Insurance Portability and Accountability Act (HIPAA) or the Payment Card Industry Data Security Standard (PCI DSS) necessitates robust disaster recovery planning to protect sensitive data and ensure regulatory compliance.

Maintaining Customer Trust: Customers expect uninterrupted access to products and services, making downtime detrimental to customer satisfaction and loyalty. Effective disaster recovery and business continuity strategies help organizations maintain customer trust by minimizing service disruptions and ensuring the continuity of operations.

Objectives of Disaster Recovery Planning

Now that we know both the goal of planning and what is potentially at stake, we can look to the actual objectives of this planning. This is where we can make these actions measurable, whether qualitative or quantitative. We can view what risks are potential, review recovery time needs and data recover needs, and even begin to develop and test these plans. This is where all the planning acts and becomes a tangible part of the business.

Identifying Risks: Disaster recovery planning begins with identifying potential risks and threats that could disrupt business operations. These may include natural disasters, cyber-attacks, power outages, equipment failures, or supply chain disruptions.

Establishing Recovery Objectives: Organizations must define recovery time objectives (RTOs) and recovery point objectives (RPOs) to determine acceptable levels of downtime and data loss. RTOs specify the maximum allowable downtime for restoring operations, while RPOs define the acceptable amount of data loss in the event of a disruption.

Developing Response Procedures: Disaster recovery plans outline step-by-step procedures for responding to different types of incidents, including data breaches, system failures, or physical disasters. These procedures detail roles and responsibilities, communication protocols, and escalation paths to ensure a coordinated response.

Testing and Validation: Regular testing and validation of disaster recovery plans are essential to ensuring their effectiveness and reliability. Organizations conduct tabletop exercises, simulations, or full-scale drills to assess their readiness to respond to various scenarios and identify areas for improvement.

Business Continuity Strategies

In terms of business continuity, we are at a very similar spot in the path as disaster recovery. The main differences here sit with the necessities of each critical component or function that is required to maintain productivity levels. The goal of this is to continue operations while the event is being addressed and ensure that losses are kept to a minimum. Keeping this in mind, let's take a peek at the strategies we will utilize.

Identifying Critical Functions: Business continuity planning involves identifying critical business functions and prioritizing their recovery based on their impact on operations and revenue generation. Organizations categorize functions as essential, important, or non-essential to establish recovery priorities.

Establishing Redundancy: Redundancy measures such as backup systems, failover mechanisms, and redundant infrastructure components are implemented to ensure the availability and resilience of critical business functions. Redundancy minimizes the impact of disruptions by providing alternative means of operation.

Implementing Remote Work Solutions: In the face of disruptions such as pandemics or natural disasters, remote work solutions enable employees to continue working from alternative locations. Business continuity strategies include the deployment of remote access technologies, collaboration tools, and secure communication platforms to maintain productivity during crises.

Security Awareness and Training

The human element remains a critical factor in ensuring efficient cybersecurity defenses, especially in today's day and age. Security awareness programs play a key role in cultivating a security-conscious culture within organizations, empowering employees, and end-users to recognize and mitigate cybersecurity risks effectively. This section highlights the importance of security awareness, strategies for educating stakeholders, and tips for creating engaging training materials and simulations. I know that I have chimed on this numerous times previously, but the human aspect of the cyber world is the most crucial in preventing or creating an incident. Proper security awareness and continuous training go a very long way to ensuring this is properly addressed.

1. **Importance of Security Awareness Programs:**

   - **Risk Mitigation:** Security awareness programs enable organizations to proactively mitigate cybersecurity risks by educating employees and end-users about potential threats and how to respond to them effectively. By raising awareness about phishing scams, social engineering tactics, and malware threats, organizations can reduce the likelihood of successful cyber-attacks.

   - **Compliance Requirements:** Many industry regulations and standards, such as the General Data Protection Regulation (GDPR) and the Payment Card Industry Data Security Standard (PCI DSS), mandate the implementation of security awareness training for employees handling sensitive data. Compliance with these regulations requires organizations to establish comprehensive security awareness programs.

   - **Behavioral Change:** Security awareness training aims to instill behavioral changes in employees and end-users, fostering a security-conscious mindset and promoting proactive security practices. By integrating cybersecurity awareness into daily workflows and routines, organizations can create a culture of vigilance and accountability.

   - **Incident Response Preparedness:** Well-trained employees are better equipped to respond effectively to cybersecurity incidents, minimizing the impact of breaches and data breaches. Security awareness programs provide employees with the knowledge and skills necessary to identify, report, and mitigate security incidents in a timely manner.

2. **Strategies for Educating Employees and End-Users:**

    - **Tailored Training Modules:** Security awareness training should be tailored to the specific roles, responsibilities, and risk profiles of employees within the organization. Customized training modules address relevant cybersecurity topics and emphasize practical actions employees can take to enhance security in their day-to-day activities.

    - **Interactive Learning Experiences:** Engaging training materials, such as videos, quizzes, gamified simulations, and real-world scenarios, captivate the audience's attention and reinforce key security concepts effectively. Interactive learning experiences promote active participation and knowledge retention among employees and end-users.

    - **Continuous Reinforcement:** Security awareness is an ongoing process that requires regular reinforcement and updates to address emerging threats and changing security landscapes. Organizations should implement continuous training initiatives, periodic assessments, and refresher courses to ensure that security awareness remains top of mind for all stakeholders.

- **Leadership Support and Engagement:** Executive leadership plays a crucial role in championing security awareness initiatives and fostering a culture of cybersecurity within the organization. Visible support from senior management reinforces the importance of security awareness training and encourages active participation from employees at all levels.

3. **Tips for Creating Engaging Security Awareness Training Materials and Simulations:**

    - **Storytelling Approach:** Incorporate real-world examples, case studies, and anecdotes to illustrate the impact of cybersecurity threats and the importance of security best practices. Storytelling captivates the audience's attention and makes complex security concepts more relatable and memorable.

    - **Interactive Scenarios:** Develop interactive simulations and role-playing exercises that simulate common cybersecurity scenarios encountered in the workplace. By allowing participants to experience simulated phishing attacks, social engineering tactics, or malware infections firsthand, organizations can assess their readiness and response capabilities in a safe environment.

    - **Multimedia Content:** Leverage multimedia formats, including videos, infographics, animations, and podcasts, to deliver engaging and visually appealing training materials. Multimedia content enhances learning retention and accommodates diverse learning preferences and styles among participants.

- **Gamification Elements:** Integrate gamification elements such as badges, rewards, leaderboards, and challenges into security awareness training programs to incentivize participation and promote healthy competition among employees. Gamification enhances engagement, motivation, and knowledge retention, making security awareness training more enjoyable and effective.

By adopting these strategies and best practices, organizations can develop comprehensive security awareness programs that empower employees and end-users to become active participants in defending against cyber threats. Through continuous education, engagement, and reinforcement, organizations can create a culture of security awareness that strengthens their overall cybersecurity posture and resilience.

Emerging Threats and Trends

Staying ahead of emerging threats and trends is paramount to maintaining robust defenses and adapting to evolving risk landscapes. This section explores the latest cybersecurity threats and trends, shedding light on emerging challenges and future developments shaping the cybersecurity landscape. Not only do we need to review the trends that are currently coming to light, but we should also take consideration of what is on the horizon.

Emerging Cybersecurity Threats:

- **AI-Powered Attacks:** The proliferation of artificial intelligence (AI) and machine learning (ML) technologies has given rise to AI-powered cyber-attacks. Threat actors leverage AI algorithms to automate and enhance the sophistication of attacks, such as malware propagation, phishing, and social engineering. AI-powered attacks pose unique challenges for cybersecurity defenders, requiring advanced detection and response capabilities to thwart evolving threats.

- **IoT Vulnerabilities:** The rapid expansion of the Internet of Things (IoT) ecosystem introduces new security vulnerabilities and attack vectors. Insecure IoT devices, inadequate authentication mechanisms, and poor device management practices create opportunities for cybercriminals to compromise IoT networks and launch large-scale attacks, such as botnets and DDoS attacks. Securing the IoT ecosystem remains a pressing challenge for organizations across various industries.
- **Supply Chain Attacks:** Supply chain attacks target the interconnected network of vendors, suppliers, and service providers that support an organization's operations. Threat actors exploit vulnerabilities in supply chain partners' systems or software to infiltrate target organizations and compromise their networks. Supply chain attacks can have far-reaching consequences, leading to data breaches, system compromises, and reputational damage for affected organizations.

Future Trends in Cybersecurity:

- **Zero-Trust Architecture:** Zero-trust architecture (ZTA) is gaining traction as a proactive security model that assumes zero trust in both internal and external networks. By implementing stringent access controls, continuous authentication, and micro-segmentation, organizations can minimize the risk of lateral movement and unauthorized access within their networks. ZTA aligns with the principle of least privilege and enhances security posture in dynamic and perimeterless environments.

- **Secure by Design Principles:** Secure by design principles advocate for integrating security considerations into the design, development, and deployment of software and systems from the outset. By embedding security features, threat modeling, and secure coding practices into the development lifecycle, organizations can proactively mitigate vulnerabilities and reduce the attack surface of their applications and infrastructure. Secure by design promotes a proactive and preventive approach to cybersecurity, emphasizing resilience and risk mitigation.
- **Quantum-Resistant Cryptography:** The advent of quantum computing poses a significant threat to traditional cryptographic algorithms, such as RSA and ECC, which could be vulnerable to quantum attacks. Quantum-resistant cryptography aims to develop cryptographic algorithms and protocols that remain secure against quantum computing threats. Post-quantum cryptography (PQC) research focuses on developing quantum-resistant encryption schemes, digital signatures, and key exchange protocols to safeguard sensitive data and communications in a quantum-enabled future.

By monitoring emerging cybersecurity threats and trends, organizations can anticipate future challenges and proactively adapt their security strategies to mitigate risks effectively. Embracing innovative technologies and adopting security best practices, such as zero-trust architecture and secure by design principles, enables organizations to stay resilient in the face of evolving cyber threats and emerging attack vectors.

Conclusion

This chapter is one of the most important of this publication, and I had difficulty placing it first or last. Ultimately, I decided to put it at the end of the book as all the knowledge built up to this point ties into the security aspect of our digital domain. This section is also of significant personal interest; it is what drew me into the field initially. Cybersecurity can affect all aspects of our daily lives, especially in today's day and age. Our financials, credit cards, bank accounts, personal social interactions, relationships, careers, educational aspirations, entertainment, and so much more rely on this to keep us secure from the risks out there. This chapter has revealed the time-proven truth that the human element is the riskiest, as well as the most crucial in preventing a cyber-attack.

We reviewed the CIA triad, Confidentiality, Integrity, and Availability, and how it intertwines into supporting all security measures within the field. This principle is fundamental to understand and utilize, regardless of experience level. I have seen this example in the most basic courses and the most advanced certifications that I have tested for. Please ensure that you thoroughly understand the meaning and purpose behind this key element. We also learned of the most common security protocols and encryption standards, at least to the requirements set forth by the

CompTIA A+ Certification Examination. With that said, that is by no means a comprehensive guide to all those details. I would personally recommend doing individual research, especially if seeking entry to the cyber field or future learning such as the Security+ exam.

As we wrap this chapter, remember all that you have learned. Think of how it ties in together and how each individual component may affect another. It is like raindrops in a puddle; the ripples will eventually overlap, and things have a much larger picture. Hope to see you once again in future publications.

Glossary

These are crucial terms to know in order to pass the CompTIA A+ certification, as well as helpful terms to understand for those looking to join the IT workforce. Please take your time to thoroughly understand each and every term to fully absorb the content material. I would suggest making flash cards and quizzing yourself periodically; this is also a wonderful last-minute study tool to utilize prior to taking the exam itself.

1. **Liquid Crystal Display (LCD):** A type of display technology that uses liquid crystals to produce images on a flat surface, commonly used in laptops and monitors.

2. **Light-Emitting Diode (LED):** A type of display technology that uses light-emitting diodes to produce images with high brightness and energy efficiency, commonly used in modern laptops and TVs.

3. **Organic Light-Emitting Diode (OLED):** A type of display technology that uses organic compounds to emit light when an electric current is applied, offering superior image quality and flexibility.

4. **Touch Display:** A type of display technology that allows users to interact with devices through touch gestures, commonly used in smartphones, tablets, and touchscreen laptops.

© Kodi A. Cochran 2024

K. A. Cochran, *CompTIA A+ Certification Companion*, Certification Study Companion Series,
https://doi.org/10.1007/979-8-8688-0867-8

5. **In-Plane Switching (IPS):** A type of display technology known for its superior color accuracy, wider viewing angles, and better color consistency compared to traditional LCD displays.
6. **Twisted Nematic (TN):** A type of display technology known for its fast response times and affordability, commonly used in budget-friendly laptops and gaming monitors.
7. **High Refresh Rate Displays:** Displays that refresh the screen more frequently than standard displays, offering smoother motion and reduced motion blur, commonly used in gaming laptops and monitors.
8. **Local Area Networks (LANs):** Networks that typically cover a small geographical area, such as a single building or campus, and are used for local resource sharing and communication.
9. **Wide Area Networks (WANs):** Networks that span large geographical areas, connecting multiple LANs across cities, countries, or continents, and are used for global connectivity.
10. **Metropolitan Area Networks (MANs):** Networks that cover the geographical area of a city or metropolitan area, bridging the gap between LANs and WANs.
11. **Personal Area Networks (PANs):** Networks designed for personal or individual use, connecting devices within a short range, such as a room or personal space.

12. **Infrastructure as a Service (IaaS):** A cloud computing service model that provides virtualized computing resources, including servers, storage, and networking, as a service.

13. **Platform as a Service (PaaS):** A cloud computing service model that offers a development platform with tools and services to build, deploy, and manage applications without the complexity of infrastructure management.

14. **Software as a Service (SaaS):** A cloud computing service model that delivers software applications over the Internet on a subscription basis, eliminating the need for on-premises installation and maintenance.

15. **Public Cloud:** Cloud services owned and operated by third-party providers and made available to the public over the Internet, offering cost-effective scalability and flexibility.

16. **Private Cloud:** Cloud services dedicated to a single organization and hosted either on-premises or by a third-party provider, offering greater control, security, and customization.

17. **Community Cloud:** Cloud services shared among several organizations with similar interests or requirements, such as industry-specific regulations or standards.

18. **Hybrid Cloud:** Cloud environments that combine public and private cloud infrastructure, allowing organizations to leverage the scalability of public cloud services while maintaining control over sensitive data.

19. **Virtualization:** A technology that allows for the creation of virtual instances of physical hardware, enabling efficient resource utilization and flexibility in cloud computing.

20. **Hypervisors:** Software or firmware components that enable the creation and management of virtual machines, providing an abstraction layer between physical hardware and virtualized guest operating systems.

21. **Storage Systems:** Cloud storage solutions that provide scalable and resilient storage for data in the cloud, using distributed storage architectures to ensure data durability and availability.

22. **Network Configurations:** The design and management of networking resources in cloud computing to enable communication between cloud components and users, including virtual networks, subnets, routing, and security groups.

23. **Scalability:** The ability of applications and workloads to scale horizontally and vertically to accommodate fluctuating demand and workload patterns.

24. **Elasticity:** The ability of cloud resources to scale up or down dynamically based on demand, providing flexibility and cost savings.

25. **Resource Optimization:** Strategies to optimize resource utilization and minimize costs in cloud computing environments, including rightsizing instances and performance optimization.

26. **High Availability and Disaster Recovery:** Strategies to design applications and architectures for high availability and fault tolerance, ensuring business continuity in the event of system failures or outages.

27. **Security and Compliance:** Measures to protect cloud-based applications and data from unauthorized access and cyber threats, including network segmentation, encryption, and compliance with regulatory requirements.

28. **On-Demand Self-Service:** The ability for users to provision and manage computing resources, such as servers and storage, without human intervention from the service provider.

29. **Broad Network Access:** The accessibility of cloud services over the Internet from any device with an Internet connection, enabling ubiquitous access to resources.

30. **Resource Pooling:** The aggregation of computing resources by cloud providers to serve multiple users, allowing for efficient resource utilization and scalability.

31. **Measured Service:** Cloud usage metering and billing based on consumption, allowing users to pay only for the resources they use.

32. **Display:** The primary interface between the user and a device, presenting information and influencing user interaction and satisfaction.

33. **Processor (CPU):** The central component of a computing device that handles computations and instructions, driving performance.

34. **Memory (RAM):** Temporary storage for data and instructions that the CPU needs to access quickly, playing a crucial role in multitasking and performance.

35. **Storage:** The repository for apps, media, and user data in a computing device, encompassing both internal and external storage options.

36. **Battery:** The power source for a mobile device, providing energy for its operation and influencing device usability and portability.

37. **Initial Device Setup:** The process of setting up a new mobile device, including language selection, account creation, and network configuration.

38. **Account Creation:** The creation or sign-in process for various accounts on mobile devices, including email, app store, and cloud storage accounts.

39. **Network Configuration:** The setup of network settings to ensure seamless connectivity and access to online services on mobile devices.

40. **Security Settings:** Configuration of security features on mobile devices, such as screen locks, encryption, and remote device management.
41. **Printer Technologies:** Various printing mechanisms, including inkjet, laser, dot matrix, and thermal printers, each with unique features and limitations.
42. **Printer Peripherals and Consumables:** Supplies and maintenance kits for printers, including paper, ink, toner, and maintenance kits, and strategies for managing printer supplies and optimizing printing costs.
43. **Printer Maintenance:** Maintenance activities for printers, including cleaning printheads, replacing ink cartridges, calibrating printers, and troubleshooting common issues.
44. **Printer Security:** Measures to fortify printers and safeguard sensitive documents against security breaches, including encryption, authentication, and security protocols.
45. **Software Updates and Upgrades:** Methods for applying patches, bug fixes, and security enhancements to software applications to improve functionality and security.
46. **Diagnostic Tools and Utilities:** Tools for software support and troubleshooting, including system logs, task managers, performance monitors, and troubleshooting wizards.

47. **Software Security Best Practices:** Measures to protect software applications and data from security threats, including antivirus software, firewalls, and secure software development practices.
48. **Software Deployment:** Strategies for deploying software applications across computing environments while adhering to organizational policies and compliance requirements.
49. **Software Lifecycle Management:** Processes for managing software from acquisition to retirement, including software acquisition, deployment, maintenance, and retirement.
50. **Cybersecurity Threats:** Security risks and threats to computer systems and networks, including malware, ransomware, phishing, and social engineering attacks.
51. **Threat Actors:** Individuals or groups behind cyber-attacks, including script kiddies, hacktivists, criminal hackers, nation-states, and insiders.
52. **Security Controls:** Measures to mitigate cybersecurity risks, including preventive, detective, and corrective controls, to ensure the confidentiality, integrity, and availability of information assets.
53. **Interoperability:** The ability of different software systems, applications, or devices to exchange data and operate together seamlessly.

54. **Bring-Your-Own-Device (BYOD):** This allows the user to bring their own personal device for use with work-related tasks. Typically, there are guidelines to follow, such as acceptable use policies and separation of applications, normally through a mobile device management solution.

55. **Choose-Your-Own-Device (CYOD):** This allows the user to choose from pre-approved devices the organization has selected for use with work-related tasks.

56. **Company-Owned-Provided-Device (COPE):** The most common method for Mobile Device Management, a device that is owned by the employing organization that is provided to the user for work-related purposes.

57. **Mobile Device Management (MDM):** An application that is used to manage work-related mobile devices, primary cell phones, tablets, or similar items. It enforces group policies for what is and is not allowed on the phone and assists with separating personal items from work-related applications.

Index

© Kodi A. Cochran 2024

K. A. Cochran, *CompTIA A+ Certification Companion*, Certification Study Companion Series,
https://doi.org/10.1007/979-8-8688-0867-8

D

E

F

G

H

I, J, K

L

M

N

O

P

Q

R

S

T

U

V

W, X, Y

Z

Printed in the United States
by Baker & Taylor Publisher Services